D1470428

Life with a Superhero

Raising Michael
Who Has Down Syndrome

Life with a Superhero

Raising Michael
Who Has Down Syndrome

by
Kathryn U. Hulings

Number 6 in the Mayborn Literary Nonfiction Series

University of North Texas Press
Mayborn Graduate Institute of Journalism
Denton, Texas

10 9 8 7 6 5 4 3 2 1

Permissions:
University of North Texas Press
1155 Union Circle #311336
Denton, TX 76203-5017

The paper used in this book meets the minimum requirements of the
American National Standard for Permanence of Paper for Printed Library
Materials, z39.48.1984. Binding materials have been chosen for durability.

Library of Congress Cataloging-in-Publication Data

Hulings, Kathryn U., 1961–
  Life with a superhero : raising Michael who has Down syndrome / by
Kathryn U. Hulings. – 1st ed.
      p. cm. – (Number 6 in the Mayborn literary nonfiction series)
  Includes bibliographical references.
  ISBN 978-1-57441-524-7 (cloth : alk. paper) – ISBN 978-1-57441-537-7
(e-book)
  1. Hulings, Kathryn U. 2. Hulings, Michael. 3. Down syndrome–
Patients–Colorado–Fort Collins–Biography. 4. Down syndrome–Patients–
Colorado–Fort Collins–Family relationships. 5. Children with mental
disabilities–Colorado–Fort Collins–Biography. 6. 0–Colorado–Fort
Collins–Biography. 7. Adopted children–Colorado–Fort Collins–
Biography. 8. Mothers of children with disabilities–Colorado–Fort Collins–
Biography. 9. Adoptive parents–Colorado–Fort Collins–Biography.
10. Mothers and sons–Colorado–Fort Collins. I. Title. II. Title: Raising
Michael who has Down syndrome. III. Series: Mayborn literary nonfiction
series ; no. 6.
  RJ506.D68H85 2013
  618.92'8588420092–dc23

                                                                    2013012748

Life with a Superhero: Raising Michael Who Has Down Syndrome is Number 6 in
the Mayborn Literary Nonfiction Series

Interior design by Robert Kern.
The electronic edition of this book was made possible by the support of the
Vick Family Foundation.

This book is dedicated to anyone who has ever loved and been loved
by a person who lives with an intellectual disability.

In loving memory of my father, Norman Udevitz
January 22, 1929–February 12, 2013

Contents

pro•gres•sive (prə-grĕs-ĭv) tense (tĕns) n. 1. A tense
of verbs used in describing action that is on-going.

Unwrapping	1
Crawling	17
Speaking	33
Running	41
Swimming	65
Playing	91
Believing	109
Learning	113
Imagining	133
Flying	139
Dancing	165
Waiting	187
Wondering	219
Wrapping	235
Progressing	241
Thanking	247
Appendix	249
Source Notes	259

Unwrapping

Michael came wrapped in layers, too many for a pleasant spring day. Even indoors, a small knitted cap was secured over his ears with yarn tied in a sloppy bow underneath his chin, brushing up against a matching sweater buttoned high on his neck. There was a small bead of sweat on his brow, but he seemed parched; a blister festered on his lower lip and, in the fluorescent lights, his skin was a dusky shade of pale yellow swirled with pasty blue. Where his head had been shaved on the sides to accommodate an IV tube insertion a few days earlier, I could see pea-green veins throb in a nervous, thirsty flow. About half an hour earlier, before I held Michael in my arms, I had met his escort, a close relative of his, who was also blanketed in perspiration from her trek through the labyrinth of Stapleton Airport.

It was not difficult to spot this small, winded woman and the quiet infant she carried on her bosom like a backwards papoose. In addition to the baby, she lugged a large blue duffel bag over her shoulder. Exiting the terminal ramp, she had a lost, searching look, not unlike a child on the first day of kindergarten who, before entering the classroom, peers over her shoulder to make sure Mommy is still there, waving her on, nodding in assurance. I was not sure if this woman, whose voice I'd heard, but whose face I'd never seen, was looking backwards for comfort or forward for closure; either way, I ached for her.

1

I had not thought to bring a sign to identify ourselves; we were a mob, all fourteen of us (my husband Jim, me, our four children, Jim's parents, my mother, my sister and her son, one social worker, an adoption exchange representative, and a good friend)—an obvious greeting party. We were all waiting with the same searching visage as the woman carrying the package we desired. When my eyes finally met the smooth, black gaze of my child's escort, my entourage faded and found a home in my back pocket, the muffled roar of jets landing and taking off resolved into a whimper, and all the bustling passengers became ants at my feet. We nodded in acknowledgment, an immediate recognition. Only three people remained in the expansive airport: my child, this woman, and I.

This is what the three of us knew: Michael's biological mother did three remarkable things in the first three days of my infant son's life. The first remarkable thing she did, perhaps as she nursed him for the first time, was notice that he looked different from her other two children. He was smaller, the bridge of his nose was flat, his tongue was large and flailing, his head was flattened in the back, and his ears protruded from his head at a ninety-degree angle. She called the doctor's attention to these malformations and demanded an explanation. She got one: her baby had Down syndrome.

The second remarkable thing she did was announce her intention never to see this child again. "Take him away," she screamed. Doctors, social workers, nurses, clergy, and the baby's father all pleaded with her to hold the baby once more, to give her heart a chance, to look into his eyes and find a connection. She refused. She could not bear to raise a child with special needs. The life of stress and suffering she foresaw was unimaginable in her reality.

The third remarkable thing she did was tell a lie of epic proportions. She left the hospital without her child and returned with her husband to her small Israeli town, her neighbors, and her two small children. And then, she told them all that the baby had died.

The adoption caseworker who handled Michael's adoption relayed the remarkable story about Michael's biological mother to me: her initial uneasiness at the appearance of her baby, the ensuing screaming, and the content of her lie. This is what I knew, based on phone conversations with Michael's female relative, the escort who eventually brought Michael to me: the biological father wanted to keep the baby—this relative wanted to keep the baby—but the biological mother was unswayable. For my son's biological mother, he really was dead.

I may have misheard the relative's lamentations over the fabricated loss of my son. I might have selected to hear a truth I could live with. I might have demonized the characters in this story so I could avoid their pain, to keep intact a narrative binary of good deeds and bad deeds, so I didn't have to linger in the abyss of grey—the place where I might have to find a moment of compassionate understanding for any of these people who were bartering the exchange of a human life. I would have to forgive Michael's biological mother for what I cannot comprehend *and* worship her for bestowing upon me my son for whom I am most thankful. A human heart can break from such aches.

Over time, I have realized that when it comes to memories, there are some we own and some, it seems, we acquire. This experience has been no different. I was not there in the flesh to watch Michael's mother's anguish. I was not with Michael's escort in the living room where bags were packed in preparation to fetch my very alive son and bring him to Denver. I was not privy to the hours I imagine Michael's biological father must have spent on his knees begging his wife to reconsider her choice. I did not hear the prayers from rabbis and family members for healing and reconciliation at her bedside. But I have imagined these scenes a million times over in my head, so many times, in fact, that I sometimes forget that I wasn't there. I find that I need to insert myself into the part of the story where I have no physical presence. I gather my emotions and let them overlay the bits and pieces of information I have received—like shellac daubed over a puzzle of one million pieces—in an effort to keep the shape from dispersing. Still, however, there remain tiny, almost imperceptible cracks in the facade of the whole. This potential for leakage, for the slippage of so many truths about Michael's beginnings, does not escape me.

The most compelling slippage, the possible truth I find most disturbing, is the moment Michael's mother forsook him, allowed him to be taken away to an unnamed kibbutz. How curious, how easy, how arrogant it is for me to use the word "forsook." It is my inchoate definition, how I define the moment she irretrievably let go of Michael, though she may, in truth, define it quite differently. Still, I have imagined through many a sleepless night under what circumstances could I have been moved to reject any of my children and agree to their being sent away to be nursed and rocked and soothed with lullabies by a communal group of strangers. My own dire poverty? My own complete and utter isolation from the world? My own instability? A drug habit? All are possibilities. In truth, I have no idea what happened to Michael's biological family, and I have no right to judge.

Even so, I sometimes feel confused when I close my eyes and see her giving Michael away to the unknown; I return to this dark place of palpitations and stomach churning, which is quickly followed by another wave of gratitude and thanks for making it possible for me to have Michael in my life. In these hazy moments, standing on the precipice of questioning interspersed with thunderous spasms of ecstatic gratitude, I am not sure where my humanity, or even my own sanity lies. Michael's story is marked by a lie, yet it is not defined by one. Instead, his story is shaped by the truths that come out of a faith in and love of life.

This is what I know alone to be true: I love Michael. He has changed me. I could have never predicted how he would make me analyze life with a mischievous, chuckling eye instead of a sad and heavy heart; or how he would make me laugh harder than I've ever laughed before; or how I would feel moments of terror I did not know existed; or, finally, how by loving me for the complete and total dork I am, he would allow me, for the first time in my life, to see myself as whole, as someone who mattered.

I did not know that soon after Michael arrived I would become deathly ill. And had Jim not repeatedly brought Michael and my other four kids to the hospital day after day and put them in my arms and on my bed, even though I was not lucid, I am not sure I would be alive today. Michael came to us on the wings of a 747 propelled by his biological mother's lie. But the remarkable fact is that sometimes a lie ends up being the beginning of beautiful truths. It is true that we offered Michael a forever family and an endless celebration of his life. It is even more true that Michael has given us more reasons to cherish life than we could have ever imagined.

♦ ♦ ♦

I know of no etiquette book that outlines the proper way to proceed with the ritual of the giving away and receiving of a child given these circumstances. There are no books with indexes and chapters suggesting how to graciously accept the gift of a human being or how to phrase a thank-you note after the fact. Celebrities have written books describing it as a blessed event, psychologists have written tomes on the statistical outcomes of adoption, and social workers and lawyers provide legal guidelines and processes. Yet, the actual moment of transfer is unknown, unpredictable territory, especially in our circumstance.

Due to the widely varying beliefs of the people involved in the adoption, there was a great deal of cautious cooperation and moral compromise. Michael was born in Israel. I live in Colorado. Jim and I are an American, interfaith couple (Jewish and Irish Catholic); my child's biological parents are Orthodox Jews. The adoption exchange was a Jewish organization specializing in recruiting families for waiting Jewish children with special needs. It was actually run by a long-lost cousin I never knew before. The adoption agency in charge of the legal mechanics of the placement and the home study was an Evangelical

Christian organization that, as a rule, placed children only in Christian homes with parents who signed oaths to raise the child to be a practicing, devout Christian. The two disparate entities' only connection was that they shared a social worker: my child's case manager. The Christian Agency grappled with our lack of Christian status; the Jewish exchange and biological family wrestled with our interfaith commitment. Jim and I were left squirming in between, trying to quickly convince all of them that regardless of the name of our G-d, whether we kneeled in prayer or swayed and davened, whether we thought Jesus was a nice Jewish boy from Bethlehem or the Light of the World, we were good people—flawed, but good.

Often times in adoption, there are long stretches of waiting time for an available child. I have read anecdotal accounts in women's magazines sharing how there is not a glut of healthy white infants who have been relinquished, but there is a high demand, plus mile-long waiting lists to adopt such children. The business of adoption is not an inexpensive one, especially for people who wish to adopt children who come with few obvious, immediate complications and are willing to pay high, five-figure sums to extend their family. There are, however, relinquished, waiting children in the world who have special needs and who often wait in vain for a family. These adoptions can move forward much more quickly, and while it is true that they too include expenses that need to be considered, the costs are usually considerably fewer. Often, these waiting children might be passed from foster home to foster home, and institution to institution, until they either become wards of the state or reach the age of eighteen and are released to find their own solitary way.

I had been waiting my whole life for Michael. As a five-year-old I read Dale Evans' book, *Angel Unaware,* which tells of Evans' daughter who had Down syndrome and died at a very young age. I told my mom I too would have an angel for a child, but my angel wouldn't die. My mom cried. Later, as a teen, I became perpetually sad and sullen as a result of watching bullies in junior high hallways torment and torture special education students who were cloistered in faraway rooms, let out only for P.E. and lunch. It seemed to me at the time that adults remained mute. It made me wonder who, if anyone, mattered.

In high school, I was often sent to the principal's office for skipping classes. I smacked my gum, blowing bubbles while he lectured, not knowing how to explain that I couldn't handle the pain I saw and felt, but could not fix. He'd always bid me goodbye with the words, "I hope I won't have to see you in my office anymore," but I knew he would. I was a truant child. I felt disembodied and helpless. I was young and powerless and was quite sure I did not matter and could not make a difference in anyone's life. I was not whole.

Twenty years later, I received a survey to fill out for an upcoming high school reunion. One of the questions asked: "What is your most embarrassing memory of high school?" I answered something about falling off my bike when I was a sophomore cheerleader riding in a homecoming parade. It was a lie. *Every* moment in high school was embarrassing. There is no other reasonable emotion to describe how I felt anytime I was silent in the face of brutality toward anyone marked by difference, or when, G-d forgive me, I enacted malice myself. A saint, I am not. Still, in that time, in my youth and in my heart, I promised G-d that when I grew up, *then* I would be truly good: do good things, say good things, and not be mute in the face of cruelty.

Between high school and my first child, I sought out goodness. I started studying dance at the University of Utah, but quickly transferred to the University of Colorado in Boulder where I studied Therapeutic Recreation and Adapted Physical Education. This field was a miraculous discovery for me—I found a way to help people *re-create* their lives and find wholeness through play! I taught creative movement and dramatics at a residential facility for adults with developmental disabilities. I went on hiking trips with clients, and I led a life-skills class where we went grocery shopping and cooked spaghetti.

Goodness came to me by the way of children when I myself was just emerging from my own adolescence: my first biological child was born two weeks after I turned twenty-one. Over the next six years, I carried and birthed three more children. At the age of twenty-seven, I was the mother of four, but I knew my family was not complete. I had been dreaming about adoption since childhood. Jim and I, a couple since our very early teens, had agreed long ago that one day we would adopt someone who needed us. This agreement was sort of a deal-breaker in our relationship. It was imperative in my life, and Jim understood that. In February of 1991, the child in need presented himself in the form of a phone call; the telephone would serve as a third party throughout the entire process, a sort of co-conspirator of chance, fate, and timing.

I put out the word to a couple of friends (one of whom happened to be an adoption counselor), that Jim and I were ready to begin what we thought would be an extended, painstaking process. Even in the schema of adopting a child with special needs, however, the process that was about to unfold was unusually rapid. Within days, my counselor friend called me to let me know that she'd received news from a Colorado social worker about a little boy, only three days old, born prematurely in Israel who had Down syndrome. He had been relinquished and was being cared for on a kibbutz; his parents wanted him placed with a Jewish family in the United States. She told us that if we were interested, we needed to make a call, and left me with the name and number of a social worker. I called that evening.

Timing is a funny thing. Just seconds before my call was placed, the social worker had been on the line trying to reach a unique family in the Northwest. They were a well-known family in adoption circles; it's hard to go unnoticed when you have over thirty children under your care, many of them under the age of three, with Down syndrome. My child's biological kin in Israel had heard of these folks and felt they would be a good match for the baby they could not keep. Thank G-d, a busy AT&T system, and whatever other forces were at work that evening, that the extension at that household was busy. Perhaps it was because the adults at that home were trying to reach a crisis hotline—within a month of that night, one of the adults had a complete and utter nervous breakdown. All the children were removed from the home and successfully placed elsewhere, except for the babies with Down syndrome—they were separated and ended up in the care of the state. My child was a busy signal away from being one of those kids. Instead, after a rushed home-study and swift preparations (talking to doctors, setting up his room, buying new clothes), my child arrived in Colorado six weeks later, in the spring of 1991, after only a short delay advised by doctors in Israel who were scared to let him travel until he recovered from a nasty, potentially fatal case of Respiratory Syncytial Virus (RSV).

Our child's escort volunteered to make the journey across the Atlantic Ocean to say goodbye to him between the airport escalators, harried travelers, and drinking fountains. After the awkward, tearful exchange, where her hands slid the weight of the infant to the crook of my elbow, we sat for a few minutes on sticky terminal furniture. She gave me a Star of David to give my son on his Bar Mitzvah, a miniature red Torah to put under his pillow to keep him safe, a blue duffel bag full of what she called "his things," and instructions on how to administer myriad medications I'd never used before to treat this still-ailing baby I held. I promised to love him, to write, to send pictures, and never to forget what she had done for my family. She gave my child one last kiss and then, with our social worker holding her steady, they disappeared around a corner to get some coffee, a tissue to wipe her face, and some cold water to keep her from collapsing.

No matter how I recall the day of my child's arrival, what angle I view the image from, I cannot forget his clothing, nor the apparatus that accompanied him. After touching his face and playing with his feet, the rest of my children went to get ice cream with their Grandpa Russ, leaving Jim and me to get to know our baby. My sister, Jane, looked over our shoulder as Jim and I sat on a stone bench, cradling our child. I wanted to relieve my child of the burden of his warmth; it was as if he had traveled wearing all his belongings, an *aliyah* in reverse; he was a wandering, baby Jew thrust into his own Diaspora, in search of a new homeland. I untied his hat and pushed it back, blew a breath of cool air on his forehead, ran my hand over his head, and dug through his "bag of things" to find a bottle. The nipple on the bottle was the kind one might use to suckle an orphaned lamb or baby calf; it was not fit for a human. Still, this baby sucked hard on the floppy nipple with a too-wide hole and not enough tautness for his developing cheeks; the dryness of his palate and his thirst helped him overcome the burden of this disfigured feeding system.

"I can see it now," Jane said.

"Me too," I whispered.

The back of his skull had that flat plateau so distinctive in children who have Down syndrome. With his hat half off, I could see his eyes were wide, chocolate brown and almond shaped, almost Asian in their placement on his face. The bridge of his nose was characteristically flat, and his ears stuck out.

"You got quite a pair of flappers there, kid!" Jim teased as he fingered the features of our new boy's face.

We named our new boy Michael, after Jim's baby brother who died after being born three months premature. Upon his mother's return from the hospital, Jim (only three or four at the time) told her that they should name the lost baby Michael because he was so brave to die, and most certainly was helped to Heaven by the Archangel Michael. His mother cried and agreed that it was a wonderful name.

As Jim and I sat on the stone bench in Stapleton, our new baby Michael kept a fix on me, never diverting his eyes. Every few seconds, his languid, oversized tongue would lag out of his mouth, until he could figure out how to retract it, return it to its resting place. He seemed to be trying to talk, to ask, "Who are you?" To help us both, I repeated over and over, "I'm your mommy . . . I'm your mommy."

The ride home was quiet. Michael sat in the front seat between Jim and me. His low muscle-tone, almost a given in children who have Down syndrome, caused him to scrunch up in a little ball in his car seat; every few moments, I had to straighten him up. His head had a stiff tilt to the left; when I tried to straighten his neck, my hands were met with great resistance. I left the tightness alone, knowing it was not normal and needed therapeutic attention. The car was completely full; there were no more empty seats. From Denver to Fort Collins, we were a new tribe of seven, each of us a little lost, each of us silently contemplating how quickly a family can change, how Michael would fit in, what new roles we would be left to play. Ten minutes into the ride, everyone except for Jim and me fell asleep.

A "Welcome Home Michael" sign was strung across our garage, scotch-taped on by friends and neighbors. I took Michael, his bag of stuff, and his medicine upstairs to my bedroom while Jim got the rest of the kids a snack and put them to sleep. I carefully laid Michael down on my king-sized bed, on a soft comforter, next to a broken-in, hand-me-down sleeper all my babies wore as a family tradition. I slowly stripped him of his hat, sweater, pullover, sweatpants, terry cloth pajamas, T-shirt, and diaper, the way I would peel an organic onion: not wanting to bruise the skin or compromise the flavor. When I was done, there, naked and engulfed in the blanket's flowers, was a sickly child. I silently sobbed, so as not to alarm the household. I wondered if Michael's layers were meant to compensate for his lack of body fat, to ease the chill from his fever, and to provide comfort from the deep, ugly cough that rattled from his lungs. The family sleeper was too big; this baby was smaller (by almost four pounds) at six and a half weeks old, than my biological children had been at birth. I put him in a fresh diaper and clad him in the sleeper anyway, rolling the sleeves three times and scrunching up the footies, so his feet would not be consumed by cotton.

Jim rocked Michael for a while, giving him a fresh bottle, as I went through his bag of things. There was miscellaneous apparel: a tiny shirt that said "I Love New York" plus mismatched tees and pants, nothing of the same size. I stuffed it all, including the garb Michael arrived in, back into the blue duffel. The only items I was interested in were the pharmacological cornucopia mixed in among the wads of shaped material. Antibiotics, steroids, painkillers, powders, and potions sat in front of me on the kitchen counter as I dialed our pediatrician's after-hours number.

"I'm sorry for the late hour, and I know we have an appointment in the morning, but I don't know what to do with all this medication," I rambled into the receiver.

"Well, well, well, you sure have bought yourself a bundle of trouble, now haven't you?" the on-call doctor snarled. He continued on, as if he were talking about a family pet. "Don't give him anything, watch him through the night and we'll see you tomorrow."

I hung up, shocked at the rudeness, the stupidity. For many years after this late-night conversation, we made sure our children saw the other wonderful practitioners at this pediatric practice, and we avoided further contact with this particular doctor.

We turned up the heat in the house, and again, I rid Michael of his covering, down to just a diaper. I dropped my own clothes in a heap on the floor and abandoned the donning of my nightgown. We slipped into bed, and I cuddled Michael, flesh to flesh, making sure his ear was on top of my chest. It was not too late for him to memorize, to recognize my rhythm; we assumed this position every night for a month, although in those first dark hours, my eyes never shut as I counted his every breath.

Kathryn cradles Michael the day of his arrival at
Stapleton Airport surrounded by family

Michael, as an infant, dressed in the oversized family
sleeper all kids wore at their homecoming

The Hulings as a new family of seven, taken two months after Michael's arrival (Clockwise from bottom left: Michael, Kathryn, Nathan, Jim, Sean, Joedy, and Edie) Reprinted by permission of Sears Portrait Studios

Crawling

I've known for a long time that my family plays hard. There's no changing that. Still, their exploits have been self-limiting. They have been slapped by the universe enough to figure out when to back off, when to call it a day, and when, maybe, to be a little afraid. The only thing for me that has equaled my kids' glee over making me quiver with worry was the loud dinnertime retellings of their foibles, follies, and adventures: "We held hands when we were jumping off the cliff into the quarry!" "We were playing hide-n-seek at American Furniture Warehouse!" "The sled was falling apart before we reached the bottom!" "We were winning the shopping cart race at Target before we got kicked out of the store!" "We were jumping the fence at the pool at midnight so we could go swimming naked!" "While we were dancing in the tent, there was a bear lurking outside!" But getting Michael to move with abandon, to act in the progressive tense (you know: verbs that end in -*ing*), to live like a superhero, and to embrace adventure and a kick in the pants as his guide—so he could also tell his story with aplomb—was not simple. Getting him to crawl was challenge enough.

♦ ♦ ♦

The first few weeks after Michael's arrival were spent subjecting him to medical tests. They were not invasive by any means, but they were stressful. It is not uncommon for children with Down syndrome to have abnormalities with their hearts, among other body systems. We were relieved when Michael's echocardiogram was normal. After we made sure he was fully recovered from the respiratory infection he arrived with from Israel, it was recommended that we begin an immediate course of therapeutic intervention. And so we began.

By the time Michael was six months old, we had a routine of sorts. Within the course of a week, we would have an occupational therapy appointment, a physical therapy appointment, a speech therapy appointment, and a play therapy appointment. That's a lot of appointments for a baby, but there were milestones to meet. There were baby books to fill, baby books that—in between the pages illustrated with rocking horses and elephants and filled with lines written in soft cursive, recording an infant's accomplishments—provided little vignettes that outlined the normal range of ages for children to reach particular landmarks, developmental goals: this is the time you can expect your baby to lift his head, to smile, to coo, to crawl, to babble, to talk, to walk, to run. It's a very long list. Parents of children who have special needs have been known to burn these books. For them, these celebratory books are a record of all that is not happening, of all that is delayed, of all that might never come to be, instead of a gala's gold lettered program of accomplishment.

I didn't burn a baby book. Frankly, I am spineless when it comes to fire. This dread of fire has been a constant companion ever since I watched a film in elementary school, when I was six years old, that dramatized various ways fires could begin in a home, and, afterwards, the emotions of the sad people who had a family member die in the ensuing blaze. I now have a fire extinguisher on every floor of my home. Our bathrooms have smoke detectors. I am terrified. And so, I figured that if Michael was going to be slow to crawl, at least it should be in a house that was still standing, rather than one accidentally burned down in a fit of lamentation.

I was, however, aware of the expected course of development in a child. And, I was not unfamiliar with the sphere of therapy. Nathan had a significant stutter at age five (which is more common than I realized); Sean didn't talk until he was two (why should he have bothered? He would point at something, and Nathan would talk for him!); and Edie was also delayed in her speech, probably due to a rash of ear infections in her infancy that compromised her hearing. All of their courses of therapy were limited. We went, we did what was recommended, it worked, and we were done. We were lucky.

In my anal-retentive mind, there needed to be a linear, overarching path to Michael's therapy: first, we needed to strengthen his neck so he could lift his head and learn to roll over; second, we needed to help him crawl; third, we needed to help him talk; fourth, we needed to help him walk; and fifth, we needed to make sure he had opportunities to use his hands and set the stage for fine motor development. I had this entrenched in my skull because even though I had not burned baby books, I had read them. Plus, I was the mom of five. I knew the routine, at least for children who seemed to be ambulatory and have all their sensory capabilities in working order. It didn't take long to realize that Michael was way off the mark.

I watched carefully at Michael's therapy sessions. To enhance Michael's balance and sense of space, his occupational therapist placed him in a therapy swing and pushed the swing in various directions, all the time saying, "Whee! Whee!" while Michael giggled. To help improve his grip, she would help him hold little balls. This exercise did enhance his grip, but it didn't help our stress levels—he popped one in his mouth more than once, sending us all into a panic. To strengthen his floppy muscle tone, his physical therapist would lay him on a therapy mat and guide him through a series of stretches followed by a massage for tight, inflexible muscles. His speech therapist would take out toys and name the parts for Michael as they played. It was all done with professionalism, the best of intentions, and it felt familiar. My Jewish-Russian Grandmother had stretched and massaged all her babies, grandbabies, and great-grandbabies during every diaper change. My mother massaged and stretched all her babies and grandbabies while pretending to make their legs ride a bicycle while she sang a bicycle song of her own creation, or made all the babies hug themselves while crossing their arms across their bodies. And so had I. My grandmother, my mother, and I had all pushed our children on swings, higher and higher, side-to-side laughing out, "Whee! Whee!" We had rolled a million balls to babies and enclosed our hands round babies' hands as they grasped a cookie or a rattle. We were talking to our babies and naming the world when they were inside our bellies or, in this case, the moment they arrived at Stapleton Airport. It was very familiar.

Let me be clear: I am in awe of the work of therapists who attend to issues of the bodies and speech of children and adults with challenges. But there was something about Michael's therapeutic experience that felt . . . well . . . different. Michael has Down syndrome, but his diagnosis is not accompanied by a list of medical complications. Again, we are lucky. And it made sense that all the therapy sessions looked familiar to me—they were medically based exemplars, some that I already knew how to do, had already had done with Michael's older siblings, and was already doing with Michael. My own challenge was to accept that Michael would have a linear path, but it would be in his own time and at his own pace.

I started paying closer attention to how our ordinary days could become therapeutic. When my sister Jane's kids and my kids played at a park near her house in Denver, she filled up Michael's socks and her son Zach's socks with sand. Michael was not yet two, and his crawling was still uncertain; Zach was about one year old. She then put the sandy socks back on the boys' feet. Jane turned to me and said, "the extra weight will strengthen his legs and make his trunk and arms work harder, too. It will help his crawling." Pretty soon, everyone's socks were filled with sand. It was blissful. And scratchy. But blissful, nonetheless.

It took me a while, but ultimately, I cashed in on the confidence and wisdom accrued from my years as a mom, my recreational therapy background, my sister, my mother, and my grandmother. Before Michael turned two, our calendar became more open. While we made sure to regularly check in with therapists and their well-honed expertise, just to make sure we were on the right track, even if it was at creeping pace, I still made an executive decision. I turned to my family and announced that *we* were now Michael's full time therapists.

♦ ♦ ♦

Our new routine was like parenting on steroids with über-sibling interaction. Jim took over the pursuit of gross motor skills. Michael had finally crawled with certainty soon after he turned two. Between sandy socks, come-and-get-it bribes from across the room ("Come on, Michael—if you crawl across the room, you'll get a Ding-Dong!"), and imitating our dogs ("See how Darby the dog creeps on the floor to get the treat? Now you creep on the floor to get the treat!"), Michael got speedily proficient at the act of crawling. So proficient, that he figured out how to climb up the stairs. The multiple stairs in our tri-level home soon became a danger zone. Jim had constructed sturdy gates made out of lattice and hinges, but in a family of seven, gates are often left open. We knew that Michael needed a safe way to negotiate a way down the double set of stairs.

At over six feet tall, Jim could not accurately demonstrate to Michael what he had in mind, so he simultaneously explained and manipulated Michael's body through the motions. Jim and Michael would sit on the landing at the top of the stairs, long, slim legs next to short, chubby legs.

"Michael," Jim would begin, "Let's turn around."

Jim would then turn Michael's body so that Michael's rear-end and legs were the body parts leading down the stairs.

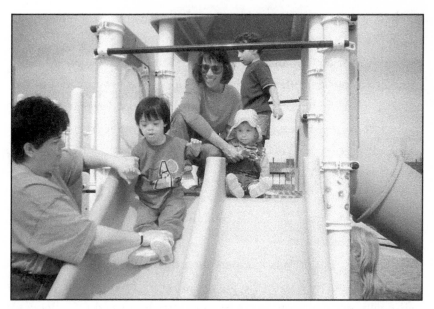

The blissful, scratchy day at the park when everyone put sand in their socks (Clockwise from bottom left: Kathryn, Michael [18 months], aunt Jane Miller, cousin David Miller, and cousin Zachary Miller)

Michael (age 4) playing in a ball pit with siblings and his cousin (Left to right: sister Edie, Michael, cousin Zachary, brother Sean)

"Get on your tummy, and make your feet go down the stairs first," Jim instructed.

He would then pull Michael's legs one at a time, showing him, through muscle memory, how to scoot down the stairs backwards.

"Scooch, scooch, scooch!" Jim would urge Michael.

When they got to the bottom, Jim would pat Michael on the back: "Atta boy!"

And then they would crawl back to the top and do it all over again. It didn't hurt that Nathan, Sean, Joedy, and Edie were happy to constantly demonstrate and, for a while, descend the stairs tummies first. Michael caught on in about two days. It took about two weeks for him to master the skill. In about a month he could go up and down the stairs so quickly it was disquieting.

When it came time to learn how to ride a bike, Jim put his analytical mind to use. Michael needed to feel secure in his balance before he could take to pedaling a two-wheeler, even with training wheels. How could Jim make this happen? He brought out the family scooter. Jim wanted to keep Michael's fear of falling at a minimum; it's much easier to try balancing when an unplanned descent can be averted by only having to put down your foot two inches. For weeks, every night after dinner, Jim would take Michael out into the quiet street in front of our house and have him try to stand on the scooter and find what he coined "the magic balance place." As soon as Michael found the magic balance place, Jim began to power the scooter by running alongside it and steering it with both his hands over Michael's while Michael stood on the scooter; soon, Michael took over the powering, and he pushed the scooter with his foot; then Jim steered with one hand; finally, Michael rode the scooter solo and . . . he fell—gloriously and completely with a requisite ugly, bloody knee.

"Hop up, buddy," Jim commanded. "We'll clean that up and try again."

With tiny hiccups, Michael got up and wiped his face and went inside with Jim for doses of Bactine and Neosporin and then the protective layer of a Band-Aid. They went back out and, indeed, tried again. A few weeks later, Jim and Michael transferred their attention to a two-wheeler; Michael entered the drill knowing the thrill of balance. Within a day, he became as bodacious as any little boy could possibly be on his bike.

Michael's siblings have endowed him with the attainment of myriad skills, including computer skills. Computers are ever-present, and we have many in our home. We purchased many computer games for Michael, but the use of a mouse and keyboard were initially impossible for him to master. But, like I've said before, we are lucky. We have resources, and we were able to obtain a touch-screen for Michael, long before they were common and widely available, so that he could play with the technical wonders of the world and not have to feel limited. All of his siblings sat by his side and played the *Arnold* book games with him. Every now and then one of them quietly turned off the touch-screen, led Michael's hand over a mouse with his or her hand, and repeatedly helped Michael's pointer finger find the power button, the backspace, the shift key, and enter. Eventually, the touch-screen just stayed off.

One of Nathan's childhood prized possessions is a large model of Darth Vader that, with the touch of a single red button, moves and emits the sound of a light saber and Darth's heavy, obscene breathing. As the oldest child (eight years Michael's senior), Nathan kept Darth on a very high shelf so that his little brothers and sisters could not reach it. Once, when asked what it was like having a brother with Down syndrome, a very young—maybe nine or ten years old—Nathan replied, "he's just as annoying as my other siblings." But Nathan also engaged in a fistfight on an elementary school playground over another student's use of the word "retarded," so I could forgive him for keeping Darth up high. Still, on those special days when Darth alit from the shelf, Nathan would sit on the floor with Michael and help him push the tiny red button with his finger over Michael's. Nathan may never fully appreciate how he intensified Michael's fine motor skills. It was more magical than anything the *Star Wars* empire could offer.

Sean, my second oldest (six and a half years older than Michael), invariably does two tricks at birthday parties: he provides the illusion of sticking a cake knife up his nose, and he pretends to swallow fire after lighting the candles. "Sean," I roared when Michael was very small, "Tell Michael that you are doing a trick! Tell him it's not real!" Sean obeyed. He pulled Michael aside and showed him the illusion, the difference between real and pretend, calming the urge to really stick a knife into his sinuses or try to eat fire and unintentionally burn down our house. "Michael," Sean would prod, "You know how to really use a knife, right?" This query was followed by a quick lesson on how to cut a cake, as Sean's hand guided Michael's down an eighth of a chocolate layer cake with frosting rosettes. Later, when Michael was older, I saw Sean teaching him how to properly handle a lighter and the importance of fire safety. I was pleased, for fire is not my friend.

Sean has always given Michael a sense of balance. While in the kitchen, washing dishes, I often heard Sean yelling from the living room, "Michael! Wanna fly?" A brief chase followed—Sean chasing Michael—and when Michael was caught, Sean lay on the floor, stuck his legs in the air, and placed Michael's tummy on his feet, all the time holding his hands. The dismount from this circus trick was Sean rolling Michael forward into a front flip, on to his feet, just beyond Sean's head. As young adults, the flying routine expanded into a skit that included Michael standing on Sean's back—comically checking his watch, miming the act of reading a book, patting back a gaping yawn—while Sean did push-ups. You can't pay a therapist to do this kind of stuff.

Joedy, five years older than Michael, changed diapers without being asked, and she threw in a little stretch and a massage. Without even so much as a nudge, in the years before she was even in middle school, Joedy could always be found in Michael's room showing him how to cut out paper dolls, or color in the lines (she is meticulous that way), or write his name, or read a book. "Let's try again, Michael. You can do it," she urged when the undertaking seemed impossible and Michael had tossed down his Crayola Student Scissors or shut tight *Goodnight Moon*. Michael often ended up in Joedy's room after lights out, just for one more story or one more hug.

Edie, only two years older than Michael, would often accompany him and me to his early therapy appointments, and she absorbed the routine. One therapy we kept as a weekly appointment was play therapy with a Special Education Professional, Patrycia Hatten. Patrycia was singular in her approach. She brought developmentally appropriate toys to our home and shared some innovative applications of play therapy. Michael—who was about three—Patrycia, Edie, and I sat on our living room floor playing with a Playskool set that had cars, people, and street signs. Patrycia thought beyond the realm of baby books and measurements. Michael was in the midst of a running phase, and we were suffering from great anxiety that he would be hit by a car. When Michael manipulated one of the plastic Playskool people across the pretend Playskool street, Patrycia made one of the Playskool cars hit Michael's little fake boy.

"Oh, no!" Patrycia yelled. "The little boy ran into the street and now he is dead!" Patrycia looked up at me and whispered, "He has to be scared of something, Kathryn. Some fear is good."

She was right, and Edie was listening the whole time.

A few years after the Playskool tragedy, Edie, Michael, and I were at City Park feeding the geese and ducks, which seem to have learned not to fly south in the winter, perhaps due to all the food offered to them by the people of Fort Collins. As always, Michael and Edie were hand-in-hand, side-by-side, throwing pieces of bread to the few ducks that were near the shore of the lake. This was a beautiful site. Edie was but a baby herself when Michael became part of the family. A week or two after Michael arrived, two-year-old Edie made clear her feelings about this small, mewling intruder. "Put baby down," Edie commanded as I held Michael in my arms. "Die, baby, die," she continued. Had Edie been my first child, I might have panicked and feared that I had raised a sociopath. This was not the case. I had five children and already knew that what we accept from siblings—both physically and psychologically—would compel most of us to seek restraining orders if enacted by strangers. In fact, I was excited. Edie had a speech delay, and this threat was one of her first full sentences. Instead of calling a child psychologist, I called Jim and shared both the good news of Edie's speech and the hilarious thing she just said.

Anyway, at the lake, I don't remember why Edie let go of Michael's hand. I don't remember why I was not within arm's reach of the two of them, especially near the half-frozen lake. What I do remember is that out of the sky a gaggle of geese that numbered around thirty or so swooped down and surrounded Michael, who still was holding pieces of bread. Michael began to screech in tones that up until that second had never been issued forth from a human larynx. He froze. He stood and screeched while the geese had their way with the bread in his hand. G-d forgive me, I began to giggle. Edie threw me a severe glare, and, even though she too was giggling (which to this day she will not admit), she ran into the geese feast and saved Michael.

"Why didn't you help him, Mom?" Edie screamed at me when she had finally chased off the geese and had Michael's hand firmly back in hers.

"I felt like he was okay, Edie. He needs to learn how to figure this stuff out. I don't want him to be scared," I responded, defending my questionable parenting.

"Mom, sometimes fear is good. Sometimes Michael can be brave, but he still might be in danger. Sometimes we need to do things for him. I'm mad at you, Mom."

We left the park and drove home in silence.

Edie, like Patrycia, was right. There's a difference between being fearless and being justifiably afraid. It was slow, this process of pushing and pulling Michael along. We all learned that every iota of progress began with our hands either on top of or entwined with Michael's hands. We all learned that the many days helping Michael—the overwhelming sense of déjà vu as we repeated and repeated and repeated the same routines until he "got it"—made us all, not just Michael, more confident and, well, more fearless than ever. And I learned that even though we had become our own team of therapists, there were—and would be—some things along the way that would merit healthy trepidation.

◆　◆　◆

When Jim and I stood over a nine-year-old Michael, who was sprawled, eagle-style, on a hospital bed in the emergency room, an observer may have gotten the wrong idea about my state of mind. The expected visage of a mother looking over her son on a gurney is one of consternation, perhaps with tears falling down her face, and a bit of hand-wringing. But I was smiling—I was ecstatic.

About an hour earlier, Michael had a little run-in with the sharp corner of a wrought-iron spectator bench at an indoor soccer facility. I wasn't there for the disaster; I was soon to arrive from a small shopping respite at the nearby mall. Jim was there. He had been enacting his expert, preternatural ability to multi-task by simultaneously keeping an eye on Michael while rooting on Michael's sister, Edie, as she slammed opposing team members into padded walls. Not to be outdone by his big sister, Michael practiced his own version of running away from the opposing team, but Michael's opponent, in hot pursuit of him, was none other than Jim. And Michael had an uncanny ability to run away while looking over his shoulder with a "you can't get me" twinkle in his eye. This time, when Michael turned his head back from taunting Jim to see where he was heading, it wasn't a cushioned wall or even a human being he slammed into. Nope. Michael turned, and his head met the edge of a wrought-iron bench. Michael took a header into the bench and came out bleeding profusely—as all head slashes are prone to doing. I arrived to a bloody Michael, an unnerved Jim, who had witnessed the event ("Stop, Michael!" he reportedly hollered in a piercing, soprano-like timbre), and a seventy-five mph trip to the ER.

Anyway, as we watched our pediatrician skillfully glue shut the one-inch gash over his right eye, we patted Michael's hand, dutifully doted—"It's okay, Michael; you're such a brave boy." And, like I said, I felt ecstatic. Ecstatic? Amidst the scene of my child's ocular pain (okay— limited pain due to Michael's healthy, continuous dose of nitrous oxide through an oxygen mask) and trickling blood, I felt ecstatic? Yes, because just a few seconds earlier, when a nurse asked if any special precautions needed to be implemented in regards to Michael's Down syndrome, our pediatrician replied, with a throaty chuckle and a wink in our direction, "Nope. Michael's as healthy as a horse! We'll probably be seeing him for more stuff like this." My little boy, like his siblings, had become indomitable!

♦　♦　♦

By the time Michael was a pre-teen, he could walk and talk and run and ride a bike and use a computer; there wasn't much he couldn't do or wasn't learning to do. But one thing had not changed—I still found fire to be scary.

I am not a wonderful sleeper. When the opportunity for sleep does present itself and my body feels like it might cooperate and be able to rest, I take it. Which is why one summer afternoon in mid-June, a couple of days after Sean's seventeenth birthday (complete with cake and candles), I was curled up in bed. The air was cool, and the skies were gray, and there was a light drizzle outside. Perfect for sleeping. The kids were all home from swim team practice, and the house was oddly quiet, so I wrapped up in a ball and dozed off.

I remember dreaming that my name was being called, and with each time I was beckoned there followed a loud, droning cry, almost a wail. It was a disturbing dream, and it woke me up, but I still heard my name, and the wails grew louder. I sat up in bed and immediately noticed an eerie orange blush, not unlike an amber sunrise, emitting from Michael's bedroom. When the form of fifteen-year-old Joedy appeared in the hall outside my room, hovering and throbbing in the glow, screaming, "Oh my, G-d! Mom! Oh my, G-d!" I wondered if I wasn't hallucinating, but the all-too-real smell of smoke in the air convinced me otherwise.

I don't recall how, but somehow I traveled from my bed to the hallway where I met Joedy outside the doorway to Michael's room. There, creeping up his beloved University of Nebraska Football jacket, the artwork on his bulletin board, and the very wall itself, was a hypnotic cyclone of flames and smoke. Michael was sitting very close to the fire with the same long-handled lighter used to light the candles on Sean's cake in his fist. One of us dummies had left it out. Michael was an enraptured, immobile spectator to what wonders could be accomplished with his new fine motor skill. Sean had taught him well!

Joedy grabbed the fire extinguisher from the wall. I reached over, wrapped my hands around the cold, red cylinder and tried to take it from her, but she did not let go.

"Give it to me!" I implored.

"No! I'll take care of it!' she screamed.

We glared into each other's eyes and begin a full bout of tug-o-war. We both pulled on the extinguisher. Meanwhile, my peripheral vision caught view of the fire, now just inches from the ceiling, and Michael reaching out to touch the flames.

"No!" I screamed, and I let go of the extinguisher.

As I swooped in on Michael, Joedy pulled the pin and, in seconds, sprayed the thick mist directly on the blaze. It was over. We all stood in a little huddle, covered in white muck.

How strange that moment was. I was teetering between two very disparate emotions. On one hand, I was furious at Michael for playing with fire after we had spent years expressly forbidding it. On the other hand, I was rather impressed with Michael's demonstration of an intricate fine-motor skill—how far we had come in our therapeutic journey! And here again was another defining moment of how fearlessness does not necessarily mean not being afraid. Michael needed to be a little afraid. After I made Michael clean up the mess, I made sure we said a hyperbolic goodbye to his ruined Nebraska jacket.

"It's gone forever, Michael. Playing with fire is very, very, very bad," I sternly lectured as Michael stood sobbing near me and the trashcan.

I knew that, sometimes, my kids needed to sob. This time, I figured maybe it could prevent Michael from turning into an arsonist. I then placed Michael in a long timeout without anything fun even remotely available to him.

"Do you understand why you are in a timeout, Michael?" I interrogated.

"Because I played with fire," Michael whimpered with tears still running down his cheeks and tiny gulps between each word.

"You got it, mister. You are in big trouble. Big, big, big trouble."

While Michael was in timeout, I hid the lighter in some nether region of our cupboards. I hid it so well, in fact, that not even I could find it for the next birthday celebration. Post timeout, I gave one more mini-lecture on the evils of playing with fire, and then I set Michael on the sofa with Joedy, who promised to watch him carefully, and together they watched the Cartoon Network.

I knew that at that evening's dinner, Michael would have a story to tell the family, loudly and with aplomb. This is what I wished for when he was very young—that he would have thrilling escapades and be able to tell the tale over meatloaf and mashed potatoes and please-pass-the-butter. Mission accomplished.

And so we were pleased, but therapy wasn't ever easy. And it wasn't over. While I hoped that Michael had integrated an iota of fear, especially regarding fire, I still wanted him to remain fearless in the face of the next fine-motor skill challenge. I knew that therapy would drag on in tedium, but I also knew it would be interrupted by unexpected triumphs. It required stamina, and I knew that come morning we would begin the routine again. But that afternoon, dinner was a few hours off, the day was still draped in a dreary fog apt for inducing sleep, and, for the moment, everyone was safe. And so, amidst the remaining aromatic traces of a burned athletic jacket and the humdrum tones of *Scooby Doo* talking from the TV, I surrendered for the day and simply crawled back into bed.

Speaking

In our family therapeutic model, I carried on with my specialty—speech. As the primary parent at home, it made sense; I talked to and with my children all day. It was a natural fit. I just talked and read and sang with Michael a bit more. During our regular check-ins with speech therapists, we focused on what we could replicate at home. But the acquisition of spoken language proved to be a long journey.

Soon after realizing that Michael could indeed crawl and walk and run and negotiate stairs, I also realized that I had begun to suppress my own fears about Michael's ability to communicate. Sometimes, it takes a keen ear and endless patience to engage in a conversation with someone who has Down syndrome. I can't say for certain this applies to all individuals who harbor the genetic anomaly, but I've spent the past twenty-plus years around enough folks with Trisomy 21—the medical term used when a person has a full or partial extra copy of chromosome 21—to make an educated generalization. Comprehensible speech is of paramount concern in the wide, wacky world of Down syndrome. At times, to the untrained ear, Michael's speech can sound garbled, like he is spewing out a great gush of nonsense. Jim often has to remind me that I easily understand Michael only because I am his mother.

Waiters at our favorite Mexican restaurant may hear Michael recite, "I'd like two ufos with macaroni," yet I know that Michael has actually just ordered "two tacos with meat and cheese only." I can barely contain my glee at this act of independence, that Michael is practicing a useful skill. I am so giddy in fact, that I usually miss the countenance of confusion on the poor waiters' faces while they try to recall if "ufos" and macaroni have recently been added to the menu. It usually takes me a few seconds, and a kick from Jim under the table, to notice the waiters' non-verbal pleas of "Please G-d, help me understand so I don't do anything to hurt this kid," as little beads of sweat gather at their temples. I have to admit that I don't make waiters' lives any easier when they finally break down and ask me to translate. No. I am cruel. I insist that Michael repeat his order, until the waiters understand. And then, I go back to my glee. It took Michael twenty years to accomplish his restaurant ordering skills, and I refuse to let a little hiccup in food service communication set us back even one iota. I am grateful for all the patient waiters who seemed to innately understand the remarkable gift they gave Michael by listening with a kind and gentle smile.

◆　◆　◆

I never crawled. When I was nine months old, I simply stood up and walked. It is also said that I never really babbled or baby-talked; at one year of age, I simply began having conversations with my mom and dad. This would suggest that I would grow into a gregarious and precocious child, but that was not the case. I had no identifiable needs, like Michael does, but I became shy and quiet in my early childhood. I made up a language when I was five and spoke it for about a year, then later, in fourth grade, I couldn't shut up and babbled nonsensically. Soon, I became quiet again. Speech has regressed and progressed like this my entire life.

Maybe crawling is one of the imperative prerequisites to healthy development. Maybe I missed something that my brain desperately needed, but I'm sure there is zero science to back this up. Maybe what I'm saying is that, perhaps, if we don't linger long enough at each mile-stone, even when those milestones are way off the mark of anything that might represent a typical trajectory in a baby book, it may set the stage for us to regress later and try to make up for lost lingering. Maybe Michael is lucky that so many of us stand by and make sure all his developmental steps are carefully crafted and molded. Even so, I worried that the tremendous attention paid to Michael's physical development would not transfer, or flow, into his ability to speak. And, in a big family, it is a good thing not only to be able to speak, but to speak loudly and quickly. Some way of talking—with voice, or communication board, or hands—has to come into play in a big family. It's a survival tool.

And so, when Michael turned two years old, and the only word he could reliably and consistently utter was "Daddy," I was panicked. I was doing everything imaginable to help Michael attain speech: therapy; educational toys; naming every fruit and vegetable at the grocery store; babbling on endlessly about my day, people's names, and the color of the sky; playing at the park; calling geese; and counting our steps as Michael and I climbed the stairs. He loved every second of my attempts to entice speech out of his mouth. But still, when I would ask him to repeat a word, say, "apple," Michael would clap his hands and squeal "Daddy!" I became desperate.

I suppose, in moments of despair, all of us can become susceptible to offers of improbable hope, especially if they appeal to some long-held fascination or desire. When Michael was two years old, I could tell by looking in his deep brown eyes that words were ready to burst through. I just didn't know how to release the floodgate. And so, I was open to such suggestions. When I finished watching a *Nightline* news blurb about one Dr. David Nathanson and his program, *Dolphin Human Therapy*, based—at least at that time—in the Florida Keys, I practically ran upstairs to pack a suitcase for Michael and me to fly out to The Keys that night. We were going to spend a week with Dr. Dave, his staff, and the dolphins! I loved dolphins! I always pretended to be a dolphin when I played in the ocean as a child! In a week, Michael would talk! In a week! Jim reined me in, however, and suggested I do a little research first. I hate it when he's right.

Dolphin Human Therapy and another program called *Island Dolphin Care at Dolphins Plus,* also in The Keys, operated from the same basic premise that dolphin-assisted therapy is a proven, scientific methodology for increasing the skills and therapeutic outcomes for children with disabilities. Numerous other programs have popped up around the world since Michael was two years old. The dolphins aren't really therapists; they are human therapists' tools. If children adequately perform a task they are given, say, counting to ten, reciting their address, or even just making the sound of the letter "B," then they are allowed to interact with a dolphin through feeding it or playing a game of ball. Free-swims with the dolphins, with life jackets and supervision, are allowed for exceptional progress. Theoretically, these programs claim that the dolphins provide a unique sense of calm and motivation, which underpins the recorded, previously unseen results in the enhanced acquisition of skills. Kids supposedly leave these programs with new abilities, i.e. speech or behavior modifications. *Dolphins Plus* also includes education programs, marine mammal research opportunities, and dolphin swims for the public. Neither program comes cheap. A week of dolphin-assisted therapy can cost thousands of dollars, not including travel and accommodations.[1]

As I raved on about the programs and how wonderful it would all be, Jim made a couple of annoyingly salient points.

"Kathryn," he said, "It's just one week. That can't compare to what you do every day with Michael. Just give him time, honey. He'll talk. Soon! Be patient."

I started to state my rebuttal, but Jim interrupted with a terse, "Sweetie—we can't afford it anyway."

And so, common sense and fiscal realities convinced me not to pursue a trip to The Keys. Instead, I continued naming everything, carefully listening to any sound Michael made, trying desperately to contextualize it, and giving Michael what I hoped were the right words. If he gurgled in glee in the tub, swatting the bubbles that floated in the air, I would gift him with language—I would say, "I love bubbles!"

When Michael crawled, I would say, "I am crawling!" We played with flash cards, watched *Sesame Street,* read all of Dr. Seuss and Eric Carle, and played peek-a-boo—I offered the beginning of "peek," and hoped Michael would respond with "a-boo!"

I had been using American Sign Language with Michael since his infancy; it is considered a valuable tool that gives kids who may have a speech delay a way to communicate until oral talking comes into play. This, too, continued. Michael knew that if he pinched all his fingers on both hands and then tapped them together, we would all understand that he wanted "more," and we would all say the word, "more!" If he took those same pinched fingers and tapped them on his lips, we would all understand that he wanted something to "eat," and we would all say the word "eat!" If he made the letter "C" with one hand and tapped it into the open palm of his other hand, we knew he wanted a "cookie," and we would all say the word, "cookie!" If he made both his hands into the shape of the letter "L" and then swooped both hands in front of his body, we knew he was saying "let's go," and we would all say the words, "let's go!" And when Michael waved his fingers, of course, that meant "hi," and we would all say the word, "hi!"

With no trumpets blaring, Michael slowly began to replace signs and sounds with words. The first sign to go was the waving of fingers. One dark winter evening, Jim came in the front door, home from a long day at work. Michael was sitting in his high chair at the kitchen table, eating some Cheerios and sipping some juice. He put down his cup, looked at Jim and said, "Hi, Daddy!"

◆   ◆   ◆

I remained concerned about Michael's speaking, and I still occasionally imagined how wonderful speech therapy with dolphins would be. And, I firmly believe that whenever I ignore the grandness of the universe—chasing rainbows instead of joining forces with the simple everyday miracles—it gladly responds by slapping me with a cosmic two-by-four. The spring that Michael turned eleven, Jim, Michael, Edie, and I went on a vacation to San Diego. Nathan and Sean were singing with a school choir in New York, and Joedy was touring Italy with a school group, so the rest of us decided to go on a little jaunt ourselves. As a treat, we arranged for us to participate in Sea World's Dolphin Interaction Program. For a pretty penny, we received an educational seminar on dolphin biology and physiology, followed by a half-hour, structured swim with a dolphin. Finally! It wasn't Florida or a therapeutic program, but it was a chance for Michael to benefit in a small way from time spent with magical dolphins!

Our morning rendezvous with the dolphins at Sea World was complicated by construction near the commercially named *Dolphin Cove*. In order to get to our appointment with Flipper's progeny on time, we were required to take a very long trek all the way across the Sea World campus. In wet suits. During a peak tourist season. I am not a small woman, and I'm positive I felt that cosmic two-by-four whack my outstandingly large *tuchus* as we walked by the sign that might as well have been announcing my arrival: *Shamu Stadium*.

Our dolphin was named Pepper. Pepper was instructed to wave hello, wave goodbye, and to roll over and let us feel her smooth, rubbery skin. Michael was terrified and spent the entire time shivering in Jim's arms. As a ten-year-old, he had no trouble saying, "Make the big, scary dolphin go away." Speech had not passed by Michael after all. Pepper also spoke to us, chattering away with a few clicks and whistles on the trainer's command. "You silly people!" I imagined she was saying. "Leave me alone, go home, and have a snack!" The half hour flew by. As I stood in the dressing room changing out of my wet suit into civilian clothes, I sobbed, not sure if I was elated or horribly depressed.

The rest of the day, we watched dolphins, whales, otters, and sea lions perform for us at Rocky Point Preserve, a concrete enclosure costumed with big rocks and man-made waterfalls. We waited for the hourly appearances of dolphins who lollygagged around the sides, pushed their noses out on to the rim and begged for fish, which tourists readily supplied. Sometimes a lone dolphin would swim in wild frantic circles, leap into the air, clicking and squealing indecipherably, and splash back down, soaking anyone—like me—who hadn't the sense to move out of the way. Afterwards, I stood dumbly in the damp San Diego twilight with salt water dripping from my hair realizing that I knew nothing as I listened to Michael and Edie talk up a storm—more about how hungry they were and how they wanted to go back to our motel and watch TV than anything magical about dolphins.

♦ ♦ ♦

Between his large tongue, small soft palate, and sometimes-discombobulated syntax, listening to Michael is a commitment of time and love, but it is always worth the effort. I know that everything my son Michael says is profound and of indescribable importance whether a listener understands him or not. I know that if people choose to take the time and listen to Michael—really listen—they will discover a charming, funny, smart young man with not only a humongous, impressive vocabulary, but a tremendous capacity for intricate, abstract thought. For instance, when I ask Michael why he wants to know something, he replies, *"Just curious, Mom."* When I tell him that we can't go out to dinner for the fourth time in a week, he replies, *"That's absurd, Mom."* The other day I muttered a frustrated "dammit" under my breath when I dropped my keys; Michael quickly, and with a devilish smile, appropriately added on a quick "Janet" to my "dammit." Someone uneducated in the ways of Dr. Frankenfurter may have deemed Michael's "Janet" as a misnomer, but my family has watched *The Rocky Horror Picture Show* and danced the "Time Warp" enough times that we know "Janet" to be part of a perfect, albeit twisted, repartee.

Michael "gets it." Some linguists assert that it is imperative to teach Standard English and all its accompanying rules and regulations concerning "correct" grammar, syntax, usage, etc., as an *additive* communicative system, and not as a system that *replaces* the native communication one uses, say with family and friends. As a parent of a child with special needs, I wholeheartedly accept that precept. Why? Because Michael uses some words a bit "incorrectly." He tells the same waiters who struggle to decipher his orders in restaurants that his mother and father are "drunk" and "selfish." Jim and I are neither of those things, yet Michael feels not a whit of linguistic insecurity while endowing us with those adjectives. Of course, the waiters are left with the task of figuring out whether to listen to (and maybe report to social services) the inebriated, egotistical parents or to the child who just ordered two "ufos" with macaroni. But things generally improve for all involved. Usually, after Jim and I are introduced as "drunk" and "selfish," Michael then commends us as "geniuses," and sometime before the restaurant closes, we all get our food, eat, and are satisfied. We've all listened, and we've all been heard. And the waiters get a very nice tip.

Running

Before it happened, the day was bucolic. I stood on the dewy September lawn in back of the synagogue drinking cream soda and eating a bagel shmeared with cream cheese. Michael, who was three years old, was sandwiched between Jim and me. Jim was in a neck brace, still recovering from an accident. A month earlier, he, Nathan, Sean, and Joedy had been in a roll-over on I-25, while driving home from a day at Water World; at the time, I was at home with Michael and Edie. After the accident, the kids were black-and-blue from seat-belt bruises, and Jim was left with a compression fracture of his fourth vertebrae. They were still achy and sore, but on that September day, they were happy to be alive, in the sun, on the grass, at the Temple.

Between noshes on my bagel, Jim, Michael, and I waved goodbye to my four oldest children as they trotted off to their indoor classrooms for the first day of Hebrew school, to learn their *alef-bet*, how to *daven* (pray), and the meaning of *tzedakah* (charity), so that dropping their allowance quarters in a charity box every *Shabbat* and each Sunday would make sense. The Rabbi stood in the middle of a swaying circle of parents and sang a lilting prayer, blessing the arrival of such a lovely morning and celebrating the future of the Jewish people, our children. A few mothers actually stopped gossiping, listened, and wiped a tear from their eyes. At any minute it would not have been impossible for all the men around me, their heads covered in a rainbow of yarmulkes, and women whose bare toes peeked out from Birkenstocks, to ask me to join hands and sing *Kumbaya*; actually, more likely, someone would start humming *Hava Negila* and pull me into a reeling *hora* (dance). Like I said, it was bucolic. Honestly, if the great *Saturday Evening Post* illustrator Norman Rockwell had a Jewish sensibility and painted *shtetls* and *yeshivas* instead of baseball fields and turkey dinners, the scene would have been a worthy muse.

Anyway, my hand perpetually rested upon the nape of Michael's neck; Jim's hand lay continually on his shoulder. I remember thinking how the next week, our youngest boy, this child we both touched, was set to begin secular pre-school in a small, family setting. Life was good. And then the unthinkable happened. I don't remember why my hand moved from Michael's neck—perhaps it was to dab at my own eyes with a tissue. And Jim can't remember why his hand simultaneously slipped from Michael's shoulder. But one second Michael was glued to us, and the next he was gone.

"Jim," I sputtered, pointing to the now empty space between my hip and Jim's thigh, "Where's Michael?" Our eyes met, glazed with shock.

"I'll go out!" Jim squawked already in motion.

"I'll go in!" I blared over my shoulder.

I raced through the synagogue, pushing aside my fellow Jews with less-than-holy shoves, as Jim bolted through the outside gate and around the hexagonal building; we met in the front parking lot. There, we watched Michael's black head-of-hair bob up and down, weaving in and out among parked cars as he headed, in a full tear, toward Drake Road, a major street congested with traffic. I wished there had been time to call out to our beloved Rabbi (who by now was walking toward us to see what was the matter), and beseech him, "*Rebbe*, please say a blessing for our dear child, to protect him from the evil eye and the Chevy Suburbans," but all that spewed forth from my mouth was "Oh, fuck!" and "G-d dammit to Hell!" Even Jim, a tender man who, when perturbed, actually says things like "good-gravy," "egad," and "dog-gone-it," was yelling his worse cuss phrase—the ones he saves for tragic situations—as a horrified, "*Oh, crap!*" exuded from his lips.

Though gentle, Jim is neither small nor weak. He stands six-feet, two-inches and, on a good day, he's a solid two hundred pounds of muscle and brawn. Thank G-d for that. Had he been less of an athlete, his broken neck might have been an impediment to his speed. He's always been a powerful sprinter, and that day he probably set an Olympic record as he tore, yarmulke flying, after our baby boy. Two steps into Drake Road, Jim grabbed Michael by the shirt, heaved him back to safe ground, swung him up over his shoulder, and headed to our car. I was right behind, but if I had been alone, or if Jim had not been so fast, there would not have been an adequate prayer to save Michael.

Jim and I agreed, practically with blood and spit, with G-d as our witness, even before our children arrived, that we would never, not for any reason on Heaven or Earth, spank our children. But, as I watched Jim smack Michael's chubby, diapered *tuchus* when he reached the car door, I let go of that vow. I apologized to G-d, but if the sting of a whack on the buns would be memorable and keep Michael from attempting such a trick again, so be it. Jim swung open the door to our station wagon, tossed a sobbing Michael in his car seat, belted him in, and screamed, "You have a timeout, mister!" And then, we both collapsed on a small, grassy slope, crying, shaking and nauseated.

"I . . . almost . . . tripped," Jim spewed between gasps for breath.

"Well . . . fuck the whole pre-school thing," I choked out.

I have a knack for being inappropriately funny at inapt times. It was strange to sit on the damp grass with Jim, both of us laughing at my joke, crying from fear, and feeling shame for losing track of Michael all in one terrifying moment. Michael sat in the car and sobbed, his bottom sore for the first time in his life. But at the same time, I could sense Michael's little brain ominously registering the peculiar excitement of escape. It was portentous. I felt ill.

♦ ♦ ♦

To say I'm tired would be an understatement. Since the birth of my first child, I have not had a good night's slumber. I don't think I've actually even completely shut my eyes. When my oldest son, Nathan, first came home from the hospital, I set my alarm to go off every twenty minutes so I could check on him and make sure he was still breathing. Sometimes, I'd wake him, just to confirm he was alive. His crying was more soothing than his silence; it brought me a modicum of rest. The fact that I became a zombie-mommy was just a minor inconvenience. This vigilance, which some may call paranoid, but I regard as perceptive, became routine for my first four kids. It's eerie; ten minutes before a child would sneeze in the night, I knew the sneeze was coming, and I would already be standing in the doorway with a Kleenex to offer. One hour before one of my darlings would wake with the stomach flu, I already had the barf-bucket at the side of their bed. Jim will tell you this is because I am just hyper-prepared for any given crisis, pointing out the first-aid kit I carry with me to travel from our house to the grocery store; regardless, I stand by my belief that you never know what might happen between home and Safeway. So, despite Jim's erudite observations, I protested and claimed security in my maternal instincts, my ability to sense danger, my parental, preemptive talents. I was bleary-eyed, but I had sure footing as far as my motherly duties were concerned.

Michael's arrival, however, wrestled that confidence to the ground and forever since has held me in a paranormal half-nelson. Michael has contributed mightily to my pre-existing repertoire of neuroses; I've grown accustomed to the constant crick in my neck and the fluttery twitch in my left eye because I always need to know his exact location. I'm not a hovering kind of mom. Really. My kids all had remarkable freedom; they flew in planes, drove on the freeway, and ate fast food. It was different with Michael, though. He was a healthy kid, who just happened to learn most things at a slower rate and have fewer inhibitions than your typical (whatever that means) kid. I fought hard to assure his complete inclusion in every facet of life, from school to recreation, but even I could not ignore some realities. I sat in rooms, at social gatherings, with parents of kids who have Down syndrome, some of us actually connected to our children with leashes. When we met, tables and chairs blocked the exits. These parents' faces were weary, and each pair of feet was tucked into running shoes. There is no scientifically proven correlation between Trisomy 21 and the desire to flee, but most parents will concur, nod their heads in universal agreement (if they have the energy), that their kids with Down syndrome like to run. Run *away,* that is.

♦ ♦ ♦

I understand Michael's penchant for running away. He and I share this need; it is our own special connection. At four, I packed my Barbie suitcase and announced I was leaving because I wasn't happy. Before I left, my dad said he would miss me and admonished me to be careful. My mom asked me if I packed clean underwear. I sat on the front porch for half an hour, and when my stomach began to growl, I went back inside and assured everyone I forgave them for whatever it was that compelled me to abscond in the first place. Then I asked for a bologna sandwich. About a week later, I packed another bag and, without declaration, moved into the backyard doghouse with my 120-pound German Shepard, Lady. My mother hollered and hollered my name, but as far as I was concerned, I had left. For good. It was amusing to watch my mother scour the surrounding yards in an effort to locate me. But again, I got hungry.

I popped out of the rickety wooden shelter and announced, "Here I am! Can I have a Pop-Tart?"

My mother, her face ashen and her fists digging into her hips, screamed, "Sonofabitch! Where the hell have you been?"

I explained that I'd run away.

"What? To live with the dog?" she yelled.

"Yep," I confirmed. "I knocked on Lady's door and she invited me to stay."

My mother's hands dropped to her sides in defeat. "Come inside," she said. "I'll make you a bite to eat."

Later, in junior high, I flew the coop a couple of times, dressed for the occasion in my red-and-white pom-pom girl uniform. I'd camp out at a construction site near our house until it got cold and dark. Mom always had dinner waiting; she knew I'd come home. For some reason, my mom and I would always fight on the days I had to wear my pom-pom uniform. There's something disconcerting about watching your daughter trot off to school with her behind barely covered. It made us both uncomfortable, I think. All through junior and senior high, I would play hooky, skip classes in the middle of the day, board city buses, and ride them to the end of the line and back. Sometimes I'd drop in on my mom at work. "Hey, honey," she'd say, and then quietly ask, "Bad day?" I'd shrug my shoulders and she'd take me out to Long John Silver's for fried hush puppies and green jello. Mom hid the truancy slips from my dad. She knew that I needed an occasional hegira.

At eighteen, during a summer break from college, I packed three suitcases full of clothes, called a cab, and announced to my dad that I was leaving because I had become territorial and desired my own space. "Where exactly are you going?" he queried. "Dunno. Somewhere," I replied. He promptly emptied the suitcases and told me they were his property. I stuffed my clothes into King Sooper's paper sacks, while he cancelled the cab. I rescheduled the cab. He cancelled the cab. Finally, with his hand on the phone he looked me in the eye and yelled, "At least run *toward* something, kiddo, instead of always running away and dodging life!" I picked up my paper bags, trudged upstairs to my bedroom, unpacked, fell on the bed, and wept.

I still run, but since that day, I always run with a purpose. I know Michael will eventually find a purpose in his running. And, like me, he will never go far, or for long, and will always return. But I have an odd sort of wanderlust. I run to Walgreens at three in the morning, sit on the floor, and read tabloid magazines. I run to Barnes & Noble at ten o'clock in the evening and read all of Ginsberg's poetry. I run to Super Wal-Mart at midnight and look at cheap furniture. I run to the park at dusk and watch the swings sway in the wind. I run to Horsetooth Reservoir at dawn and guess the depth of the water. I run to travel agencies and plan trips to Tahiti. I run to prestigious neighborhoods and pretend I'm rich. I run to trailer parks and count the front yard whirligigs. I run to empty stadiums and cheer for ghost teams at the top of my lungs. I run to my bathroom, lock the door, put on tons of make-up, and wonder what it feels like to be pretty. I run toward *something* every day. Michael will, too. We are the same.

♦ ♦ ♦

It's odd to think that just one year before Michael pulled his shenanigans at the synagogue, we sat in an orthopedic surgeon's office worried that, at age two, Michael had yet to take a step. I should have seen what was coming. Even without walking, he was incredibly mobile. Just by crawling, Michael had perfected the art of hiding in laundry hampers, in kitchen cupboards, in toilets, in empty boxes, and under beds. I stopped needing exercise; worrying became aerobic. The moments spent seeking him out provided enough rapid heartbeats to make me a model cardiovascular specimen. I put locks on the refrigerator and freezer even though Jim promised me that modern appliances had inside latches that assured easy egress if trapped inside; I wasn't going to take any chances.

Still, I wanted Michael to walk. We set up a vigorous routine of activities that naturally integrated physical therapy, like swimming and mom-tot gymnastics. I even engaged in questionable parenting by setting up Hostess Ding-Dongs across the room, telling Michael he could have them only if he walked to them. There's an old Yiddish folk saying: "If you want to give G-d a good laugh, tell him your plans." My G-d has been remarkably entertained. Before Michael turned three he truly did learn how to walk. And, very quickly, he began to run. He ran everywhere, all day. He ran in the mall, through the grocery, and to the front of movie theatres to dance while the credits rolled. He ran in the direction of hotel elevators, stairs, crosswalks, and sink-to-sink at the dentist's office. I lost all shame. When Michael would run and disappear in Target, I would stand in the middle of the Misses' section and unabashedly shout *"Michael!"* at the top of my lungs, until he would emerge from a rack of clothes dressed in women's panties and coyly exclaim, "Peek-a-boo!" Sometimes I could actually hear G-d giggling.

Jim has the enviable talent of being able to stick his fingers in his mouth and produce an ear piercing, uniquely distinguishable whistle—a very nifty skill for a married father of five. Wherever we go as a family, if we become separated, all Jim has to do is continually whistle, like a human foghorn, and we all eventually gravitate back to his high-pitched beacon. Our whole neighborhood knows Jim's whistle; it took on a new meaning, however, when Michael discovered running. Michael would wait until we were occupied with cooking, homework, bathing, or day-dreaming, and then, he would make tracks. Someone, a sibling or parent, would try to manage the initial fright and shakily announce, "Michael is gone." Whoever was home would calmly disperse on bikes, in cars, or on foot, Jim whistling the whole time. Sometimes, if it was early in the morning, I canvassed the blocks barefoot in a sheer nightgown; there was no time to dress. No one seemed to care. Neighbors, having heard Jim's whistle, would come out of their homes and join the search. Michael would be found in any number of places: in a tree, under a bush, visiting a friendly dog, ordering a Popsicle from the ice cream man, on his way to Rolland Moore Park, or at the neighborhood pool.

Michael loves the pool. All my kids were competitive swimmers and swim team was our second family. Whenever Michael ended up at the pool, someone would take over, give me a call, and bring him home. At swim meets, all I had to do was yell, "Where's Michael?" and hundreds of people would immediately start climbing fences, poking under towels, checking showers and combing the concession-stand. He was always located within minutes. Finally though, with the potential of drowning heavy on my mind, I sternly told Michael he could not ever go to the pool without me. He was not happy. He was so unhappy, he called 911, a skill I had taught him just a week earlier, and reported to the operator in a sorrowful voice, "My mom is very mean." A fire engine and two police cars arrived at my house to investigate. Michael explained to our friendly Fort Collins paramedics and law enforcement officials that the reason he called was because I wouldn't take him swimming. For a second, his running seemed preferable to his new talent of dialing the phone.

The first time Michael vanished after dark was a full out mêlée of panic and dread. Jim woke me up, around eleven, quivering, and said, "I can't find Michael." We looked everywhere. Inside. Outside. In the back yard. In the front yard. Around the block. In the closets. Just as we were ready to call the police, we heard a little peep from our daughters' bedroom. "Here I am!" Michael had climbed into the top bunk to sleep with his oldest sister and hidden under the covers. It became imprinted in cement that nights were no longer meant for relaxation. My eyes consistently felt as if they were held open by toothpicks. It was official: I'd never really sleep again.

◆ ◆ ◆

I'm not a litigious person. Bad things happen, and I believe most of them have no direct source to blame; they are usually the result of unfortunate meetings of mistimed events. But before the start of kindergarten, I became a little tense. Every year, in the months before a new school year, my kids got physical exams. After the poking and prodding, I paid the doctor while they sat, recovering, in the waiting room. The spring afternoon of Michael's pre-kindergarten check-up, he didn't agree with the sitting part. In the time it took to swipe a credit card, he was gone. A bearded, bespectacled man stood peeking out the blinds of the office window and muttered "Well, look at that! A little Down's boy is running away!"

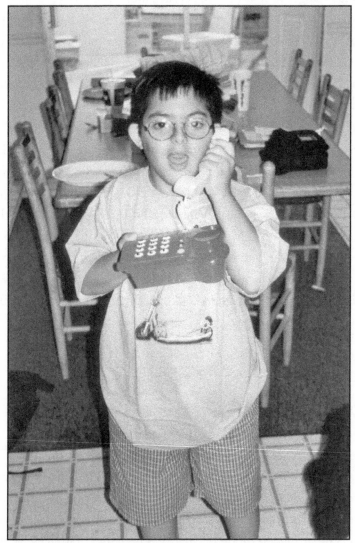

Michael (age 10) practicing how to call 911 on a toy phone

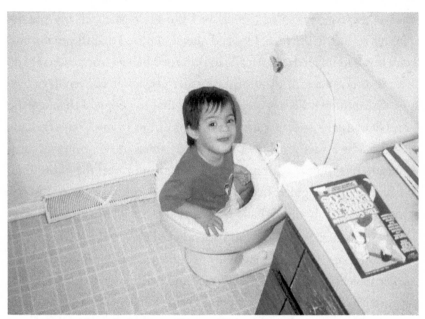

Michael (age 2) showing off one of his many creative hiding places

"Holy shit!" I shrieked and dashed out of the building to catch my wayward child. At this time in my life the actual physical act of running had become very difficult for me, but run I did. It was also the time of my life when I was desperately seeking alternative medical solutions to unsolvable medical problems. That week it had been recommended to me by an unconventional healer that my choice of an underwire bra was contributing to my lack of good health. I burned my bras that night. What I didn't consider was the fact that nary a soul would wish to see me walking, let alone running toward them without the constraints of a bra. As I ran after Michael, my breasts were hitting me in the face. I looked ahead, relieved that three cars and a city bus had formed a barricade to prevent Michael from entering the street. It was not a funny moment, but all those involved were trying to stifle their guffaws. Flying breasts will do that to people. I thanked the Good Samaritans with my arms crossed in front of my body. Perhaps they thought I was praying. I buckled Michael in our minivan, and we headed for home, with me blubbering at the wheel the entire time as I repeatedly imagined his lifeless body underneath a car or thrown across a street. I shouldn't have been driving.

The very next week, Jim and I attended Michael's Pre-K, Individual Education Plan (IEP) meeting with his new teachers, principal, social worker, psychologist, and both physical and occupational therapists. All of us squished into a teeny-tiny room, in chairs that left us knee-to-knee, around a big rectangular table. I had only one thing on my mind: I had to communicate—no—I had to shove down their throats the fact that Michael was bound to run away. I told the story about him running from the doctor's office, sans the part about my breasts. I needed them to join my campaign of hyper-awareness and über-cautiousness. I now know that I became every educator's nightmare parent. I insisted that a gated fence be built around the school, preferably one that Michael could not unlatch, and that they provide an extra para-professional. The principal explained the ins-and-outs of inadequate funding and suggested I come to school and take over a staff member's Xeroxing duties so they could more capably watch Michael. The special education teacher, who later became a close friend, asked if we might consider training our Border Collies to herd Michael on the playground.

After a brief moment of silence, Jim asked, "Are all the other children herded at school? Wow! Is herding a school tradition?"

I quickly jumped in and, while miming the action of weighing things on a scale, asked the principal, "Mmmmm . . . pursue creative financing or face a lawsuit . . . what to choose . . . what *to* choose . . ."

We were inexcusably obnoxious. I look back at our behavior and cringe. At the time, however, I would have done anything to keep Michael from running. Anything.

Despite our ugly aggression, it was promptly agreed upon that a fence would be erected and a Para would be hired. When the meeting ended, I took flight, ran *toward* Baskin-Robbins, ordered a banana split, and stuffed my face, unsure if I was ashamed, relieved, or both.

◆ ◆ ◆

The summer before Michael entered kindergarten, I decided to go on the lam. It was planned and had spousal approval, but it was running away, nonetheless. Before we journeyed on a family vacation to Disneyland, where Goofy, Pluto, and I (in my pajamas) roamed the halls of the Disneyland Hotel looking for an elusive Michael, and after my family traveled to the badlands of Montana in a rented motor-home to camp with Jim's five million Irish-Catholic cousins and two priests on their ancestral O'Connor family ranch, I wanted one week for myself. I flew out to Coos Bay, Oregon for a writing workshop with the poet Marvin Bell. I stayed at Captain John's Motel and filled the mini-fridge with yogurt and apples. In the morning, I sat upon huge, slippery rocks, pulled off my shoes and dipped my toes in the icy water. I walked the sandy cove before dinner and skimmed rocks into the bay. I watched seaweed float. I was silent, intentional, and feeling very poetic as I read

Robert Frost and tried to write in the styles of Marge Piercy and Rita Dove. I pretended to be literate.

When Jim called me in my snug little room, the glug-glug of waves hitting the pebbly shore clearly audible outside my window, I assumed it was to see how I was enjoying my respite. He sputtered out a few niceties, a little small talk, and then, he sprang the news. That morning, around seven or so, Michael left the house on his red tricycle, crossed a busy street and found his way to my friend Roni's house. He declared he was hungry and was hoping she could feed him breakfast. Roni called Jim, waking him up.

She chirped, "Good morning, Jim! How's Michael?"

Jim, responded, a bit groggily, "He's great. Sound asleep."

Roni seized the moment, suggesting to Jim, "Do me a favor and check on him, okay?" Jim complied—there is not a being on earth who argues with Roni. Of course, Michael's bed was empty. He ran back to the phone, praying that Roni's sometimes warped sense of humor was at play.

"Roni . . . " he began to implore, his voice cracking.

Roni interrupted with a terse, "Calm down. He's with me. We're having pancakes."

That evening, I skipped the nightly poetry reading and, instead, ducked out to a little restaurant overlooking the bay. A freshly-caught fillet of salmon, rice pilaf, and steamed vegetables were placed before me, but I was more enamored with my bottle of white wine. It poured beautifully, the sunset catching the rim of my glass, the sparkle of my wedding ring bouncing off the walls as the goblet touched my lips over, and over, and over. Sated and tipsy, I walked back to Captain John's, glad for the brisk sea mist. I changed into my robe, sat down on the bed, picked up the phone, and changed my plane reservations. Even in Coos Bay, I could not sleep; I left three days early, and did not travel solo out of the state for many years after. When I got home to Fort Collins, Jim installed keyed deadbolts we could lock from the inside on all our exterior doors.

◆ ◆ ◆

Elementary school was a cacophony of wonder and terror. Michael would hide in the temporary buildings, conceal himself in bathroom stalls, run away from teachers on the playground, and slip out of class. Yet, at the same time, he grew and matured and told all the right people when a good friend got into a strange car. He learned how to do TouchMath—a licensed program that uses multisensory approaches to teaching— how to read, and how to play soccer at recess. Most of the time, he was a good boy. As the years progressed, so did Michael. He ran less and less. When he did take off, it was at least with a purpose; he would leave the library to visit the principal; step away from the cafeteria line to check on a friend in the nurse's office; or, while on an errand for a teacher, he'd go give one of the school's therapy dogs a treat. His running was no longer aimless, albeit thrilling meandering. Michael was running in a specific direction. I still didn't trust him, though.

Toward the end of Michael's elementary school career, his Grandpa Russ died. Michael was sad and confused. I worried he might revert back to old habits as he often did in bad times: stress meant wetting the bed, sucking his thumb, and talking like a baby. To celebrate Grandpa's life, all the Hulings traveled to Bayfield, Wisconsin and then to the family cabins on Sand Island in Lake Superior. The island is a rugged, sticky, uninhabited, dense forest of trees and flora. It is either stifling hot or bitter cold, depending on the season. We were there in midsummer, but it was still damp and chilly. Scattered across the island are various rustic cabins the family has built over the years. We had a magical time, with frigid dips in the lake, good food, fine wine, cold beer, bonfires, silly songs, fireworks, and tales of Hulings' lore. When we retired to our cabins, with only moonlight and the stars to guide us, I was acutely aware of the rumored bears that rustled in the brush; no one heard them but me. I knew, given the adventurous treks we'd taken across the island and the sailing we had done that morning, Michael would be tempted to explore on his own that night. Explore, with bears as company.

I do not lie to my children. I tease and I make up absurd stories that I later recant, but I don't lie. I withhold information they do not need, but I do not lie. I avoid answering some difficult questions by responding with my own questions, but, again, I do not lie. However, the image of Michael's entrails hanging from a brown bear's mouth convinced me that sometimes a good old-fashioned lie is a good thing. Before we climbed into our cots and covered up with sleeping bags, I took every shoelace from all our shoes, securely knotted them into one long rope, fashioned it into a belt, tightly fastened it around Michael's waist, and then wrapped the rest around my chunky waist. Then, I told a very big lie. I took the thing I knew Michael was most terrified of and I used it to my sick advantage.

"Michael," I whispered as he snuggled up to me trying to get as comfortable as two people tied together can get.

"What, Mama?" he murmured back.

"Michael," I continued, "There are many, many, many monkeys on this island." Chuckles filled the room.

"Shut up, everyone," I insisted.

They knew I was serious and suppressed their laughter. Michael was crying. I do not know why, but he was and still is horrified by monkeys. He cannot watch *George of the Jungle* without requiring the hall light on at bedtime for the next month. I pressed forward.

"If you leave the cabin, Michael, the monkeys will get you."

Michael trembled. The rest of my kids soon fell off to sleep, as did Jim, but Michael and I stayed awake all night; he listened for monkeys, and I made sure he stayed tied to my body. In the morning I stole away and stomped down the worn trail that led to the beach, entreating G-d to forgive me for my lie.

◆ ◆ ◆

The family getting ready for a frigid dip in Lake Superior off the shore of Sand Island, where Kathryn told Michael (age 10) there lived many, many, many monkeys (Clockwise from bottom left: Michael, Jim, brother Sean, cousin Danny Kramer, sister Joedy, Kathryn, sister Edie)

It is said that Jesus lived with his mother until he was thirty years old before he ran off—with her blessing, I imagine—toward something new. If it was good enough for Jesus, I think it might work for Michael. After all, they're both nice Jewish boys. Jim has built an eight-hundred-square-foot addition onto our house with his own two hands. It is a creation of love. We actually had a barn-raising complete with pizza and beer when the frame went up; it was more than just extra square footage that made us rejoice. The new walls gave hope, committed us all to the future. The security of the walls tempered our desires to run. I cannot regularly negotiate stairs anymore, and the new space lets me do most of my living on one level. It also freed up our entire garden level for a sort of bachelor pad for Michael to reside in, until he is capable of independent living. I do not know, however, when that will be.

On Michael's first day of seventh grade the kids had to fill out a questionnaire that asked, "Where do you see yourself in ten years?" Michael wrote down that he saw himself in Boulder, where his older siblings attended college. My throat closed up when I read that, for it's bittersweet raising a child with special needs. At first, I wanted Michael to run, unencumbered by limitations. Then I grew weary of always having to chase him. Soon after, I wanted Michael to settle down near me and only run in planned ways, only toward something meaningful and attainable. A dear friend once told me, "You have a forever-child, Kathryn. Cherish him." And I do. G-d knows, I do. But it's a curvy road 'round a perilously steep cliff that I traverse. And sometimes, I have wondered how long Michael and I can run without tripping and falling into a chasm of heartbreak and disappointment when we both fully realize that not everything is possible, or, perhaps, we both discover possibilities we have not yet imagined.

These fears of tripping and falling, and our hysteria over Michael's well-being, subdued after elementary school, but junior high was not without concerns. The school was connected to a park that called Michael's name more than once, and, accordingly, he ran to the slides and the jungle gym, ignoring the staff's demands that he return. The principal, a big bear of a man, was known to show up at these times and give Michael a solid reason—as in six feet, five inches, and 250 pounds close on Michael's heels—to increase his speed and agility across baseball diamonds and jogging paths, dodging and weaving his way to freedom. Often, the staff would have to hide their giggles when Michael left the principal in his wake, bent over, hands on his thighs, trying to catch his breath as Michael hopped on a swing and whooped out in glee. Sometimes being chased is just plain grand. But sometimes it's not.

One very special teacher took the thrill out of the chase. She dedicated her time to insisting that Michael go running with her (she ran in pumps!) around the school's football field until he grew . . . well . . . sick of running. Some concerned citizens (and my neighbors) on a leisurely walk saw Michael's teacher running in her professional finery, dragging Michael along and yelling, "You wanna run? Okay, then. Let's run!" My neighbors called me and asked if I knew about this unusual exercise regimen. I assured them that I did. "Sometimes," I confided in them, "We have to do goofy things to keep Michael safe." Since Social Services never came calling, I figured that my neighbors trusted me and the crazy, high-heeled, running teacher. These creative running drills, and detention, thankfully solved the problem; Michael did, and still does—usually—respond to appropriate consequences. Still, once a day, Michael was hot footing out of class, finding a phone and calling me to make sure I was home, while staff anxiously paced the corridors in search of him. His teachers and I promised that all he had to do was ask and he could call me whenever he wished. He didn't have to be sneaky. He heard us. He asked and called every day, at the same time, for a mommy check-in.

Michael actually loved school. So much so that in seventh grade, in the pitch-black of pre-dawn, he slipped out of the house, without our knowledge, and walked to school, crossing a major thoroughfare. I must have been catching my nightly two hours of tossing and turning. I didn't hear a thing. When Michael discovered the school uninhabited, he turned around, crossed the street again, and came home. The creaking of the door woke up Jim. Most mornings I do not need an alarm. Michael comes into my room, rests his cheek on mine and pats me on the back. "Wake up, Mama," he says. That morning I woke to Jim loudly berating Michael, "Don't you ever again leave this house in the dark! Ever! You could have been hit by a car, or kidnapped by a crazy person!" I wanted to add the potential of encountering monkeys, but Jim seemed in control of the situation. "But, Dad," Michael interrupted, "I left a note." And, he most certainly had. It read: "*dear mom I go to sklo luv Michael.*" At least his running away had become responsible. Still, that day, we installed indoor alarms on all our doors.

There were things that bamboozled me. In the hubbub of junior high, Michael put his sister's car in reverse and backed it down the driveway. He was catching on—there were endless ways to run. Since then, I've had to explain to Michael daily that he will probably never be able to drive. I tell him that instead he has a cell phone, his own computer, a cool bike, a bus pass and maybe, one day, he can even get a Moped. In the meantime, Jim has arranged times to visit a go-karting facility where Michael drives himself silly, without danger. There, he is just like all the rest of the adult world, driving in circles, going nowhere in particular, just enjoying the rush of speed and the illusion of breaking away.

And the rush of life began to offer more tangible treats. Michael had his first girlfriend in junior high. She was a darling, complex motor mouth with significant developmental delays. When the two of them entered a room, the chance of hormonal combustion was entirely possible. He was a walking erection and she was in the middle of blossoming. Michael couldn't take his eyes off her chest; they'd known each other since kindergarten, and Michael was well aware that something about her had changed. Their inhibitions were freewheeling with a definite unpredictability. It was just like any other, normal junior-high romance, but safer. These two were always being watched. Always. At school they held hands underneath coats. She called on the phone five times a day to remind Michael what he needed to bring to school, what his schedule looked like, and how much she adored him. Before Michael hung up from their conversations he cooed a soft "Goodbye." We never left them alone, even though their relationship was akin to something one might see between second-graders on the playground. Their boyfriend-girlfriend status was brief; they quickly returned to just being pals. Nonetheless, life had irrefutably transformed; Michael now had solid motivations to run, aside from the sheer, kinetic joy of movement; he had people to see, places to go, and an adolescence to explore.

One bleary junior high day, Michael was home sick from school. I gave him ginger ale and crackers, tucked him in on the downstairs futon to watch cartoons, and retreated to my room to study. I closed the door, something I usually only do when Jim is home. Ten minutes later, the phone rang; it was Michael's high-heeled teacher, Tracy. "Kathryn," she said reassuringly, "Don't worry. Michael's with me." As the mother of teenagers, I had navigated the twilight zone a few times before, but this time I was completely lost. "Tracy," I replied, "Michael is downstairs watching cartoons." I was wrong. Barefoot and sneezing, he decided he felt better, decamped, and returned to his academic haven and his favorite teachers. Tracy drove him home, and I greeted him with a hug. I pleaded, "Please don't scare me like that, Michael. Please don't run away anymore." He tucked his head under my chin. "Oh, honey," I sighed, "I'm just exhausted."

♦ ♦ ♦

G-d willing, Jim and I will grow old. We have planned for this. Before we can't remember our names, our children own stock in Depends, and the only way to describe us is as positively balmy, we are going to buy a little condo for Michael and the woman he marries. It will be across the street from the neighborhood we call home, from the house Jim and I want to die in. Before we're too forgetful, we'll help them set up housekeeping and we'll get them a dog. We'll disable the stove and teach them how to live a microwave life. We'll take care of all the governmental red tape and jump through fiery hoops so they can receive services, Medicaid, and support when we are no longer able to serve. We know that, eventually, someone else will have to help them balance their checkbooks and grocery shop. A trustee will manage their special trust fund so they can take a trip to Florida or Disneyland. Good people will have to make sure Michael and his wife go to movies, compete in Special Olympics, eat at their favorite restaurants, get bi-annual dental exams and yearly physicals, get their flu shots, bathe regularly and cut their toenails. Benevolent bosses will have to patiently guide them on how to get to work on time. Michael's four siblings will be named as his joint guardians and assure all is well. That's what our will instructs.

Of course, Jim and I will take care of Michael as long as our bodies cooperate. But age will get the best of us. Still, I will occasionally run away from home with a purpose: Michael's condo will be so close that if I put on an attractive housecoat, preferably with a daisy flower print, a pair of taupe, knee-high hose, and a pair of fuzzy yellow slippers, I will be able to steer my mobility scooter across Taft Avenue on a chilly evening to deliver challah and chicken soup to Michael if he has the sniffles. Remember, he is my forever-child. His wife, no doubt, will be annoyed when I show up on their porch because she and Michael will be busy having sex for the fourth time that day. Later, though, she'll be happy not to have to make dinner.

One day I will die. I imagine all my children and Jim gathered 'round my deathbed, hopefully giggling over some extremely dirty joke I just told. I don't want tears. I will take each child's hands, and for the last time, like all Jewish mothers do, I will tell them exactly what they should be doing with their lives and that each of them is my favorite child in their own, special way. I suppose that for the first moment in many decades my lids will feel too heavy to keep open. But before they shut for the last time, I will open my eyes wide, take one last look, and whisper, "Where's Michael?" But no one will scatter to seek him out.

No. It will be Michael's voice that answers. "Mama," he'll say as he lays his cheek against mine and drapes his arm across my back, "I'm right here." And then, with nowhere left to run . . . I'll go to sleep.

Swimming

There is a certain look that can be passed from one mother to another; it is a singular look, and it is saved for specific moments. It is not a pleasant look. It is more like a sneer of contempt. A scoff. The upper lip slightly curls, and teeth are not quite bared—still, the possibility is real that fangs may appear—the eyes redden and then close into razor-sharp slits, and the chin ever so slightly lifts to expose the pulsation of the jugular vein. This look can be seen at Target when another mother's child pleads and wails like a banshee for a squirt gun. It can be seen at a restaurant when another mother's child has tossed crumbled saltines over the back of the booth into a dining patron's hair. It can be seen at a movie theater when another mother's child moans for Milk Duds and threatens to hold his breath and then throw up if a box is not purchased immediately. Once received, it is unforgettable, for nothing says "you suck as a mother" better than *the look*.

Around 1997, when Michael was six years old, I received a variation of *the look*, en masse, from a sea of females who were simultaneously growling and grunting as they rampaged toward me. Clad in bikinis, one-piece swimsuits and, I think, a sundress or two, they waded—no, they tsunamied—toward me, creating a splashing, cyclonic mess out of the two feet of water that filled our neighborhood baby pool. It didn't help that I started giggling. No, it didn't help at all. For this version of the look transcended the traditional telepathic message, transmitted by the curled lip, slit eyes, and throbbing veins, that I was a sucky mother. The images that were being throttled my way were *the look* times ten with wide gaping mouths and tsking tongues wagging every which way and screaming: "Aren't you going to help your son?" "My G-d, what is *wrong* with you?" "Oh-My-G-d, he's going to die!" This very special look said, "You are a *horrible* mother. *Horrible. And,* you suck!"

Sometimes I have waited until the last minute to help one of my kids who might have been in a jam because I wanted to make sure he/she really needed to be rescued before I swept in to save the day. Maybe that caused some anxiety in my kids. Maybe it also built for them some genuine confidence and courage. Maybe I have misjudged some of my timing in deciding exactly when to step in and lend a helping hand. But I'm not a horrible mother. And I don't suck.

I know that my parenting style is different from the norm. And, in no way do I offer myself up as the paradigm for parenting. Still, I was okay with the multiple *looks* I received when I attended to three-year-old Edie's temper tantrum at *Target*. Edie had thrown herself to the ground in the toy aisle because I said "No" to one of her requests for a *Barbie* or a spinning top or something like that. She threw herself down, flat on her back and, while kicking her legs and flogging her arms at the air, she let out staccato whoops that made her sound as if she were being attacked by a giant, ugly man with knife. I had no choice but to be a good mom. I joined her on the floor, on my back, and I too, kicked and flogged and whooped. Loudly. With zest.

Edie sat up in an instant. "What are you doing, Mommy?" she asked.

"I'm doing what you're doing, Edie," I replied in between my kicks, flogs, and whoops.

Six-year-old Joedy and Jim appeared in the aisle. "See, Daddy? See what Mommy's doing?" Joedy said.

"Yep," Jim replied. "I see. C'mon, Joedy, let's go look at bikes," Jim replied.

"But, Daddy! People are staring!"

"Yep. Mommy once did that for you, too, sweetie. Now, let's go," Jim repeated as he and Joedy left the scene.

Edie watched them leave, her face contorted into a grimace of confusion; her nose crinkled, her brow furrowed and her lips pursed.

"Stop it, Mommy. Everyone is staring. Stop it," she implored. Edie was right. I was in the cross-hairs of many *looks,* from many mothers, from many different directions, all aiming for my heart.

"I'll stop, if you stop," I offered.

"I did stop," Edie pinged in my direction.

"I mean stop forever. As in never, ever, ever do this again," I ponged back.

"Okay, Mommy. Okay. Just get up!"

Edie never kicked and flogged and whooped again. Never. Jim and I learned that parenting for our kids needed to be memorable. And meaningful. We solidified that concept once and for all for our kids. We took many, many, many road trips as the kids grew up. Road trips can be painful. And loud. Hair gets pulled, Nilla Wafers fly through the air, names get called, and sweet sing-along lyrics turn into choruses about leaving a bra in boyfriend's car and ninety-nine bottles of poop on the wall. It was entertaining for a while, but Jim and I were carrying precious cargo, and there came a point where the mischief was too distracting. We took action. We selected a sunny summer day on the way to a swim meet to get serious about the kids' behavior in the car. We knew we could count on them to cooperate and act like doo-doo brains. And, as soon as the decibels of naughtiness reached the level of being heard from outside the car, Jim and I pulled the car over and parked. We parked and we began to make out. I'm not talking about a sweet little kiss on the lips or mere lusting into each other's eyes. Nope. I mean the kind of making-out Jim and I used to enjoy in the backseat of his 1967 Camaro when we were in high school. The kind of raunchy, raw, clumsy, unforgettable slipping and sliding of thighs and breasts that precedes teenage sex.

When we were ten seconds in, Nathan, thirteen at the time, began to audibly gag. Sean, twelve, covered his eyes and rocked his body. Ten-year-old Joedy began to lecture. "This is not fair. I wasn't doing anything. I shouldn't have to watch this. Oh, gross, gross, gross," she yakked. Seven-year-old Edie stared and giggled. Five-year-old Michael kept playing with his White Power Ranger. When Jim and I came up for air, Jim asked the kids, "Are you done making this trip miserable?" Too traumatized for words, the kids just nodded. There were many more road trips after that—not one was marred by our kids' silliness going completely out of control.

This sort of parenting works for me. Jim and I have found that when we used these techniques of humor and theatrics, our kids learned something about the importance of how they present themselves to the world and about the natural consequences of acting like an fool. Our methods took more time than, say, a swat to the tushy or the use of harsh language, but the effects were long-lasting and lessons were learned. Our kids were left less than enthralled and somewhat discomfited dealing with our oddness, instead of a sore bottom, a diminished sense of self-worth, or a growing resentment and fear of us as parental units. At times, it was an uneasy trade-off.

And, I have been less than stellar in my parenting. And there was never a good excuse. I regret each instance. Some of my kids, at times, may have thought—as the old joke goes—that their middle name was "G-d-dammit," as in "Edie, G-d-dammit, what the hell were you smoking in the back seat, and who was driving your car?" I also know that I called at least one of them a "little shit," as in, "Joedy, you little shit, I don't wanna go to Walgreens to get you poster board for the project that's due at 8:00 am—it's three in the morning!" And I once threw soft pillows at Nathan when he was about fifteen because . . . well . . . I don't remember why. I just remember the flying pillows, him ducking, and my terrible shame. It is true: I am incredibly flawed and extraordinarily peccable and gloriously imperfect. Still, I have never accepted my parental foibles as tolerable. Never.

Nonetheless, for better or worse, Jim and I never really adjusted our parenting skills for Michael just because he has Down syndrome. When that gang of dripping wet, angry mothers once stampeded toward me across the baby pool, I was simply allowing one of Michael's idiosyncrasies to play out to its logical conclusion. Michael has astounding breath control. That day, he was seeing how long he could hold his breath. He showed me this trick in many venues: the baby pool, the bathtub, with his face in the sprinkler. I encouraged this practice; I knew it would be valuable in swimming. He was never really in any danger—I promise—but my timing may have been off, and my giggling didn't help. Looking back, I suppose that Michael did indeed look stone-cold dead, floating lifelessly, face down, in the baby pool. And even though it's never fun to get the *look,* I loved those mothers by the pool for their über-concern about Michael's welfare. It was, after all, what I had wished for.

◆ ◆ ◆

As a child, growing up in hot California summers, my family didn't have a pool. It seemed like everyone else had a pool. We dipped in the Pacific with jellyfish and sea lions, and we could swim at neighbors' homes, but I wanted to arise at 9:00 a.m., walk out our own sliding glass door, jump into the undisturbed, waveless water of our very own pool and displace molecules of stillness with a sense of ownership. During my teen years in Colorado, I rode my bike or grabbed a ride from my mom to travel two miles from my house to swim at a local pool, but, again, I admit to neon, lime-green envy for the kids who only had to roll out of bed and cross the street to take a dip. I know that a swimming pool was—*is*—an unnecessary luxury. Really. I do. Still, I wanted a pool for my kids. I wanted a twenty-five-yard, chlorinated pool with sparkling blue water, a diving well, a high dive, a low dive, and lawn chairs. I wanted it to be filled with beach balls and noodles and rafts and flippers and goggles and endless rounds of Marco Polo; to be surrounded by scantily clad lifeguards wearing Speedos and Oakleys and whistles 'round their necks, and flocks of mothers all looking out for one another's kids. *I wanted a pool!*

And Village West—the neighborhood where I raised my kids—had a beautiful pool. It was the main selling point for us. In 1986, Jim and I made a bid on the cheapest house for sale in the neighborhood. It was small and run down and needed repairs that we knew we could not afford to make. The paint was peeling inside, and the outside paint was an army-green mess spattered on rotting siding. The carpeting was the color of sand and dirt and was marred with cat scratches and the greasy years of heavy footsteps. The garden level bathroom had zebra-stripe wallpaper and checkered linoleum. The windows were single paned, and the slightest wind whistled eerie hisses through them. The fence was decaying and coming apart, and the next strong gust threatened to expose our backyard, which, in actuality, happened several times. We didn't care. We were young, we were in love, we adored our kids, and— praise G-d—Village West had a swimming pool. Until we began the construction on the eight-hundred-square-foot addition to our home in 2000, we managed to raise our five kids in that fifteen-hundred-square-foot, squeaky, tattered house with one working bathroom. We were squished in every space, no one had an iota of privacy, and it was always loud.

But we really loved our pool. Each of my children swam competitively from the ages of five to eighteen for our neighborhood's Village Green Summer Swim Team and for our local senior high during the school year. My kids were pool rats whose skin turned five shades darker in the summer, whose hair turned green and orange and brittle. Jim and I were rat parents, and we had rat friends. We were one big, ratty community. And so, at three months old, Michael became a pool rat, too.

◆　◆　◆

I produced and adopted swimming babies, but I was not a hale and hearty pregnant woman. I miscarried. I spotted. I lost weight from hyper-emesis. I became a gestational diabetic. After Edie, our fourth child, was born, I could not recover. I bled heavily, non-stop, for two and a half years following her birth. This pathological bleeding could neither be explained nor curtailed. When I was twenty-nine, my doctor declared that he found massive fibroid tumors in my uterus—that was the answer, the reason for all that had gone awry. If I was ever to be well, I needed a hysterectomy; I'd tried everything else.

In between this news and my surgery, we adopted Michael. As adoption was my life-long dream, and Jim had agreed to share that dream with me, I experienced minimal grief over losing my ability to conceive biologically. I did need to get well, though. In early May of 1991, when Michael was three months old, I went in for surgery, not knowing that my surgeon was probably flying high as a kite when he made the first incision in my body. I did not know that one year later, he would be put on medical probation for self-prescribing Percocet; or just how many complaints had already been filed against him; or that there was not one fibroid in my uterus; or, that in the end, he would have his medical license revoked. I knew nothing.

The first word I spoke to the Post-OP nurses when I came out of anesthesia was raspy and strained: "Pain," I said. "Pain." And I knew pain. I spent seventeen years as a ballet dancer, bending, splitting, leaping, and twirling my body in unnatural ways as my skin tore and my muscles cried; I'd delivered a 9 lb. 5 oz. baby; I'd had an emergency C-Section; I'd had carpal tunnel—caused by lifting baby carriers with my right hand for years—so bad that I couldn't lift a spoon. When I awoke from that hysterectomy, though, I felt as if a sliver of glass was being raked inside my abdomen, back and forth, up and down, in spirals, and then incrementally plunged into the small of my back.

"Pain," I croaked.

Over the course of five weeks, I became a fixture at my doctor's office.

"I hurt," I said.

"You're fine," he replied.

"I have a fever. I feel like I am being stabbed," I'd repeat.

"You are grieving the loss of your uterus. It's all in your head. Get therapy," he muttered while tapping my chart with his pudgy hand. He prescribed a mild antibiotic and sent me on my way.

And so, I pushed through the pain as I continued to push Michael and Edie's double-stroller to the pool every day, pausing every five minutes to double over. As my vision doubled, I wondered if my grief would also continue to double and double and double. I sat at swim meets watching my older children race and commune with other fish-like people, sprawled out on sleeping bags, playing cards, telling jokes, painting toenails, and grooving to tunes as they waited for their next event. I did not, however, stand to cheer when they hit the water. I knew I might collapse, lose my footing, or audibly wince when the pain shot through my body. I didn't want to call attention to my weakness. I was beginning to think that perhaps the doctor was right; maybe I was insane.

We traveled all four corners of Colorado to attend swim meets. In late July of that summer, we journeyed to Estes Park. As most summer weekends are in Estes, it was temperate with a slight breeze that smelled of juniper and lake water. I had chills. At the Saturday swim meet, I shivered, which is unnatural in the steam and humidity of an indoor pool. At dinner, I cut into my fresh trout and moved the food around my plate. At our rustic hotel, I locked myself in the bathroom and lay on the floor, trying to find a position of comfort. My belly raged and was hot to the touch. I scanned the Yellow Pages looking for Urgent Care medical facilities. As I searched, though, I remembered what the doctor told me, that this—the shivering, the chills, the nausea, and the sore belly—was actually grief; no Urgent Care doctor would be able to help me. While Jim and the kids went to a movie, I stayed in the hotel, silent, hopeless, curled up in the bed.

On Sunday, before we started the drive home to Fort Collins, the kids clamored to go down the Giant Slide at one of the tourist entertainment traps. I felt guilty for not going to the movie, so I agreed not only to go, but to sit my bottom on a carpet square and fly down the peaks and valleys of plastic and steel with them. The ride was swift, almost too swift, and I gained too much momentum. At the bottom of the slide, I ran into what felt like a steel barrier. In fact, it was only the regular padding that everyone hits at the end of the ride. I remember my vision going black for an instant. I tasted salt and bile on my tongue and felt each atom in my body begin to twitch and dig and collide. I stood up from my crash landing and Jim was giggling.

"Jim," I said, 'Let's go home."

"But we have more tokens, more rides—" he resisted.

I stared at him hard. "Home," I repeated. "Now." I do not remember anything about the drive home.

The first thing I did after that hour-long trip was check the fridge and cupboards. "This won't do," I thought. "I am going to die tonight, and the kids will need food." I drove to the grocery and filled a cart with only Ding Dongs and Spaghettios. Home, I pulled in the bags, sat on the couch next to Jim, and went into what I now know is called rigor—severe shaking during a high fever that can actually cause damage to muscles and unintentional biting of the tongue. Jim had never seen rigor before. He thought I was cold and poured me a hot bath. When the shaking became worse, he put me to bed and took my temperature. 106 degrees. We did not call a doctor because I thought I was insane, and Jim comes from a background that values self-care and working through even the worst of illnesses on one's own. So he brought me cold cloths and a handful of Advil. When I drifted off, he thought I felt better, and he, too, went to sleep.

In the morning, he found me in a fetal position. I only moved to vomit. I remember deciding to die. I was an animal. I wanted dark and privacy. I wanted to die, alone. Jim took my temperature. 108 degrees. I heard him on the phone talking and talking. I remember he told me my doctor said that my situation was no longer gynecological; he said I probably had the flu. He told Jim to take me to an internist I'd never seen before. I didn't respond. I was too busy with the act of dying. Jim carried me to the car.

I could not walk or sign papers. I incessantly chattered, trying to make sure Michael didn't catch what I had. All I could think about was that whatever was attacking my body could possibly kill him because, as another side effect of Down syndrome, his immune system was not as strong as a normal baby's. There were tests and whispers and doctor after doctor after doctor pushing on my belly and inserting fingers in my orifices and asking me about the pain. Everyone looked small and distant. I was not crazy after all. There had been a tubal-ovarian abscess the size of a grapefruit in my abdomen. When I hit the bottom of the slide, it burst. I was septic. My entire body—my very bloodstream—was filled with the slime and refuse of a massive, ten-week-old, festering, infection. Before I was rushed into surgery, I told Jim to get the kids to gymnastics that evening and to make sure they didn't miss swim team practice the next morning. I wanted Jim to leave. I didn't want him there when I died. He nodded in agreement with my agitated, foggy demands, but he stayed. Soon after, I was opened from belly button to pelvic bone, and the cleansing began.

Even in recovery, I had no intention of fighting for my life. Something deep inside my very sinew, my cells, told me that my body was ruined, told me that it was not me who had come out on the other side connected to tubes and more tubes. "You are the sickest patient I've ever seen in all my years," said one of my older nurses. Doctors brought medical students on rounds to look at me. "She's a very lucky young lady," the doctors would tell the wide-eyed students. "She's a miracle." Still, I wanted to die.

Jim stood at the side of my hospital bed.

"Get better," he barked. He pushed aside all my tubing and put Michael in my flaccid, hot arms. He sat all the kids on my bed, not caring about the pain caused by the shifting and shuffling.

"Get better. Fight."

He was angry. He was drowning in guilt for not getting me to the doctor earlier, for not refuting the ongoing diagnosis of depression and uterine nostalgia. It would take a while for Jim and me to reconcile his guilt with my eventual anger at him, the world, and my body for what seemed like betrayals of epic proportions. Specifically, it took one evening of my throwing every glass object in our garage at Jim's feet—not particularly caring which one of us got cut—accompanied by an hour of my guttural, primal screams, followed by five years of therapy for me to appreciate that there were no betrayals in my life. I grew to understand that I was not exceptional, that the universe owes me nothing, and that all bodies are imperfect. This could have happened to anyone. I learned that Jim was simply acting out the ancient family script on which he was raised. That script said that when sick, it is best to tough it out and hope for the best.

But that day, in my room at the hospital, he violated the script. Jim barked and yelled. He insisted that whatever was to come, whoever I would become, that I was needed. He graced my arms with Michael, who was only five months old.

"Get better," Jim snarled in my face. "This baby needs you." And in that moment, Michael began to save my life.

Jim then graced my bed with Nathan, almost nine; with Sean, only seven; with Joedy, almost six; and with Edie, barely past two. That was too much grace to ignore. My family needed me. My family saved me.

"This will humble you, Kathryn," said a dear friend when I returned home from the hospital. She was right. In the beginning, I was humbled by the rush of comfort. Those ridiculous people who traipsed with us all over Colorado, who loved swimming pools as much as I do, and who saw reflections of life in water filled with children—those soaking wet folks helped us survive with food and babysitting, rides and love.

My lessons in humility continue. Over the past twenty years, I have been repeatedly operated on to remove internal scar tissue, called adhesions, which can wreak havoc on the body. Adhesions glue organs to the abdominal wall, to each other, and they can cause painful bowel obstructions. All those organs are supposed to slide softly, moistly, past one another. When they don't, the pain can be like living with testicles squeezed in a tightened vice or breasts perpetually stuck in a mammogram machine lined with daggers.

I have been operated on to clear out new abscesses, to remove blood clots, to correct a bowel obstruction, and to cut out more organs that became infected and failed me and were rendered completely useless; luckily, they weren't necessary for life. I still have adhesions, and every day hurts. I also experience partial bowel obstructions. I know what it's like to have the elastic of a waistband or the hem of a cotton shirt that brushes on my abdomen be tantamount to hundreds of wasps stinging and stinging and stinging, digging deeper and deeper and deeper into the tender skin of a baby. My foot makes contact with solid ground and a pulsation of heat, a straight line of derision, aims for my belly and quakes my inner body into spasms of rebellion while nausea leaves the taste of feces in the mouth.

But I refuse any more surgery. I am protecting Michael. Surgery buys me only about six weeks of limited relief, and then it all comes back with a vengeance as the adhesions reform and haphazardly reconnect to places they do not belong. My body is not meant to continually tolerate assaults of scalpels and forceps and the disappearance into anesthesia. So I manage. I wait out my partial obstructions. I pray they will resolve on their own. So far, only one has required me to endure an emergency surgery. I pray they will never become complete obstructions. I keep my fingers crossed.

I am still getting to know the new me. And there are days that feel untenable. In moments of pain that I cannot reconcile, moments that challenge my vow to celebrate even the most terrible days, to daily drop to my knees and give thanks for my children, my spouse, my family, my friends, my dogs, my teaching, my writing, my life—it is then that I spiritually leave for thirty seconds or so, no matter where I am. I take a breath, and sometimes I wrap my arms around my torso to ground me in reality and assure my safe return. I slink behind my eyes, through the retinas, through a viscous place tacky with sand and grit, until I watch a spring of lucid water and gaze at the languid opalescence of lily pads and fairy moss. Then, when my belly sends forth a signal of calm, a synapse of dopamine, I return. A lot can be missed in thirty seconds. More, I have learned, can be gained.

When I am awake, I hold my body in set positions that keep the worst at bay. I take elevators, roll my backpack on wheels, catch rides so I do not need to lift my foot to accelerate or break. Sometimes I hide and curl up into that old fetal ball. But movement of the night, the involuntary tossing and turning and rearranging, is brutal. Some nights, when my abdomen screams, I see a muted apparition of suicide lying between Jim and me. But then I turn on the light and wake Jim. I tell him that the specter of death is haunting me. He responds with a sweet joke to make me laugh—"Does it look like Rick Perry?" Then, before we turn out the lights, he issues a stern admonition, "Don't you dare leave me." In the dark, I stare at the outline of a child's picture on the nightstand, or I listen to Jim's sweet snoring, or I pat the head of a dog who's whimpering while dreaming, or I rise when Michael calls out for a glass of water and, just like I have since he came to me, I bring him a drink to quench his thirst.

When I do sleep, my brain tries to make sense of pain. It tries to protect me, to give me a modicum of rest. Every night, I dream that I am in labor, and my temporal pain is given purpose in the ether of chimera and terror. A baby is born, I hold the tiny form to my breast, I stand, and I place her in a wicker bassinet. I stand, and the pain is still there, even after the baby is born, the placenta expelled, the cord cut. I turn from the bassinet—the baby sleeps—and there is a pool of blue water, still and cold. I walk down concrete steps into the wet, and my feet touch a bottom of smooth sand. I lower into the deep until my thighs are covered, my belly is submerged, and my shoulders are doused. Then I let my head sink under.

◆ ◆ ◆

Michael entered the water early. As an infant, Jim and I would hold him to our chests and bob up and down in the shallow end of the pool. He did not protest, usually because he fell asleep. Michael's siblings were well into the process of freestyle and back floats by the time they were three. Things move at a different pace for Michael. The summer of his third year, I enrolled Michael and myself in a Mom / Tot swim class taught by Marty, a seasoned coach and instructor, and Trevor, an occupational therapist in training at Colorado State University. Marty, Trevor, and I passed Michael back and forth in the shallow end for half an hour. We floated him in front of us, his hands clenched in ours. We cradled his neck and shoulders in our arms and provided the buoyancy he needed to drift on his back. Often, Michael would spend the thirty minutes emitting a low-pitched moan similar to a car that won't start on a cold winter morning. Sometimes, there was nothing low-pitched about his screams. And, his repetition of the word, "No," was hard to mistake as anything but, well, "No!" I kept Michael in the water, though; I don't let my kids wimp out of anything.

The Mom / Tot class became my déjà vu for three summers—that and wading in the baby pool. Finally, in 1997, the same summer that Michael performed the eloquent dead-man's float, I figured with that sort of breath control, he was ready for big boy swim lessons in the big pool. Finally, I could sit in a lawn chair, let its plastic straps leave my rear end indented and sweaty, sip iced tea, shoot the breeze with other moms, and watch Michael learn how to swim. Beginning-level swim lessons at our pool utilized a specific technique. Long steel tables with an adjustable height mechanism were lugged to the edge of the pool and lowered into the shallow end. Tiny children stood on the tables, in the water, and held onto the wall while they waited for instructions on how to place their faces in the water and blow bubbles. The tables removed the obstacle of even the shallow water being too deep for tiny tots to successfully negotiate. It was genius in action.

Marty was Michael's teacher, of course. Things began well. Michael held on to the wall, and his feet remained on the table. He was at the end of the table. The *end*. I was watching, so proud that Michael was in the big boy class, watching his smiling face peek at me over the rim of the edge, my head nodding approval and encouragement in his direction. And then Michael was gone. He stepped off the table—the end of the table—and sunk downwards, silently, except for his thrashing arms. Marty's back was to Michael; he was helping another child. No matter. My voice and about ten other female voices—a high-pitched frenzy of motherly love—spouted in petrified unison: Marty! Marty! Marty! Marty, who, in his blonde haired, blue-eyed, chiseled existence, was quite easy on the eyes, might have thought we were cheering for him. That confusion was quickly shattered as the same ten women, me in the lead, charged the full four feet from our plastic chairs and iced teas to save Michael from certain death. Marty looked up at us and, with a smirk, simply reached down into the water, pulled up Michael by the swim shorts and plunked him back on the table, before I, fully clothed, could jump in and do the same.

All, however, was not well. Michael was physically fine, but the fruits of three summers of Mom / Tot classes and the endless wading and breath holding in the baby pool disappeared. Michael climbed out of the pool and would not get back in. Getting him back in the water was like competing in a tractor pull. If we walked too close to the big pool, Michael dug in his heels and would not budge. If I carried him within close proximity to the big pool, he would grab my neck, dig in his nails, and almost choke me. I had to redefine my views on wimping out. All was not well, that is true, but all was not lost, either. Jim decided to capitalize on the fact that Michael still loved the baby pool.

"Michael," Jim said. "You may not go play in the baby pool until you let me take you into the big pool."

Michael is no fool. When Jim stepped in to fix the damage, he knew which parent he was dealing with. This was Dad that Michael was dealing with. No-nonsense Jim. *The man*. The parent who always means business. "Michael, I'll hold you tight," Jim promised sternly, but lovingly. And he held fast to that oath. Jim took Michael into the big pool, holding him impossibly close to his chest. Each day, Jim added a challenge and a condition.

"Okay, Michael," Jim said. "Today, if you want to play in the baby pool, you need to do whatever White Power Ranger does." Jim took Michael's beloved White Power Ranger action figure and, at first, would just make it splash. Michael, then, would need to let go of his strangling grip on Jim's neck and splash a little. A few days later, Jim would make White Power Ranger put his face in the water. Ditto for Michael. Jim exclaimed how brave White Power Ranger was whenever he did some new water trick. When Michael copied the trick, Jim would extol, "Atta boy! You are so brave!" Soon, Michael and Jim were diving to the bottom of the big pool—in the shallow end—to scoop up White Power Ranger who needed rescuing. Michael's fear evaporated under the guile of games and, of course, bribes. He resumed big boy lessons in the big boy pool four weeks after the steel table incident, but he was not yet a true swimmer.

June of 2001, when Jim's father, Russ, died, was a mournful, bleak time. In late July, the Hulings family, in its extended entirety, gathered in Bayfield, Wisconsin at the home of Mary Rice, one of Jim's cousins, before we all sailed to Sand Island—and threats of monkeys—for a couple days of reflection, introspection, and celebrating Russ' life. There, in Bayfield, something magical happened. Mary's house has a back-porch swimming pool entrenched in the landscape of a slope that tumbles and trips down toward the shore of Lake Superior. It is both surrounded by and spectator to flora I cannot name; I just know it was lush and beautiful and vibrant.

The weather was uncharacteristically cloudy and wet and chilly, but that did not stop Joedy and Edie from taking a dip in Mary's pool. Of course, Michael tagged along, no longer frightened of any depth or expanse of water, but still unable to actually swim; he rode the edge of the pool, never letting go. Jim and I wrapped ourselves in sweatshirts and blankets, sat in some wicker chairs, and watched the kids in the pool on the hill. And then the magic unfolded. The pool was miniature in its size, perhaps only as large as our baby pool in its width, and no more than six feet at its deepest. Twelve-year-old Edie and fifteen-year-old Joedy placed themselves at either end of the pool and took to passing ten-year-old Michael back and forth with gusto. When he arrived in each sisters' arms, they gave him a little swim lesson. Joedy reviewed how to fully move the arms through the water. Edie reviewed how to turn the head to the side, take a breath, and then return the face to the water, blowing out bubbles the whole time. They both yelled at him to kick, kick, kick. Back and forth, sister to sister, until Michael swam. His arms moved over and under, his legs kicked in rhythm, his head turned to the side and returned to face down, and he eschewed his sisters' arms. From edge to edge, Michael swam and swam and swam.

♦　♦　♦

Michael's (age 10) first honest-to-goodness swim with
his sisters at cousin Mary's home in Bayfield, Wisconsin
(Left to right: sister Edie, Michael, sister Joedy)

A year later, at eleven years old, Michael joined the Village Green swim team. The only requirement to join was being able to swim a twenty-five-yard freestyle, with freestyle being the operative word. Thank goodness. Michael could traverse the pool's length at morning practices by executing a crawl / dog paddle / back float / treading water ballet thing-a-ma-jig of a stroke. There: *freestyle*. We had to get permission to allow Michael to swim in the "8 and Under" category at meets since kids his age always swim more than twenty-five-yard races, and that's all Michael could do. Permission was granted, but success did not immediately follow. At meets, Michael jumped feet first into the water—the diving blocks were too scary, too slippery, too high—and was immediately disqualified because his feet hit the bottom of the pool. No matter. The next five minutes were spent watching Michael execute the crawl / dog paddle / back float / treading water ballet thing-a-ma-jig of a stroke with multiple stops to hang on the lane line, wave to me, shout out a "Hey, Dad!" to Jim or, sometimes he put his forehead on the side of the pool and whimpered an unconvincing, "I—am—drowning!" After his five-minute performance, I'd give Michael a high-five and tell him I was so proud. Jim would roll his eyes tell him to stop being a drama queen.

These high jinks, high-fives, and eye rolls continued all summer. At the last home meet, Michael had an air of manliness about him. He strutted to the diving blocks for his heat. He climbed the block on his lane. *The block!* When the starting gun roared. Michael flung his body—*headfirst*—into the pool, landing in a glorious belly flop. And then, he swam. *Swam!* Michael swam a real freestyle crawl. He took breaths by lifting his head up instead of to the side, but no one cared about this tiny technical glitch. The entire swim team and parents and coaches and the whole other team gathered around the pool and started to chant, "Michael—Michael—Michael!" The eight-year-olds finished their races and waited for Michael at the other end. They, too, chanted his name. Michael, having finished his first twenty-five-yard race without touching the bottom, was met with rolling applause, ridiculous cheers, and even a high-five from Jim. The rest of the meet, folks kept on buying Michael treats from the concession stand. Michael received his first ribbon at that meet. It was unofficial and he did not place, but it was his ribbon. Michael now has a box overflowing with ribbons from seven years of swimming for Village Green. The cheers never really stopped.

There was more patience and leeway granted to Michael than any other swimmer in the entire history of Village Green swim team. I thought this was due to kindness and the spirit of inclusion, but later I found out there may have been another reason. A swim team mom once communicated to me that my kids had a *reputation*. Her son was feeling a bit left out of the social circle, and I offered my help and the help of my kids to help him ease in and feel more comfortable.

"Thanks," she said. "It's always so easy for your kids. That must be nice."

"Easy?" I asked. "What's easy for them?"

"Oh, Kathryn," she continued, "Everyone knows that if you mess with one Hulings, you mess with them all!"

I wasn't sure whether to be proud or alarmed that I had raised a gang of thugs. What had happened? I am a pacifist, except for when I am not. I am all for peaceful dialogue and civil disobedience and Rogerian Argumentation. I admit though, that if my kids are threatened, I am ready to rumble. It's primal. Of course I don't actually maul my fellow human being; I always find some common ground in my protective moments. Still, if I had to fight to keep one of my kids alive, I am quite sure I wouldn't turn my other cheek.

My kids are not bullies; I am sure of that. They are not bullies, but they are well equipped to handle themselves in a scuffle. My daughters have told me that often, the first thing they considered when meeting a guy was whether or not they could take him in a leg wrestle, or crush the guy with their thighs. Somewhere along the line, I must have communicated to them that this was important. Michael's brothers are big boys—so is Jim—and while I have never seen them initiate a fight, I have seen them, and their sisters, physically defend folks who have been at the mercy of some tormentor on the playground or a park or a street corner. I didn't chastise them for forming blockades with their bodies. I didn't specifically condone these actions, but I also was okay with the fact that my kids were not content to be oblivious bystanders to oppression and victimization. Somewhere along the line, I must have communicated to them that this, too, was important.

Michael, like all folks with special needs (especially females), could be an easy target of abuse. Fortunately, no one has ever hurt Michael; my other kids made sure of it. All of my other kids' friends and parents have been helpful and supportive; many have even shared with Jim and me that their lives and attitudes about disability were changed by knowing Michael. Michael was always included in everything his siblings did with their "typical" friends—swim team especially. Michael swam, sat on towels, played cards, ate junk food, partied at spirit dinners, and engaged in horseplay. He made friends. Swim team was a model of what inclusion and acceptance can look like. It didn't hurt that Michael's siblings were all lifeguards, too (with Oakleys and whistles but, thank G-d, not Speedos) and all the pool was often under their watchful gaze. But the world as a whole is not as highly evolved as I might wish for it to be. Taunts of "retard" can still be heard on playgrounds across the world, and maybe even at some swimming pools. But Michael has been safe. He's a Hulings, and if you mess with him, you mess with all of us.

◆ ◆ ◆

Michael (age 11) sporting a funky hat and giving another
swimmer a thumbs up at a swim meet

Michael (age 12) and his sister Edie mugging for
the camera at a pre-swim-meet pep rally

Michael (age 15) taking off from the block with his inimitable dive / belly flop

Many of our old friends—our pool rat community—have moved out of Village West into patio homes on golf courses, mountain cabins, condos, or mansions. Some have died. Some remain, but I know nothing of their lives. Jim and I have stayed. We watch as young strangers with pregnant bellies and strollers and puppies and mini-vans and vegetable gardens move in. I am no longer the very young mom with five kids; I am now the sweet, eccentric, pleasantly plump, middle-aged woman who lives on the corner with the barking dogs. I am most often referred to as "Michael's mom." All the names are accurate.

I assume that the folks who nursed us through my near-death have forgotten the whole incident. I say "assume" because in the years since getting sick, I have become a bit of a social hermit. I made sure that my children stayed entrenched in the business of neighborhood life; a child's life without the benefit of community can become void of success. It can end poorly. A child could drown in such loneliness. But not me. I pulled out of communal life, focusing only on caring for my kids, for Jim, for my dogs, for my extended family and a very few friends;

on writing; and on returning to school and teaching to at least keep my head in working order. I pulled away from neighborhood teas and gatherings and chats by the pool with other women. I never returned to the buzz and hubbub of my neighborhood. I realized I had become an uncertain friend; my heart was always in the right place, but I cancelled plans at the last minute, I didn't chat on the phone, and I didn't bake cakes for parties. In the beginning, my pain made me reactive and moody and unpredictable, so I began to hide in my house. I knew I needed solitude to fix myself, so I chose to grow into full adulthood alone. It became a habit—I remain a loner.

I would be grateful if the people from my past have forgotten it all; grateful to not be eternally identified as ill; grateful to be able to help instead of being helped. When I do see folks from my neighborhood at the grocery or on the street, and we wave a perfunctory hello, I never think to remind them of the past. I don't want them to know how that incident still has no physical or psychological end in sight.

Things have changed for Michael, too. Michael's last two swim team seasons were a bit lonely. His siblings had all moved on to other summer pursuits both by desire and logistics (eighteen is the cut-off age for swim team). Plus, swim team goes in cycles. Sometimes it is over-run with teens. Sometimes, it is overrun with a younger set. Michael's last two seasons were in the company of a majority comprised of the ten-and-under crew who could all out-swim him. Michael's friends were mostly the coaches. Still, we didn't let him quit. In fact, Jim took over as the swim team president and navigated the way for Village Green as it changed from a USS Swim Team that, despite its summer-only status, competed against year-round swimmers, to a recreational team that only competes against local teams. It was done. No more trips to Estes Park. No more hotels. No more road trips. The change was needed; swim team numbers rose from the low thirties to over one hundred swimmers.

The old guard had faded. Moved away. Grown old. Grown up. Only Michael, Jim, and I were left. At the end of every summer, swim team has a slide show that recaptures the *oohs* and *ahhs* of the season, with a musical soundtrack and subtitles, ice cream and gooey toppings, and a late night swim. Jim and I produced six years' worth of those slide shows. At our very last slide show, in the summer of 2009, I realized that I hardly knew a soul in any of the pictures. We had been part of Village Green Swim Team for twenty years. The name Hulings remains on the pool's record board; some of my kids still hold some of the fastest times in Village Green history. Still, it was time to go.

Michael's summers are not lonely. He and Casey (his fiancée), spend inordinate hours together. Once or twice a week, they go swimming. Twice, in the past two summers, Michael has feigned drowning and had to be "rescued" by a nubile lifeguard. Maybe he wants the attention. Maybe he misses the cheers. Maybe he wants Casey to rescue him. I don't know for sure. On afternoons when Michael isn't with Casey, Michael occasionally takes solo trips to the pool. He doesn't always swim. Sometime he just sits and listens to music. Maybe he reminisces about his races and friends and his siblings who have all moved away. On one of the rare days that Michael and I went to the pool together, when Michael was twenty, he had a request.

"Mom, I have something to say," he began.

"What's up, Michael?" I asked.

"I want you to sign me up for swim team," he said, looking up at me with serious eyes and a hopeful, upturned smile.

"Oh, Michael," I answered. "Remember? You're all grown up now. You're too old for swim team."

"Oh. Right. I remember," he said.

I watched Michael as he flipped in the water, and I thought to myself, "*I'm* too old for swim team. I'm just too old."

◆   ◆   ◆

Sometimes, in the off-season, on a snowy day, I'll drive to the pool, stand near the entrance, close my eyes and inhale the imagined residue of soda ash and ripped lycra swim caps. I grip the chain link fence and try to convince my body that even though I cannot remember the suppleness of my youth, I still can understand hope. I know that summer always returns. I hear the ricochet of starting guns and bullhorns and shrill whistles and slapped water and cheers still chiming inside the cracks of the walls. In this landscape of grass and trees, of brick and wood, all surrounding a covered hole, half-filled with water, I meet the helix of my existence as it swirls together in hues of red pain and blue waves and Michael's café au lait skin and a White Power Ranger in Jim's hand and grey silhouettes of all my children.

On hot summer afternoons, every now and then, I still go to the pool, and I watch the young moms with their kids. I admire their energy and their trim figures and their shiny hair. I envy the time of life they are immersed in—their newfangled entanglement with their children and the mystery of their still fledgling marriages unfolding into even greater mysteries they cannot imagine and their falling apart houses they cannot afford to mend, but give no heed to, so enraptured are they in caressing and nurturing and making mistakes. And when one of their children does something inane—as children will—I try to not give them *the look*, even if a small profanity passes through their lips. Or if a small, soft pillow flies though the air toward one of their older kids' bodies. If it makes sense, I smile, I lightly wade across the baby pool, and I offer them a hand. Maybe I'll hold a baby while a mom chases down an escaping two-year-old who has taken to running toward the big pool while screaming, with glee, "I'm a big girl! I'm a big girl!" Or, I'll dig a much needed diaper out of a bag when a mom's attention is fully occupied with doling out sippy-cups and cookies so the rest of her clan is safely engaged for the one minute it will take her to change her baby's poopy bottom. When I've served my purpose, I quietly move away and leave the mother and her children to figure out all the rest in their own special, glorious, imperfect way. I wish for them health. I then walk to the edge of the deep end, and I dive in. I keep swimming.

Playing

The past few years, I have started to type a fan letter, but I always end up hitting delete, even before I print it out to see how it reads on paper, to see if maybe my words look less creepy on an 8 × 10 sheet graced by sunlight than under the starkness of office lights and the glare of my computer screen.

I'm a middle-aged woman, and I swear that I've never written a fan letter to any celebrity. Never. Not to Oprah, not to Baryshnikov, not even to Treat Williams. I admit, I did wax poetic my adoration for Bobby Sherman on a piece of construction paper spritzed with *Love's Baby Soft* perfume when I was eight years old, and I swooned over the life-size poster of his boyish frame that hung on my closet door. I never sent that red crayon confession of undying worship, though; I think I was unsatisfied with sending my innermost thoughts to a fan magazine and, unable to find Bobby's personal address, I deep-sixed that love-letter in my flower-power trashcan.

Since that time, I have been consistently unimpressed with the juvenile antics, the self-obsessed posing, the ridiculous salaries, and the self-proclaimed-pseudo-political-expertise of the silver screen jet set. That, and I am probably a bit envious. But now, I am going to have to eat crow. I am going to have to put aside my prejudices and admit to having a fanatical fancy for a Hollywood icon. And so, here it goes: *Adam Sandler . . .* this one's for you.

♦ ♦ ♦

Dear Adam,

Most of my life, I've hated golf. Hated it. I mean, there was nothing wrong with golf in terms of its potential ill-effects on world peace, and if folks wanted to put on goofy clothes, lug around big 'ol bags, drive bumpy tin carts, hit little balls with sticks, and traipse through shorn grass in stupid shoes with itty bitty spikes, for hours on end, I wasn't going to stop them. But still, I hated it.

Maybe I hated golf because when I was about eight years old, I was traumatized by my father on a miniature golf course one warm summer evening. We were at one of those places that perpetually smell like salted pretzels, yellow mustard, cherry Slurpees, and blue cotton candy, and where families can go-kart, putt-putt, or jump on in-ground trampolines (which can beget a disgusting kaleidoscope if done after eating salted pretzels dipped in yellow mustard that have been washed down by Slurpees and finished off with a blue cotton candy dessert). Somewhere between trying to putt our neon orange putt-putt balls into a clown's nose and making them air borne to escape the plastic croco-diles in a chlorine saturated, concrete pond, my older sister and I got the giggles.

My dad could be unpredictable. That particular evening, he de-cided that our giggling would interfere with my future. "Kathryn!" he yelled as he approached me with a royal blue, hard plastic, child-sized club hoisted on his shoulder, "We need to talk!" And there, in front of toddlers plunking putt-putt balls in their mouths, kids trying to wade in the crocodile pond, and parents who were walking funny from jumping on trampolines for the first time in twenty years, Dad told me exactly what my problems in life were. "You could be an outstanding miniature golfer, if you'd put your heart into it," he growled. At this point, my sister walked away, overcome with laughter, because . . . well . . . it's funny to see a father intently concerned with his daughter's putt-putt skills. Dad continued with the lecture, which all the people who had stopped playing miniature golf—meaning everyone—were now privy to. Standing toe-to-toe, grown man to little girl, my Dad preached down toward my lowered head. "Kathryn," he began, "if you practiced playing putt-putt enough and decided to be serious about where the orange ball goes, you could have an amazing future in the golf world. Now shape up and get those balls in the holes." When Dad wasn't looking, I shoved the little balls into their Astroturf holes with my feet and repeatedly muttered "I hate golf," in a sing-song falsetto hoping to entertain my sister, but neither of us had any giggles left.

♦ ♦ ♦

I avoided anything that had to do with golf for many moons after the putt-putt fiasco. Which is why, Adam, it was slightly odd that over forty years after giggling away my chances at ruling over a golf dynasty, I chose to drive across town one crisp, fall, Sunday morning in 2008 to Link-n-Greens and fork out five bucks for a bucket-o-balls. My son, Michael, has an unusual ability to sway my thinking; it was he who wanted to hit the driving range. And, Adam, it's your fault.

Michael loves movies. Loves them. I have continually psychoanalyzed his affection for all things cinematic, and it's not too hard to figure out the attraction, at least on the surface; as a family we are movie junkies and may have single-handedly helped send all of Steven Spielberg's kids to summer camp with our reliable Cinemark ticket purchases. But I think it goes much deeper. Movies provide an innocuous testing ground for Michael's fantasies. Having Down syndrome is, by definition, limiting; movies, by definition, proffer infinite sources of the impossible. It is a match made in Hollywood heaven: Michael plus movies equals a chance for him to temporarily suspend not only his disbelief, but also his constraints. He can play make believe, and, for a couple of hours, pretend that anything is possible. He can, and has, become obsessed with some characters and the need to integrate them into his daily routine. Michael loves your movies, more than any others. And, even though he knows, say, *Happy Gilmore* may not be a real person, Michael still believes Happy's sophomoric antics are worthy of emulation beyond the silver screen. Thanks, Adam.

Happy posed a conundrum for the Hulings family. Over the dinner table we vacillated between various options: Should Michael be encouraged to ape Happy's stick-in-the-face ice maneuvers and his lack of country-club etiquette? We pondered what to do. Hockey or golf? Missing teeth or plaid pants? Pucks or balls? The dialogue continued.

"Michael," I queried. "How about we sign you up for some skating lessons?"

"I hate getting cold, Mom" he blubbered with his lower lip sticking out. "And the skates are too tight. And I don't like to fall. And the music is stupid."

"So . . .you don't want to be like Happy Gilmore?" I asked with a modicum of hope.

"I want his clothes. And I really wanna play golf."

As a compromise, I bought Michael a replica of the Bruins hockey jersey Happy wears in the film, but still, his sport of choice was—G-d help me—golf. Michael inherited his older brother Nathan's cheap set of golf clubs, which he dragged up to his room and propped the bag up against the wall. The bag was right next to a life-sized mural of Luke Skywalker that his older sister, Edie, had painted. I tell you this so you don't get too carried away with yourself, Adam. Other movies announce themselves as part of our home décor and daily rituals, too. Michael's room is a shrine to the *Star Wars* saga and the *Spiderman* industry; our family room boasts another *Star Wars* poster, plus homage to *Billy Elliot*, *The Wizard of Oz*, *It's a Wonderful Life*, *My Dog Skip*, and *ET*, all professionally framed and huge. Like I said, we love movies.

And so, on that fall morning, I sat down in a plastic lawn chair, with an iced tea, under the covered patio, outside Link-n-Greens pro shop and watched Jim and Michael head out toward the driving range. I don't play golf, not ever, but I will watch my Jim and my kids do anything, anytime. Jim toted the bucket-o-balls while Michael walked and swung his club. Michael was dressed for the occasion; he donned an orange t-shirt, layered with a plaid shirt, and a Nebraska baseball cap set backwards on his head. Sound familiar, Adam? From my chair, I watched the equally fantastical worlds of film and golf swirl and mesh as Michael morphed into Happy Gilmore Junior.

Michael took his position in front of the tee and spent the next five minutes looking first at the ball, then re-positioning his grip on the club, then gazing out at the driving range, then wiggling his bottom back and forth, then turning to wave at me while I sipped my iced tea. Jim stood nearby tapping his toes on the bucket-o-balls. I knew something was up when Michael broke the looking-re-positioning-gazing-wiggling-waving routine and vigorously began to scratch his rear end. Unexpectedly, he took five big banana steps backwards, away from the tee, and then—oh, Adam, you would be so proud—Michael executed a perfect, ice-hockey-style approach toward that tiny, unsuspecting golf ball and, executing his version of a slap-shot, slammed the hell out of the poor thing, sending it a whopping one hundred feet. Of course, even for one hundred feet, I let out a whoop and a holler. "Whoo-hoo!" I screamed. "Way to go Mike-Man!" I was elated when Michael turned toward me and did an awesome little victory dance. I was so elated that for a moment, I started to think that maybe golf wasn't so bad after all, but I was a bit surprised when all the other golfers turned to stare at me, including Jim, who put his pointer finger up to his lips and hissed "shh-shh-shh" repeatedly as he rushed toward me. "Kathryn—golf is not a loud sport. It is a quiet sport," he whispered to me before he took a sip of my iced tea. I recalled that I wasn't even allowed to giggle on a putt-putt course, so not being able to voice my enthusiasm on the driving range for my son who had just hit his first golf ball made odd sense. There was only one thing to do. I stood up, raised my arms over my head and gave another strident cheer. "Yee-haw!" I bellowed. With a wry smile, Jim shook his head and scolded me. "You're impossible," he teased as he headed back to the range and an hour of instructing Michael how to stand, how to unlock his arms, and how to watch the ball, all in between Michael's next fifty slap-shots.

"Okay, Mike," Jim would patiently instruct. "Stay loose, Mikey. Look at the ball."

"Like this, Dad?" Michael would ask before proceeding to once again cream the poor little golf ball into smithereens.

"Way to go, Mike-Man!" Jim would say as he gave Michael an atta boy pat on the back, all the while biting his lip and shrugging his shoulders in my direction. Jim is a beautiful father. He even hit a few balls while Michael inappropriately, but hilariously, mimed the action of humping the golf club for my amusement. I remembered to laugh quietly.

Afterwards, I told Jim that I thought he and Michael could handle nine holes, and maybe Michael could even drive the golf cart. I was pretty sure golf would have to be father-son activity. My behavior was unlikely to improve on an actual golf course: wider spaces meant a heightened potential for more ebullient guffaws to emanate from my un-golf like personality, which ultimately translated into really annoyed golfers which would just end badly for all parties, all around. "The two of you could have a jolly good time," I joshed. "We'll see," Jim replied. "We'll see."

◆ ◆ ◆

Oh, Adam. Happy isn't the only matinee idol you've given Michael. Nope. Our life is a montaged simulacra of your on-screen exploits. Watch:

MONTAGE—MICHAEL EMBODIES ADAM SANDLER

—INT. JUNIOR HIGH—DAY—Michael drops down on one knee in the middle of a class and sings "Grow Old With You" to a young girl he thinks is cute.

—INT. MICHAEL'S BEDROOM—NIGHT—KATHRYN sits on the edge of MICHAEL'S bed and tucks him in for the night.

KATHRYN

Michael! I know she's cute, but you hardly even know her. What were you thinking?

MICHAEL

It worked for Adam Sandler.

KATHRYN

How's that, honey?

MICHAEL

You know! Like Adam Sandler in *The Wedding Singer*. He sings to a girl!

KATHRYN

Oh, right! Silly me.

—EXT. —MICHAEL'S BACKYARD—SUMMER—DAY—Michael pees on the outside wall of the house, while KATHRYN watches from the kitchen window.
—INT. —MICHAEL'S KITCHEN—SUMMER—DAY—KATHRYN and MICHAEL sit at the kitchen table.

KATHRYN

Michael! We don't pee in the yard. We don't pee on the house! That's what dogs do. You're a person! You pee in the bathroom. What were you thinking?

                    MICHAEL

It worked for Adam Sandler.

                    KATHRYN

How's that, honey?

                    MICHAEL

You know! Like Adam Sandler in *Big Daddy*. They
pee on the wall!

                    KATHRYN

Oh, right! Silly me.

—INT. —MICHAEL'S HOUSE—DAY —MICHAEL walks
around the house with a TV remote, points it at
KATHRYN and desperately presses buttons.
—INT. —MICHAEL'S FAMILY ROOM—DAY—MICHAEL and
KATHRYN sit on the sofa. KATHRYN holds the remote.

                    KATHRYN

Michael! Why are you pointing the remote at
me and pressing all the buttons? I asked you to
do your chores, and instead you're being really
rude. What are you thinking?

                    MICHAEL

It worked for Adam Sandler.

                    KATHRYN

How's that, honey?

MICHAEL

You know! Like Adam Sandler in *Click.* I thought
if I could make you go away for a little then I
wouldn't have to do my chores.

KATHRYN

Oh, right! Silly me.

END MONTAGE

And so, Adam—you became the usual suspect in our house whenever Michael and mischief would surreptitiously meet. I never put it past Michael to find a way to include you in his impish machinations. Using his keen technological skills, Michael covertly figured out how to pause our VCR on a scene from the Bruce Willis flick, *The Fifth Element,* which focused on impressive cleavage, and then took a still-life photo of said ta-tas with his Dad's fancy camera. When I discovered the pictures, I wanted to ask Michael about their . . . well . . . meaning and understand their origin. I didn't inquire though, because I feared that he might calmly explain, "They're from *Hooters,* Mom! You know! Like Adam Sandler says in *Big Daddy!*" I didn't want to be in the position of having to once again say something inane like, "Oh, right! Of course that's where they're from. Silly me."

♦ ♦ ♦

Yes, Adam, a range of your characters infiltrates the narrative arc of Michael's life, but Happy remains his number one guy. Nowhere is this more apparent than on athletic playing fields. It's not that Michael has juvenile temper tantrums at sports events. No—it's an attitude that Michael exudes and shares with the later, more evolved Happy. It's that, "I'm gonna do it my own way, in my own time, and have a blast doing it," kind of thinking. And, it's often public. As one of his high school's football team managers, Michael danced—literally—up and down the line of players, giving them high-fives, hugs, drinks of water and telling jokes even when the team was being routed; it made the opposing team wonder what surprise might be lurking with the next snap. At high school swim meets, Michael boogied down on the starting block before his race; amused, distracted opponents were known to look rather shocked by the blare of the starting gun and falter on their entry dives. Happiness can often psych people out.

But it's at Special Olympics where the spirit of *Happy Gilmore* reigns supreme. Michael has been a Special Olympian since he was eight years old, and he probably will be for life. It is majestic, the empire of Special Olympics. Adam, even without your ubiquitous presence in our lives, I think Michael would have found worthy role models within his Special Olympics family for the proper ways to have a rockin' good time. I dare anyone to find a Special Olympics event that doesn't sing with peals of laughter.

But having Happy Gilmore—having you, Adam—in his life hastened Michael's process of integrating fun with competition, and of understanding what it really means to "win." I suspect that every Special Olympics venue offers the same types of soul-healing treats for both athletes and spectators that I have witnessed over the years. I can bet my life on three things happening at least once during the events Michael is engaged with: athletes totally wiping out, then rising to their feet, joyfully proclaiming "I won!"; athletes stopping the game to check on a fallen member of the other team; and, without fail, Michael providing some form of ridiculous entertainment. At floor hockey matches, Michael runs after the puck and wields his stick with mighty swings—that sometimes hit fellow players instead of the puck—and when Michael makes a goal—*or not*—he always performs a dazzling knee slide across the gym floor and bellows out "I won!" even if he missed the goal by yards. I have patched enough knees on his jeans and sweat pants to prove true his gift of sliding and making merry. At soccer games, Michael will find a way to hog the ball—he is fast and sneaky—and then carry out a Marx-brothers-worthy comic routine of mimed kick and chase. He will kick the ball and then run a circle around it pretending he doesn't know where it has gone. He will sometimes run with the ball and dramatically check his watch as if he has all the time in the world, since no one can take him down.

But as I mentioned before, if a fellow player falls in an attempt to steal the ball, Michael, and every other athlete on the field, will let the ball roll away—into a pond, a street, a gulley, a ditch—and they will gather round the fallen comrade with water and a shoulder to lean on as together they limp off the field. At basketball games, Michael often shows up, ready to rumble, sporting dark shades, a backwards cap, and the sleeves on his t-shirt rolled up *a la* Danny Zuko. No one cares. "Hey Michael," a fellow athlete will call out. "I dig the shades, bro!" Michael blocks people, making sure to whistle while he's waving his arms in front of their faces, and skips to follow their paths. Really. He skips. And then someone shoots the ball, misses, and the whole gym cheers, because it's the shooting that counts, not the scoring. It's all good. Everyone plays without a care in the world, not worrying what anyone thinks if they fall, slide, channel Harpo, or mimic Happy Gilmore. I've lived long enough amongst folks with unique challenges to know that sometimes what might seem odd or inappropriate to the rest of the world, is, in fact, the only sane thing to do.

This is partially because Special Olympics—along with the entire realm of life with special needs for that matter—is not without its sorrows. The kids who participate in Special Olympics are often medically fragile. Sometimes they become sick and sometimes they die and it's difficult to explain to Michael—to anyone—why they can't return to play. And it's not just on playing fields. It's everywhere. In 2006, one of Michael's childhood friends, Randy, who had Down syndrome, became ill. Our families connected long ago at our synagogue and through a mom's group for mothers of toddlers who have Down syndrome, but we had not been in contact for a while. In May, Jim and I noticed that Randy wasn't at that spring's Special Olympics soccer games, but we chalked it up to a busy schedule or taking a season off (which we all sometimes do). I didn't call to see if all was okay.

That December, I read Randy's obituary. He was seventeen years old and he died from Leukemia—a cancer that haunts all families who love someone with Down syndrome. Scientists do not know exactly why, but people who have Down syndrome are protected from getting almost all cancers, except for Leukemia, which occurs at a much higher rate in people who have Down syndrome than in the general public.[2] I am sure that none of those facts mattered to Randy's parents. After his death, they had a memorial where they served his favorite foods and celebrated his life. I wrote a note to Randy's parents and his sister, thanking them for giving Randy the most remarkable life. He was a regular kid: he climbed fourteeners with his parents, he skied, he rode horses, he went to school, he attended religious school, he helped at his mom's day care, he loved sports cars and football, he giggled regularly—daily—and he was a Special Olympian his whole life. The laughter and the camaraderie of Special Olympics—even when it's evoked by my son acting like a complete and utter fool—becomes even more remarkable, even more of a marvel, even more necessary when the shadow of death sits in the bleachers and the sidelines, always. It's sanity at its best. Randy's parents know this. A few months after Randy died, they made an appearance at a Special Olympics basketball banquet and announced the advent of a special award, in Randy's name, to be given every year to an athlete who has shown extraordinary courage and perseverance. They made a brief speech, gave out a few hugs, and then quietly slipped out the door.

◆ ◆ ◆

Michael (age 10) as a Special Olympic basketball team member

Michael (age 8) posing for a soccer team picture

Michael (age 14) showing off his floor hockey style

Michael does watch other folks' movies, Adam. Especially sports themed flicks. Take *Angels in the Outfield* for instance. Michael was obsessed with this film. One day, at a local restaurant, Michael turned to me and began an impromptu conversation just as the waiter was about to take our order. "Mom, do you believe in angels?" The waiter stood by our table, pen in hand, slightly stymied by the direction our conversation was heading. Before I could get all spiritual and mystical, I—we all—realized that Michael was parroting dialogue between characters in *Angels*. Since Michael—and, by default, the whole family—had watched the movie five million times by this point, I was prepared. The waiter was not.

"Well . . ." I began, "there are a lot of amazing things in life that just can't be explained."

At this point, Michael's older sisters, Joedy and Edie piped in as we all recited the remaining dialogue.

"I believe in the possibility of miraculous things happening; it's what makes every day of our lives worth getting up for. So, yeah, I guess I do believe in angels."

"Yeah," Michael cooed. "Me too."

After waiting one cautious moment to make sure our movie moment had elapsed, the waiter took a deep breath and asked if he could take our order. I imagine he was relieved that we didn't break out into the "Hallelujah Chorus."

But somehow, Adam, you always creep back into the picture. Sometime later, while watching—again—*Angels in the Outfield,* Michael turned down the volume on the TV and asked me, "Do you think Adam Sandler plays baseball?" That day, I remember, I had Michael's upcoming Bar Mitzvah on my mind. So, even though I couldn't speak in the affirmative about your potential talents for baseball, I could vouch for some of your other lovely attributes.

"I don't know if Adam plays baseball," I began, "But I do know that he's Jewish!" Michael sprang to his feet, and jumped around jubilantly exclaiming, "He's Jewish?!? Adam Sandler is Jewish?!? Adam Sandler is Jewish! Adam Sandler is Jewish!"

To make the moment even more singular, I played Michael "The Chanukah Song." Well! Angels, schmangels! Forget about baseball! Michael had more important things on his mind. "Mom, can we invite Adam to my Bar Mitzvah?" he pleaded.

"Oh, honey," I backpedaled, "I don't know where Adam lives. But he'll be at your Bar Mitzvah in our hearts." My answer, luckily, sufficed.

♦   ♦   ♦

You don't know this, Adam, but on March 8, 2003, you were comfortably ensconced in Michael's heart (and in my heart) as we davened and sang in my family room which was temporarily converted into a synagogue, with our entertainment center serving as an ark for the Torah we borrowed from our local synagogue. Michael and his older sister, Edie, had a shared B'nai Mitzvah officiated by our dear friend, Rebbe Jack Gabriel, who graciously agreed to perform the ceremony in our home, with just immediate family and a few very close friends. I was recovering from a surgery, and I couldn't put on the regular extravaganza of a B'nai Mitzvah. When it came time for Michael to talk about what his Bar Mitzvah meant to him, Rebbe Jack stepped back and Michael, wrapped in his new *tallis* (prayer shawl), took over the room. He addressed each person by name, shared what his or her role in his life was—grandma, grandpa, cousin, uncle—and then told some astonishing, hilarious anecdote about that person.

"Grandma Marsha, I love the potato chips at your house."

"Aunt Jane, I would like to live with you. My mom won't mind."

"Uncle Bill, you are so tall and handsome!"

"Edie and Joedy—you are beautiful women. And you are my sisters."

"Cousin David and cousin Zach, I wish you could live with me. Your mom won't mind."

"Sean, you are the best brother."

"Nathan, *you* are the best brother."

"I wish Adam Sandler was here."

His adoration oration lasted about twenty minutes. He then told us all about his life, from Special Olympics, to his favorite movies, to his devotion to *Happy Gilmore,* to his great adoration of mashed potatoes and spaghetti. We laughed and cried and then laughed some more.

Later, over matzo-ball soup and *kugel,* Michael made sure that everyone knew you were Jewish, which made you his brother, and that one day you were going to visit our house. Adam, for as much time as you've already spent with us, you don't even have to knock; you can just walk in whenever you wish. For all practical purposes, at least as far as Michael is concerned, you're a bona fide member of the Hulings family. Michael believes he's your greatest fan, but he's wrong about that—*I'm* your greatest fan. You are a *mensch,* a truly wonderful human being, and you've given Michael the gift of delight and slap shots and silliness and Hooters and magical remotes and a very expensive Bruins jersey and a Jewish "bro" and a backwards-baseball-cap-fashion-sense and permission to celebrate life in his very own, big-screen, inimitable way.

I do love you, Adam Sandler. Truly, I do. But I still really, really, really hate golf.

With all my heart,
Kathryn

Believing

Read to Michael on his Bar Mitzvah

People always want proof:
　　　　　DNA, a fossil, a fingerprint,
　　　　　a burning bush.
　　　　　This science of faith
　　　　　eludes me;
　　　　　to those who doubt,
　　　　　I offer the authenticity
　　　　　of you:

I tell them to look closely,
　　　　　to see the curvature of your head,
　　　　　the way your glasses slip down your nose,
　　　　　the pools of sweet chocolate
　　　　　melted in your eyes,
　　　　　the chubby legs that quickly
　　　　　make a break,
　　　　　your smile, unfettered by worry
　　　　　or the nagging feeling
　　　　　you might look silly—

"See!" you whoop. "Life is *always* silly!"
        I beg the cynic to listen,
        to hear the voice
        whose first words—"hi, Daddy"—
        marked a hallelujah, marked a genesis,
        marked the beginning of a trillion hellos
        to a trillion sleeping people
        in lines, cafes, offices,
        stores, hallways, and parks,
        all people who woke up,
        seemed alive for the first time,
        all at the sound of your greeting.

I take the skeptic's hand,
        and we try to follow,
        hope we can see your world,
        where the colors of skin
        are no more than hues of crayons,
        where bodies mimic the shapes
        of blocks, all useful,
        all part of the building,
        where war is a card game,
        and G-d is everyone's friend—

I've watched head-shakers
        slow their wobbling when you sing
        in a key of your own making,
        and dance to your own music—
        their bodies begin to sway—they whirl with you
         and Woody, (Spidey, The Man of Steel, and The
        Caped Crusader too),
        each of you a hero.

I offer not an exact analysis
        or a methodical deduction;
        I offer just you,
        a simple certainty, dear and true,
        just you—a way to believe—
        my undeniable proof,
        my sweetest declaration
        of G-d.

Learning

I wrote and hand delivered a letter to Michael's elementary school principal after he brought home a project on Native Americans, complete with a Crayola picture of a chief in feathers and war paint, and a story scratched out in his emerging block print. The project was intended to provide a sample of his work, proof of progress or not, and a prompt for discussion at his upcoming Individual Education Plan (IEP). And, what a piece of work it was. The first and only line read, "*My name is Crazy Horse because I like to act crazy.*" My letter to the principal suggested, that perhaps, just maybe, it might have been a good idea to teach the kids that Crazy Horse was a courageous Lakota named for his father, to talk a bit about Little Big Horn, and to mention the monument in South Dakota. I wrote quickly, because I didn't want this issue to cloud my son's IEP which was within a week. I wrote deliberately, nearly breaking my pencil as I pushed words onto paper. I wrote stoically, because I believed the warrior I was becoming needed to refuse to cry.

The response was speedy—a retreat of sorts—yet unsatisfying. As Jim and I sat across from the principal in his chilly, cramped office the next day, his pale skin was embellished with two rosy, embarrassed circles, the size of half-dollars.

He remarked, "*Maybe the teachers thought it would be cute.*"

The sting of Jim's foot landing on my toes compelled me to swallow the lava that was about to spew from my mouth.

I replaced the venom with a terse, "Hmmm…It's **not** cute."

That evening, I received a call from one of the teachers, apologizing for her insensitivity. She explained, "I was in a rush. And, anyway, we let special education kids fill in their own blanks. We just thought funny Indian names were a good way to go. Nothing else fit into the schedule. We have a large number of kids and we had to get done what we could in the special-ed room." In that moment, as I pondered the plight of children with special needs, I understood an iota of Crazy Horse's fury at the denigration of his people and the push to remove them from their lives and their land. I lost it. Speaking in decibels louder than, say, a Stones concert, I left this teacher unmistakably aware of my views. In between my sputtering and pontificating, that teacher may have heard me claim that special education students deserve historical truth, scientific facts, and the same information as typical students; that we should not let any child erroneously fill in blanks; that the special education teacher's challenge is to adapt curriculum in a ways to achieve IEP goals in a general classroom; and, that schedules must accommodate learning and change accordingly. She may have caught on that I didn't want my child coddled. She probably sensed that I wanted to throw up at the notion of my child being patronized. She most likely—despite the deafening volume of my voice—heard me beg that I just wanted my child included, but only in meaningful ways. I regret the tantrum. I do. It was not me at my finest. But the anger was real and had been mounting for quite some time.

♦ ♦ ♦

It is amazing, how strong and direct a projectile a phone can be; the same object that in one moment is cradled between ear and shoulder, can, in the next flash, be easily grasped and hurled toward the ground. The phone can become a weapon for no real human target, but rather for a metaphorical destruction of words uttered by someone, invisibly, via the courtesy of electric wires. I've seen the insides of a phone tumble out of its protective casing and expose batteries, buttons, and circuit boards. I know it's an overdramatic analogy, but it resembles what I imagine my heart might look like if it were dismantled from my body, then frozen and crushed; indeed, this process was cold and heart-shattering.

And it's true: I've hurled a phone . . . or two.

You see, it took months to find a preschool that was willing to include Michael. It took hours of pressing odd combinations of numbers on phones, hoping for someone friendly, someone educated, to answer on the receiving end. I hoped for a chance to make exciting plans for Michael's education. Instead, I might as well have been greeted by: "Good Morning! You've reached 'We Prefer Perfect People Playhouse.' May I help you?!? That is, if you're *perfect*, may I help you?!?" For this is the dialogue I repeatedly encountered, complete with the many, many, many exclamation points these preschool people often use:

"Hello! This is [ ] and [ ] Preschool! How may I help you?!?"

"Hi. My name is Kathryn Hulings and I am calling to ask about openings in your preschool's three-year-old program for the Fall."

"Well, let's see . . . tell me a little bit about your child!"

"My son, Michael, is three-years-old, he is a terrific kid, and he has Down syndrome."

At this point, the sound of crickets at dusk permeated the phone line for what felt like five million hours, until the receptionist's voice chimed in with her insect-like reply.

"Oh, my! I'm looking at our registration charts here and we seem to be booked for the fall! Booked, booked, booked! We're sooooooooooo sorry! Call again next year, okay?"

In my head, my reply was something akin to "Don't count on it . . . bitch!" In the mouthpiece of the phone, I usually just replied, "Well, thank you for your time." *Usually,* that is.

Somewhere around my twentieth phone call, my patience had worn thin; okay—it was transparent. My fingers tapped out the Lone Ranger's musical theme as the phone rang.

"Hello! This is [ ] Preschool! May I help you?!?"

"Yes, please. May I speak to your director?"

"Is there a problem?!?"

"No. I just have a few questions."

"Hmmm! One moment, please!"

I'd learned to go straight to the top to get my answers; that approach left little room for granting any benefit of the doubt to a front desk operator. The directors, most often, promptly came to the phone.

"This is [ ]! How may I help you?!?"

"Hi. My name is Kathryn Hulings and I am calling to ask about openings in your preschool's three-year-old program for the Fall."

"Well, let's see . . . tell me a little bit about your child!"

"My son, Michael, is three-years-old, he is a terrific kid, and he has Down syndrome."

"Is Michael toilet trained?!?"

This question gave me pause. It was the first time I'd gotten beyond the crickets and the rudely polite, "No, we're booked!" response.

"No. He is not. This is not unusual for a child with Down syndrome."

"Who, exactly then, do you expect to change his diapers?!?"

I immediately understood why the crickets were silent: there lurked a large, growling grizzly bear in the deep, dark woods waiting to pounce.

"By law," I begin, my voice cracking, due to my vocal chords being unaccustomed to the chance to vibrate, "Michael cannot be denied admission to any school, proven his inclusion does not elicit any undue *financial* burden. Look, there is an itinerant team of specialists from the school district who will follow Michael and provide any additional services you might need. Michael is a kid like any other kid. He just needs a *little* more time, a *little* more help. I will come and change his diaper if necessary. And," I fatally added, "I'm sure one of your staff has changed a diaper before."

"Mrs. . . . . Hulings, is it?!? My staff is comprised of teachers with advanced education! None of us obtained Master's degrees so we could change the diaper of a retarded child!"

If G-d had come down from the heavens and commanded me to send Michael to this particular preschool, I would have refused. I was furious. "G-d-dammit!!!!!!!!!!!!!!" I screamed into the phone, finally finding my own use for exclamation points. I slammed down the receiver a few times—to make sure the director knew I had hung up—and then heaved the phone toward the ground. Something had to be destroyed. The phone sufficed. I won't lie; it felt good. Really, really, really good. But it solved nothing. In the end, I ended up feeling ridiculous and embarrassed.

Still, the damaged phone be damned, I marched on. I dressed Michael in his cutest toddler outfit and together we visited a preschool in person. We took the linoleum foyer of the school for tiny noisy people and, if we'd owned a flag, we would have rushed the doors and planted it smack in the middle of a pile of Play-doh.

"Hello!" sang the male director of the preschool as we approached the reception desk. "How can we help you?!?"

I took a deep cleansing breath and in one great spew of verbiage exclaimed: "My name is Kathryn Hulings, and this is my son, Michael. He has Down syndrome, he's a great kid, and we'd like to enroll."

The director eyed Michael and me and took his own deep breath, "And this Down syndrome . . . Is it contagious?"

A kinder person may have taken the time to offer a Genetics 101 lesson, but I wasn't feeling . . . well . . .kind. "Yes!" I whispered. "It *is* contagious." And, before Michael and I made our dramatic, foot stomping exit, I added, "You should be so lucky to catch Down syndrome!"

I knew that my battle for inclusion was not without some degree of authority. I was trained as a recreational therapist, and even though I can never return to the profession—it requires more strength and stamina than I can muster—I still keep myself informed about the field, its practice, and the disability laws passed that have made it easier for therapists to help folks with special needs.

So, I continued to seek allies. Busy Bee Preschool met me in my struggle. The program was based in Cindy Banfield's home in Southeast Fort Collins. Cindy had a B.S. in Early Childhood Education and was seeking a M.S. in Special Education. The enrollment was limited to six children, and Cindy was committed to making sure that one of the six kids was a child with special needs. When she announced her intentions to the community, I heard her bugle call. In 1994, Michael was to be *that one* child.

But when Michael ran away from our synagogue and toward Drake Road a few days before he was to begin at Busy Bee, we all had a change of heart and a change of plans. Instead of the diverse, accepting pre-school milieu at Busy Bee, I chose to enroll him in a school district sponsored therapeutic playgroup populated exclusively with children who had challenges, in a contained environment. The teacher-child ratio was practically one-on-one, so I knew there would be little opportunity for Michael to run. Plus, the teachers were top-notch.

The playgroup wasn't horrible, nor was it magnificent. The kids created a little craft, ate a little snack, sang a little song, and then went home; it was not unlike a bazillion other preschools in form. But this playgroup was based on the precept of exclusion, of separatism, of perpetuating the belief that people needed to be categorized, then compartmentalized, and their ability to intermingle be censored. In 1994, not everyone agreed that children with developmental disabilities belonged in academic settings side-by-side with typical children.

The next year, in 1995, Michael did attend Busy Bee. Every Monday, Wednesday, and Friday morning, Michael again created a little craft, ate a little snack, sang a little song, and then went home. But this time, he was included.

Inclusion is so easy with small children. Choices are concrete: It's either grape jelly or strawberry jelly; you either have to poop or pee or both; and you either need to wear a coat or you don't. Little kids haven't yet learned to believe that differences signify anything more than mere differences; they don't equate the markers of disability—say, how the large tongue of a child with Down syndrome might interfere with speech—as markers of inferiority. Parents are a different story. It seemed to me that the Busy Bee parents gave an appropriate nodding to Michael's inclusion, but it hurt when they made afternoon plans directly in front of us, while we all departed from Busy Bee. Five of the children spent their days after Busy Bee eating ice cream, playing at the park, swimming, or climbing on backyard swing sets while their mothers sipped lemonade and gossiped. The sixth child, Michael, went home and played with his mother, and repeatedly asked, "Where did the other kids go?"

After a few months of being left out, once again I pulled my pen out of its sheath and wrote a letter. I explained that Michael was fully aware of being left out. I shared that Michael was fully capable of eating ice cream, playing at the park, swimming, or climbing on backyard swing sets, and that I was not "the mother of a child with special needs;" I was simply a mother. I suggested how much their children were missing by not embracing Michael as an "after-school" friend. I signed the letter, "warmly." Only one mother responded; she was apologetic, abashed, repentant, and immediately wanted to make play-day plans. Her son and Michael became great friends, and she and I enjoyed a little lemonade. They played together but, still, separate from the other kids. You just can't legislate kindness.

My campaign for inclusion was given a joyous bolster in 1996. Fort Collins Parks and Recreation has offered a program called Funtime for over forty years; past students send their kids, who send their kids. My four older children all were Funtime participants and had a ball. It's a program steeped in tradition and fun. It proudly advertises itself as more of a social time than an academic regimen. You know: mud pies instead of multiplication for four year olds. At the time, Miss Geri was running the program (and had been for the past thirty years). When I asked if Michael could enroll, she replied: "Why wouldn't he be able to enroll?" 1996 was glorious. There was not an iota of exclusion. The Funtime group far exceeded Busy Bee's six children, but Michael made a multitude of friends, made a mess of mud pies, finger-painted with chocolate pudding, learned how to handle a pair of scissors, and brought snack once-a-week. Miss Geri never called attention to Michael's challenges, so neither did the kids and parents. If Michael faced an obstacle, another kid would step in and help. Little kids are usually innately inclusive; that is, until an adult shows them the grown-up alternative.

◆   ◆   ◆

When a child in Fort Collins is born with Down syndrome, an experienced parent is called upon to visit the new family in the hospital as support. I have been told that this is a role I will never occupy, that I am not part of the *esprit de corps*; it is felt that I am not capable of sensing the burden of sadness, or dealing with the perception of tragedy, because my child was a choice; I only feel joy about Michael. It has been indicated that my overwhelming enthusiasm is unrealistic and possibly more harmful than helpful. At first, I responded, *"All children deserve a happy welcome; what damage could that possibly do?"* I see now that my question was proof of my naïveté. Over time, I have accepted that there is an emotional difference between my situation and theirs that I cannot comprehend and one I must respect.

What I do share with most parents of children with special needs is the donning of armor necessary to enter the arena of academic negotiations, the realm of the Individual Education Plan (IEP). We are all gladiators for our children, whether we are in mourning or not. At times, it had been impossible not to prepare for battle before Michael's IEPs. Jim and I armed ourselves with a tray of donuts, fruit, cheese, and juice, all brought to the table as a peace offering to please and subdue the opposing sides. We also came equipped with a list of Michael's accomplishments and positive milestones. We fortified the room with heart-felt compliments to everyone involved. Still, things often got heated. I wish I could have included shots of vodka in our arsenal to ease the pain of wounds I sustained when Jim nudged me under the table or pinched my thigh as a spousal cue to restrain myself from sarcasm or abusing my right to free speech.

At an IEP, people sit around a rectangular table or in a circle, with large adult rear-ends stuffed into small students' desks; it is much like trying to squeeze a square peg into a round hole. The fit is awkward, but the arrangement is useful. I appreciated being able to maintain eye contact with whomever was speaking and being able to gaze out the window thinking how lovely it would be to smash open the panes and let a soft breeze quell whatever seasick sensations might have arisen. There is unavoidable tension when the future of any child is being discussed in any room, anywhere.

My own tongue has permanent, self-inflicted teeth marks from my own attempts at self-control not to scream at the illogic that can pass from mouth to mouth at an IEP. I've learned that being a resolute seeker in the quest for the holy grail of inclusion is not for the faint-hearted. I've learned over and over that my initial sense that true warriors don't cry is often true; instead, they plot and connive, and press forward with nerves of steel and punctured tongues. I've learned that in the IEP process, children risk becoming numbers in the worst of ways, both on paper and in the classroom; if an IEP is not added up carefully, with all the work double-checked and then checked again, children with special needs can be easily erased from a school's environment. Their inclusion in society can be threatened. These children truly can be left to fill in their own blanks.

It's curious how so many well-intended individuals heard reveille and sallied forth to determine my child's needs, often without asking Jim and me our views. Like, for instance, what our position on commodes might be. On one language assessment, in about third grade, Michael was asked to engage in a word association exam specifically geared toward objects and their proper locations; if given a word like "stove," the correct response would be "kitchen." When presented with the word "newspaper," Michael, positively and unflinchingly, cheered, "Bathroom!" The examiner marked his response as unequivocally wrong. But he was right, given his home-life; our family's best reading is done in the bathroom, where piles of newspapers are stored until they are left on the curb on Thursday mornings for recycling. Our family motto is thus: "The pot is meant for thinking!" Still, there was no space for Michael's particular, perfectly acceptable response on the answer sheet.

Even with such bogus testing, the quality of Michael's first few years of public education and the success of his school day were gauged on scales of happy or sad, excited or tired, struggling or triumphant. His IEP was, by law, numerically based, but his teacher's communication of plans was like a love letter, listing all the ways we could help Michael make his relationship with the world blossom and grow: create a circle-of-friends; cast him in the school play; make sure he had a library card; let him have cold Spaghettios for lunch; make sure he never missed the school carnival and a chance to dunk the principal in a tub of water; or let him dress as Santa for the winter choir concert and bellow "Ho! Ho! Ho!" Michael was encouraged to play CD's of his older brother's collegiate a cappella group while working on projects, and his teacher let him take dance breaks. She showed up and cheered at his summer neighborhood swim meets, soccer games, and Special Olympic events. She adapted lessons so that Michael's inclusion in the regular classroom was truly participatory and not a token experience; he changed the date on the calendar, recited poetry, made models of Egyptian pyramids, and mastered TouchMath side-by-side with his peers who memorized their multiplication tables. His teacher knew what the State required of her and didn't balk from filling out forms and issuing evaluations, but the final, neatly typed document was never her bible. She thought on her feet. She brought us times of peace and understanding.

Learning was fun. One or more of this teacher's three therapy dogs were always present and participating. It was commonplace to walk into the room and catch her giving a math lesson with Clara Faye, her chocolate lab, lying on a table, and the students gathered 'round. They counted her paw pads and received a wet, sloppy kiss in return, regardless of the percentage of correct answers. Learning stayed fun. Michael got to feed fish as a way to learn colors and train dogs as a way to learn sequence. Students not identified with special needs served as tutors for Michael; in turn, Michael helped other students with even higher needs than his as a way to increase his own verbal and leadership skills. Once, a child in his class—who had a brain tumor and was terminally ill—needed to lie down because of pain and exhaustion. Michael soaked some washcloths at the sink, brought them over to this child and gently placed them on her forehead. His teacher knew that there are no tests, no numbers to measure this kind of learning.

Things changed in grades five and six. Michael was assigned a veteran special education teacher with over twenty years of teaching under her belt, who, at his IEP, lamented, "I yearn for a return to the days when children were placed according to their I.Q. scores and not by their neighborhood school. Inclusion," she continued, "is a horrible thing. And, Michael doesn't belong here. He belongs in a contained classroom." Jim immediately held me tightly by the waist with both hands; he knew I was about to climb over the table and strangle her. Instead, I excused myself from the meeting, went outside, and threw up. Outside, sick to my stomach, I realized that if a teacher in the twenty-first century were to have said that she wished black children were still segregated in separate schools, she would be fired on the spot. Since then, whenever people ask me if perhaps I am not seeing the full picture of the effects of inclusion, and maybe I should back off a bit, I simply ask them to remove all adjectives from the inclusion debate that say "developmentally disabled" and replace them with "Black," or "Mexican," or "Asian." This tactic usually clarifies my point.

This veteran teacher called me at home and asked me if I would consider training Michael to have bowel movements at specific times, like, she explained, "a well-trained dog." She complained that his frequent bathroom visits were stressful. I suggested she let Michael take a kitchen timer set for ten minutes into the bathroom, and then he would have a cue that it was time to finish up and return to class. She said she didn't know where to get a kitchen timer. I sent one with Michael the next day, and the bathroom crisis was solved. I wanted to tell her what another special education teacher confided in me: An M.S. in Special Education stands for Master of Shitology, and if you can't deal with bathroom issues, special education is not the place for you. At Michael's mid-year IEP, Jim and I desperately wanted to synchronize the alarms on our watches to chime at regular intervals, at which time we would leave the room, explaining that "It was time to take a poop!" But we managed to resist.

The same teacher insisted that Michael go directly from fourth grade into sixth grade, so that he would not be a thirteen-year-old in an elementary school sixth grade class, making him one and a half years older than the other kids; she feared he would engage in inappropriate sexual behavior because he had Down syndrome. Her concern wasn't outside the sphere of possibility. There are documented cases of inappropriate sexual behavior by some people who have developmental disabilities in elementary schools. But inappropriate sexual behavior has also been documented in "typical" kids, and in general classroom teachers, principals, coaches, counselors, and special education teachers. If Michael had shown any aberrant sexual behavior at any time we would have listened and made sure to take appropriate action, but there was no such evidence. Nonetheless, we found out two years later that this veteran teacher convinced another family to send their child to another school because she feared some sex might go on between Michael and their daughter.

At an informal meeting to discuss Michael's progress, she told me she didn't have a clue what to say to Michael when his hand went into his pants (a common occurrence in special education where there may be some lack of inhibitions). I suggested that a simple, privately bestowed direction like: "Michael, take your hand out of your pants," might do the trick. I told her to tell Michael that when his hand came out of his pants he could then join the group and do whatever they were doing, and then to quickly make sure they started doing something really fun, like eating candy or watching a movie. "Oh, my!" she replied, "Will that work?" She arranged for a sex education seminar for parents of children with special needs. The facilitator, hand-selected by the veteran teacher, instructed the parents to never, never, never let their children masturbate. At Michael's mid-year IEP, I tried to convince Jim to take an announced masturbation break after his "take a poop break," but he stubbornly refused.

This veteran teacher made sure that not only were Michael's improvements, goals, and accomplishments expressed numerically on paper, but now his movements and behaviors were also recorded in *percentages* for an official, daily, running record. His school plan was expressed as a diarrhea of numerals. The new scales measured increments of superfluous nonsense instead of substance and humanity. We were told that if 80 percent of the time Michael was "able to follow two-part, non-routine directions," "complete tasks," and "begin to make evaluative statements about his work," then we could all breathe a collective sigh of relief and celebrate success. All of a sudden, his ability to perform tasks imperative to an accomplished life—like stacking chairs according to specific, anal directions—was of paramount importance, and was noted in a full-page document of heavy fodder for the next IEP. *Stacking chairs! Good G-d!*

I sensed this veteran teacher had not met any older teenagers. If, 80 percent of the time, my older teenagers obeyed when I asked them to, say, take out the garbage, clean their rooms, do the dishes, throw in a load of laundry, do their homework, or call their grandma to say hello, I would have been over the moon. If they completed those tasks without mixing red t-shirts with white underwear in the washer, actually exceeded monosyllabic communication with grandma on the phone, or cleared a visible trail from their bedroom doors to their beds, I would have had palpitations. If their evaluative statements about their jobs had the ring of "I'm proud of my work," instead of "well, it sucks, but I did it," I would have covered them in kisses. Their progress, success, and motivation in these areas was dim, yet nowhere did the school system require a daily chart mapping the highs and lows of their normal, teenage, sloth-like attitudes. As the new teacher outlined the endless percentages and averages, I heard a far sounding *shofar* calling me to prepare my defense, say a prayer, and sharpen my sword.

She babbled on. We were told that if nine times out of ten Michael made "appropriate comments about others," we should have a party. Specifically, he was not to say "Hey, baby," or "You're hot," to a girl. Any girl. I wondered if his veteran teacher got out very often, had strolled past a construction site, been to a bar, or walked the halls of a senior high in the past decade. I imagined what the veteran teacher's punishment would be if she ever became my prisoner of war; I would make her watch MTV, twenty-four-seven, the volume on high, until she begged for mercy.

Hindsight is painful thing. After I spent two years taking on the job of adapting Michael's schoolwork for his incompetent, veteran teacher, I found out that she was on probation in the district. I spent two years taking phone calls from Michael's veteran teacher and explaining how to work kitchen timers. I spent two years convincing myself that I let Michael stay at this school because he had friends there, and it was his home. I spent two years missing the fact that this veteran teacher decided to keep Michael in from recess for *two years*, after just one occasion of mild misbehavior. I have spent years wondering how I let this happen, given my eagle-eye watch on this teacher and Michael. When I recount *my* mistakes, I wish I could disappear into a foxhole.

At Michael's transition IEP from elementary school to junior high, the table was fuller than usual. In addition to all the regular participants, the special education teacher from our neighborhood junior high and her para-professional were in attendance. In retrospect, I recall hearing a heavenly choir singing when they entered, but I shook it off as an auditory illusion and a symptom of my overwhelming sense of depression and mistrust of special education at that point. I was still reeling from the veteran teacher's suggestion that we check out a life skills program at a far-away school. I knew in my heart this wasn't an option, but I wanted to be able to claim experiential knowledge when I refused to enroll Michael in said school. The teacher at the life skills school told us that a half-hour of every day was spent on grooming skills; the kids sat in front of a mirror and practiced combing their hair. Then, the kids practiced pouring juice. Before I said a tearful, disturbed goodbye, I told the teacher that Michael could make all his own meals and manage his own personal care, and, even if he couldn't, it was my job to teach him those tasks. I explained that I was more interested in his reading, writing, learning how to ride the bus, and being able to balance a checkbook. Then, I ran to my car.

The veteran teacher spoke first at the IEP.

"I want to say first off that I know Michael belongs in a contained classroom with a life skills program," she asserted again in mousey peeps. "He is just too hard to teach. And, he stays in the bathroom a lot. And he puts his hands in his pants, and I think, in the bathroom, he's, well, you, know . . ." she stammered as her face turned crimson.

Tracy Gefroh, Michael's junior-high-teacher-to-be, piped in.

"You think he's *masturbating* in the bathroom?" she queried. "That's perfectly normal behavior for a special education student who is bored, isn't being given a correctly modified curriculum, or feels excluded. He may well be *masturbating*, but we don't want to make dirty a common, healthy activity like *masturbating*."

She continued on, not missing a beat.

"What needs to be addressed is what else is going on in Michael's life that would compel him to need that sort of release, like *masturbating*, during the school day."

The room was silent as Tracy punctuated the word *masturbating* every time it passed through her lips, which were coyly smiling the whole time; Jim and I finally broke the silence with gleeful, uninhibited giggles. Finally! A sense of humor! Gifted teachers! Hope! Perhaps the heavenly choir wasn't a figment of my imagination after all.

◆   ◆   ◆

Michael (age 9) on a first day of elementary school

Ah . . . junior high. Slowly, I was able to shed the metaphorical armor that had dug deep grooves into my shoulders. Michael's teachers made sure his curriculum was adapted in meaningful ways. He used the same textbooks as his classmates. The majority of his day was spent in general ed classes with very little assistance. Tracy Gefroh and her para, Molly Kechter, set the bar exceptionally high in terms of expected behaviors from all students, whether they were diagnosed with a disability or not. She held general ed teachers to an even higher standard; she helped teachers who thought they couldn't handle special education students in their classrooms become some of the most adept educators at adaptation and inclusion in the school. Inclusion wasn't a concept to be attained, it was a way of life; it was the rule, not the occasional exception. And, Michael's hands were never in his pants.

Friends played coveted roles in Michael's life. Peers competitively volunteered to help him with schoolwork. The gangster-wannabe-hood-rats at school stole other people's lunch money and gave it to Michael. Other kids helped Michael navigate the Internet in computer lab and find YouTube segments of people farting jingle bells. Boys need silly things like that. Kids came over to our house to play X-Box and eat pizza. He played on a slip-n-slide at Molly's house and went to Water World with Tracy. Nothing was off limits. He played percussion in band. He ran on the track team. He attended school dances and boogied down with everyone. He was a star in the all-school talent show and received a standing ovation for a spectacular dance routine filled with head rolls, hip-hop moves, and Elvis inspired maneuvers. And, Michael rarely took extended bathroom breaks. Sporadically, he'd have a rotten day and make a stall retreat, but Tracy would boldly enter the boy's bathroom, talk through the issue (a fight with a friend, a failed test, a tummy-ache), and they'd return to wherever Michael had absconded from.

Unfortunately, however, there is no Eden, and no perpetual peace on Earth. During ninth grade, I knew that my truce with special education was coming to an end. Part of Michael's curriculum required bi-weekly visits to a place called Cooper Home. Cooper Home is an actual house where special education students used to go to practice cooking, cleaning, laundry, shopping, and housekeeping skills. These jaunts never went well for Michael, who had been deeply engaged with cooking, cleaning, laundry, shopping, and housekeeping since he was three years old. He hated Cooper Home. He could never quite figure out why he had to go to a strange house and s-l-o-w-l-y be taught things he already knew how to do. Finally, he declared a revolution. During a Cooper Home shopping trip to Safeway, Michael ran away from the occupational therapists who facilitated the program.

"Come back *now*, Michael," they demanded, "or you'll never be invited back to Cooper Home!"

Michael is smart. Very, very, very smart. And he knows how to get what he wants. Michael reframed the occupational therapists' threat into a welcome invitation.

"*I hate this shit!*" he shouted with great delight up and down the aisles of Safeway. He was systematically banned from Cooper Home and, as such, was supremely satisfied.

◆   ◆   ◆

What exactly does inclusion mean? I've read beaucoup definitions over the years in textbooks, academic studies, and social work guides, and none of them completely reconcile with one another. Some call inclusion a utopian illusion. Some call inclusion an imperative societal goal. Some debate the semantic difference between inclusion and mainstreaming. Sometimes words just plain get in the way. So . . . here's my take: Every person, each child and each adult, should be included in the ways that are best for that singular human being. It's simple: we need to figure out who the people in our lives are, what they desire, what they need, their aspirations, the skills they have, and the skills they must acquire. This is equality. This is called caring for our fellow person. It won't always look fair, because no two of us are the same, but, taking each person for who they are and acting accordingly is the only way to truly enact societal equity.

And, I am a damn hypocrite. In the summer of 2007, I sent Michael to a camp with his sister, Edie, who was serving as a camp counselor. Even though I knew Michael would be fine with Edie there, Jim had to give me a paper bag to breathe into as we drove away; I was hyperventilating from the separation anxiety. It was an odd reaction. The camp was founded to grant opportunities not normally available to individuals, ages three to twenty-four, with developmental challenges. As part of the teen camp, Michael spent seven days rafting, shopping, riding a zip line, riding a gondola, rushing down an alpine slide, taking hikes, and sitting 'round campfires, all with folks who were decidedly not typical. He hated every minute, save the ones he spent with his beloved older sister, Edie. He found the pace to be slow. He thought the food was icky. Plus, Michael had come to expect diversity; the homogenous nature of the camp's population confused and scared him.

So, why did I send Michael to a contained camp? Because I was testing the waters. Because I was scared of the transition to high school that was looming in the fall. Because I was slowly re-arming myself for the inevitable fights, battles, and emergency vomit breaks that came with IEPs. Because I had already needed to challenge and rewrite Michael's pre-determined high school class schedule to include general ed classes. Because I wanted to see how Michael fared in exclusive situations. Because I was scared that junior high was an anomaly. Fortunately, I was wrong.

In Michael's first year of high school he served as a football team manager, worked on the technical crew for the high school musical, swam on the boy's swim team, attained a 3.7 GPA, kept up with Special Olympics, joined a community dance troupe, fell in love with a very special girlfriend (who has become "the one"), and filled his cell phone with friend's phone numbers. He was even featured in a school newspaper article. People are evolving. Times are changing. I still had to nudge and cajole, push and insist, educate and support, but I didn't feel quite as combative. I was resolute, but not desperate.

On September 27, 2007, Jim and I escorted Michael—who donned dress pants, a silky teal shirt and an awesome tie—across the gym floor of Rocky Mountain High School at the Homecoming Pep Assembly to honor his nomination as sophomore homecoming royalty. When his name was announced, the students rose to their feet, and their deafening cheers rose from the bottom of their hearts. He didn't win that year, but he still got to walk out on the football field at the homecoming halftime, again to raucous cheers, and while we stood with the other nominees and their parents, waiting for the winners to make their walk, Michael entertained the fans with a little dance and a Tai-Chi routine. And there, in the crisp fall air, on a damp football field, in front of hundreds of good, kind people watching Michael be nothing more than himself, it was impossible to explain to my completely happy son, who happens to have Down syndrome, why his completely happy mommy, and sometimes warrior, refused to stop crying.

♦   ♦   ♦

Not once before this moment have I mentioned Michael's capabilities as measured by tests and percentages and standards used for old-school special education placements. Here are the stats: Academically, Michael performs on a second-grade level. Emotionally, he acts about the way you might expect an extremely immature (but sweet) ten- to twelve-year-old boy to act. Socially, he shares the interests and obsessions of any typical young man: his girlfriend, cars, music, and sports. If an archaic placement system, that did not encompass the ideas of inclusion had been implemented, and educational services were based on his "stats," Michael would have spent junior high and high school imprisoned in a contained, exclusive classroom, combing his hair and pouring juice.

Imagining

I have a bone to pick with what the mighty and powerful at Walt Disney Studios have allowed, specifically the machinations of the darling pixies who toil away so diligently at their hugely successful offshoot, Pixar. You see, they complicated my parenting skills, especially with Michael. Now, I know that masters of the cartoon genre have long been known to work on two levels: one for the pure imagination of a child and another for the pure as the driven snow recesses of the adult mind. I suspect it has always been an industry fueled by inside jokes, winks and nudges, but now, I'm convinced that the small world of the Magic Kingdom has, shall we say, enlarged; it's become a fully engorged, phallic fantasy land designed to have penetrated and complicated my existence.

They are endlessly entertaining—yes—but those jovial workers at Pixar went a frame too far when they chose to impact my life. They made it personal. They left me with agonizing moments of public humiliation and, I'm sure, near-miss encounters with concerned social workers from my local child welfare agency. See, I too can be an "imagineer," the lovable moniker endowed upon the Disney geniuses who have given us classic movies and endless family treasures and probably adopted by those Pixar poops. I imagine most of the animators employed by Pixar to be guys between the ages of twenty-five and thirty. They are probably the exceptionally smart guys in high school who sat silently in the last row and, at just the right moment, cracked the kind of joke that ended class with uncontrollable laughter. Guys who had the time and inclination to develop a refined sense of humor based on male anatomy. The same guys Michael loves to hang out with. Those very guys surely were capable of concocting the vast conspiracy meant to punish me, by creating a main character in a blockbuster film and naming him *Woody*.

There are so many fine and worthy names influenced by so many different cultures: James, Omar, Shepsel, Zachary, Igor, and José, just to cite a few. But the tongue-in-cheek gel masters at Pixar, could not be content with the meat of a strong storyline and multi-dimensional characterizations in the movie *Toy Story*. No, they had to, absolutely *had* to, name the lead player *Woody*. Of course, they could defend the name as a proper one for a western cowboy. Right, I say, much in the same way Johnny Cash lamented "A Boy Named Sue." There are some things so obvious they hurt, so tantalizing they tingle, so truly deviant that one must do whatever he or she can to get away with the dirty deed. Had one of these devious Pixar guys been in Target the day I yelled at Michael to "put down [his] Woody and listen to me," I'm sure they would have whistled a very merry little tune at work the next day. It's complicated: Michael is now in his twenties, but when he was sixteen, he still frequently played with his Woody doll. I often had to do a bit of imaginative explaining: *Thanks, Pixar!*

The thrust of the matter is not how much milk must have spewed from the noses of these guys upon their creation of Woody, but the torment they inflicted upon me. It's not like every time I wanted to tell Michael to do something with his plastic and cloth Woody I could calmly say, "Please dear, remove that nice little character from that sweet movie *Toy Story* from your hand and hop in the car." Nope. It came out more like "Quit playing with your Woody, and buckle your belt." The looks from passersby were vile; what kind of mother could possibly speak to her child in that tone, with that word? I'll tell you what kind of mother: the same one who called a million toy stores asking if they had

"Woodies" for sale when Michael lost his beloved toy; the same mother who allowed her son to make Woody dance on his grandma's shoulder at cousin David's Bar Mitzvah, chanting "Woody, Woody, Woody"; and the same mother who shushed her husband, not her son, at the same Bar Mitzvah, when the following loud conversation ensued at the same holy moment the Torah was lowered from the ark:

"Daddy, where's my Woody?" Michael queried as a silent congregation turned to see just exactly where Woody was hiding.

"Call it a doll!" Jim blurted out, just as the Rabbi, thankfully, began chanting the *Shema* over a microphone, but not before I shouted, in a synagogue appropriate whisper,

"Sha! Woody is in *my* lap!"

♦   ♦   ♦

Michael (age 10) making Woody dance on Grandma Marsha Udevitz's shoulder at his cousin David's Bar Mitzvah

I suppose Woody is not all bad. Michael had made him into sort of a family mascot, you could say, and we all grew accustomed to Woody's presence. He sat at meals with us. He was tucked into bed at night. He watched TV by our sides. I suspect that in the dark of Michael's teenage bedroom it is entirely possible that Woody defiled the naked Barbies that Michael sometimes snuck into his room. Woody was a permanent fixture in our household, but, he was not a silent partner in the deal; he can speak, you know. He has a string that comes out of his back. A string, that when pulled, elicits commentary from Woody: creepy, strangely appropriate commentary. Woody's opining can happen anywhere: even on a short road trip.

One frigid, winter evening, we all piled into the minivan after eating dinner at a soup–n–salad joint. Jim and I both were at the tail end of a yucky flu, so we weren't exactly feeling like Ward and June. Think of us as more like Roseanne and Dan.

"Get in the car, kids. Now. I'm tired and I wanna get home," Jim mumbled through his congested nose.

"Come on, guys," I entreated and coughed. "Listen to Daddy, okay?"

There was a bit of the expected pushing and shoving to jockey for preferred seats—nothing out of the ordinary really—but the kids actually did get into the car. Cold weather has its merits. Once inside, though, things heated up.

"It's cold. It's always cold. Dad, why can't we get the heater fixed? It takes too long to get warm," whined Sean.

"Shut up, you dope. Some poor people don't *ever* have heat! They suffer and they are hungry, too," retorted Joedy.

"Mom, I gotta get home, cuz I gotta take a dump. Let's go. Make Dad drive fast," said Nathan.

"Mom, Daddy shouldn't drive fast. Even if someone has to poop," chimed in Edie.

And then, all our voices commingled into a globbety–gluckety din of "poop-dump-daddy-cold-poor-people-mommy-heater-I-feel-so-sick-does-someone-need-a-time-out," all squished into our own biblical "family of babble." Somewhere in the middle of it all, there was a moment of stillness in which Michael (who had remained quiet during the commotion) pulled Woody's string, breaking the momentary hush with Tom Hanks' chirping, suitably whiny voice declaring, "There's a snake in my boot!"

I don't remember who guffawed first, but the laughter in the car grew exponentially. A passerby might have been alarmed at the rocking car with steaming windows filled with seven people crying and howling. I think I loved Woody that night. And, I loved Michael for knowing when to pull that darn string.

♦ ♦ ♦

Love fest or not, the saga of Woody continued. Michael had a proclivity for sneaking toys to school, a definite and big no-no, especially for kids in special education. It's distracting. Nonetheless, in junior high, he stowed Woody in his backpack. As lunchtime grew near, his teacher was not going to be available to watch over the kids and needed to inform another staff member as to the peculiarities and specifications of this group of kids.

"Please," she implored, "I want you to make sure Michael doesn't pull out his Woody and dangle it in front of the kids." The other educator stared back in disbelief.

"You want me to what?" she choked out.

Impatiently, Michael's teacher quickly recapped her instructions: "You know. . . Woody! Make sure he doesn't take out his Woody and dangle it."

The lunchtime substitute sputtered a raspy, "Excuse me?"

The light bulb took a second to spark, but finally flickered and began to glow over Michael's teacher's head. After a moment of embarrassment she explained about the doll, the movie, and my son's attachment to his very own, personal Woody.

◆   ◆   ◆

I do not begrudge those industrious, artistic Pixar souls who work as busily as the little rats—I mean mice—sewing Cinderella's dress. No, not me. I exalt their ingenuity and creative endeavors, the way they make me smile whenever a new movie or toy comes out. And, G-d bless 'em, they do have a gift for endowing the world with some darn cute characters. I admit, Woody was a loyal companion, confidante, and security toy for Michael. Woody traveled with my family across the United States, to every grocery store in Fort Collins, to malls all over Colorado, to the park, to the doctor's office, and to every school my kids have attended. When my family rose for the pledge of allegiance at high school sports events, I suspect Woody stood erect also. Imagine that. Yes . . . I suppose, in some ways, I am grateful for the folks at Pixar. Just please, for the love of Pete, I hope they never feel the need to name a character . . . Dick.

Flying

For a moment, suspended over an expanse of nothingness, their collective breath only a speckle in the span of totality, my family flew. Of course, I wasn't with them; I am permanently grounded by my abdomen full of internal adhesions. So, when my family took to the skies without me on a clear summer day in Southern Colorado, it was meant to be a secret. It was a secret for more reasons than just a kindness to spare me any feelings of envy; those motivations would become clearer as the story unfolded. Regardless, I wasn't supposed to find out—but all covert adventures eventually find a voice. Someone always rats.

Michael, who was fourteen at the time, was the rat of this particular frolic in the wild blue yonder.

"Mommy," he whispered into the phone from the comfort of a cozy room at a Holiday Inn, "I have a secret."

Michael, Jim, and Edie had traveled to Cañon City to compete in the Summer Swim Club State Meet. They'd left me home to relax, to find my bearings after a hot, sweaty July filled with physical challenges. Yet, at the moment of that long-distance call with Michael, I didn't feel exactly, well, relaxed. I remember my stomach churning acids that I knew my nighttime dose of Nexium would not touch, the portent of an ulcer.

"Honey, where's Daddy?" I queried. No Response. Never a good sign.

"Honey, does Daddy know the secret?" I heard Michael inhale and giggle before he uttered in unabashed glee, "Mommy, this is my secret: *I—am—Superman!*"

"Superman?" I probed.

Michael rattled on with an enthusiastic, "Yes, Mommy! And do you know what?" I wasn't sure I wanted to hear, but offered the obligatory, "What, honey?"

I could sense Michael was looking over his shoulder to make sure no one was eavesdropping.

"Mommy," he stealthy confided, "I can fly! I can fly, *and* Daddy says I scream like a girl!"

The stomach acids were now at volcanic proportions as I added up the evidence in my head: a secret, Cañon City, Jim, Michael, flying, Superman, screaming like a girl—it all came together.

"Oh, Shit!" I began in my most serene oh-my-G-d-I-can't-believe-this-is-happening voice. "Find Daddy—NOW—and put him on the phone," I commanded.

"Okay, Mommy," Michael obeyed, then cupped the phone with his hand and found his father the way most kids find their parents: He bellowed. His insistent, "DADDY! MOM WANTS TO TALK TO YOU!" reverberated, I imagine, through the entire Holiday Inn, if not through all the phone lines of the Front Range.

In seconds, a new voice came through the line. Jim piped in with a cloying, "Hey, hon—how's it goin'?"

"How's it goin' my ass," I thought; I didn't have time for niceties, for small talk. I dove right in.

"You took Michael and Edie on the Royal Rush Skycoaster at the Royal Gorge, didn't you? How could you do that? Now, life will be Hell. Hell! You all could have died and why, oh why, did you tell Michael he screamed like a girl?"

Silence. Again, never a good sign. After he let loose a deep, annoyed sigh, I got Jim's reply cloaked in his most oh-aren't-you-cute-when-you're-mad-but-get-a-grip-cuz-it-was-fun-and-I'd-do-it-again-nana-nana-naaaa-na voice.

"It was Edie's idea!" he explained.

"You gotta be kidding, Jim. She's sixteen. She dyes her hair crimson."

"Kathryn," he rambled on, "We were strapped in good and tight and the ride is safety checked three times a day and I'd never do anything to hurt the kids and yeah, I told Michael he screamed like a girl, and I said it in front of a lot of people because I was screaming too, but I scream like a guy, and I didn't want anyone to think the high-pitched banshee wailing was me—it was a joke—and Michael knew that. Michael laughed. Hard. It was a joke."

I started to cry. Jim hates it when I cry. It means I'm more scared than mad and he doesn't like scaring me.

"But Michael could have fallen off the cliffs—you know how he wanders—he could have fallen into the river and died, alone and scared," I sobbed.

"I had a back-up plan, Kathryn. I decided that if Michael fell, I would just jump off the cliff right after him and die a fast death, which I knew would be much preferable to the tortuous, drawn-out one, the one full of dismemberment and vicious verbal assaults; you know, the horrible death I would have suffered at your hands."

"Oh, Jesus, Joseph, and Mary!" I countered. "That is so—"

Jim interrupted with a boyish, "Hey, hon—we got a great video of the whole thing. You'll love it, and it's really funny hearing Michael scream!

I beseeched, "My mother must never, ever, ever see that video. She must never even know it exists. She will have a heart attack and drop dead, and it will be your fault. Never, Jim, never! Promise me!"

So a promise was made, but it was what was left unsaid that was unsettling. Just a week earlier, for about five minutes, I was convinced Michael was dying. He had a strange red rash creeping over his chest; it had an ugly, smeared appearance, the kind I guessed would indicate scarlet fever, the Ebola virus, or the onset of anaphylactic shock. Closer examination revealed the huge red sore to be a backwards "S" drawn on by Michael himself, in front of his bedroom mirror, with a red permanent marker.

"Why'd you do this, sweetie?" I asked.

He looked at me as if I was asking the most ridiculous question ever posed in the span of history, and matter-of-factly said, "I'm Superman, Mom. See? "S" is for Superman. See?"

Michael's fantasy of being a superhero was not birthed while free-falling twelve hundred feet above the Arkansas River, harnessed in and released from a gigantic, eighty-foot-tall swing-set, relying on the ridiculous apparatus to keep him alive, all while screaming like a girl. For over a decade before that momentous occasion, Michael had been dabbling in visions of the extraordinary, feats of superheroes and comic book characters, and exploits of residents from galaxies far, far away, all from the confines of his bedroom, our backyard, and the neighborhood park. Figuring out ways to explain that his action figures, movies, and books were imaginary had become a constant conundrum because Michael would not fully accept that premise. The Royal Rush Skycoaster incident complicated matters more. Now that Michael had tasted the exhilaration of flight, I wondered if the already shaky line between real and imaginary had been uneasily extended, its edges now irreparably, perpetually blurred.

♦ ♦ ♦

Michael (age 14) flying with Edie and Jim in the Royal
Rush Skycoaster at the Royal Gorge in Cañon City

Long before becoming Michael's mom, I was well-acquainted with attachments to make-believe heroes. Quite a few years back, in my early twenties, *The Denver Post* stopped running the comic strip *Prince Valiant,* and my father threatened to cancel his subscription. He was willing to cancel his subscription to the paper at which he labored for almost twenty years as Chief Investigative Reporter and won a Pulitzer Prize, all because Prince Valiant riding some damn steed into the sunset, with a stupid Buster Brown haircut, saving damsels in distress would be absent. I grew up watching the Prince and Dad begin every morning together, in some Arthurian fog, bonding over coffee and cigarettes, crossing moats, and affirming their code of heroic chivalry. Valiant's pen-and-ink deeds somehow improved my father's sometimes curmudgeon demeanor. I felt sorry for my Dad and his potential loss of camaraderie and a sidekick to help him fight the actual bad guys, the real ones with guns and hit men, the ones he tracked down and exposed for a living. So what if the Prince's support was all in his head! Some things, I realized, were just more important than the news.

I had my own childhood fixation. And, because of his own, active, ding-dong of an inner-child, my father had no qualms about my mania for *Batman and Robin.* Weekly, we watched the 1960s TV series together, on the couch, eating Bon-Bons and drinking lemonade—always at the "same Bat time," on "the same Bat channel." Dad guffawed at the campy overtures of the mega-conservative, totally nerd-driven parody of the tumultuous 1960s; for half an hour, the police were led by the hapless, but well-intentioned Commissioner Gordon, a cop temporarily unburdened with the era's popular moniker of "pig." But I took the Dynamic Duo very seriously. And, if my father was amused by the endless array of criminal fetishes (umbrellas for the Penguin, riddles for the Riddler), and ridiculous dialogue ("To the Bat-pole, Robin!"), I was inspired with optimism. Heroes existed! Men wore tights! Dad always told me I was a dynamo, so how far was that from contributing to the creation of a Dynamic Trio? Didn't I dare to jump off the edge of my porch, five feet from the lawn, and not even wince when I'd hit the ground rolling? Wasn't I worthy of a black, flowing cape?

Things change, though. It wasn't long before my Dynamic Duo was replaced by an immersion in *Star Trek* and the voyages of the Starship Enterprise. But I retained a soft spot, not only for heroes drawn in primary colors with balloon bubbles permanently affixed above their heads, but also for anyone who carried a superhero in their heart *and* could recite dialogue from any *Star Trek* episode. If a man knew what I meant when I'd say, "I feel like Captain Pike today—get me to a doctor!" he practically had me in bed.

And this is why I married a man whose favorite cartoon is still *Johnny Quest*; Jim can scat the jazzy theme music on demand. I married a man who has a life-long enthrallment with anything Spiderman; we both had memorized our favorite Spiderman theme song. Mine was from Spiderman's somewhat creepy, silent appearances on *The Electric Company* ("Spiderman, nobody knows who you are"), and Jim's was from the Spiderman cartoon series of the late 1960s ("Spiderman, Spiderman, does whatever a spider can"). I married a man who believed in Superman and the possibility of always saving the girl from distress. Yes, the man I married would not think twice about squeezing into gold lamé tights if it meant becoming endowed with a sudden surge of out-of-this-world powers.

This all explains why, since 1978, we've repeatedly settled into movie-theater seats, right next to each other (with whatever number of children we had at the time), munched popcorn, and, whenever Clark Kent pushed up his thick glasses in a Superman flick, we too would make sure our aviator-style frames were properly situated on our faces. It clears up why every time Chewbacca appeared in *Star Wars*, my family would join in with our best Wookie imitations. Jim and I are the annoying couple, who, after every special effect loudly says, "Awesome!" or "That's so cool!" and then briefly sums up just how George Lucas and Industrial Light and Magic accomplished the miraculous deed, just in case our fellow cinema buffs missed the action and were curious. It also removes any of our adult neighbors' possible confusion as to why through the early nineties we religiously sat in front of the TV, on the family room floor, folding the laundry amassed from five children while watching *The New Adventures of Superman*, both of us secretly wishing a bit of those powers could somehow help us fold five million pairs of socks at the speed of light and rinse off the day's dirty dishes with one mighty toss of water. It gives an ounce of clarity to the fact that we were not above scheduling our week around *Star Trek: The Next Generation*: "Drinks? At 7:00?" we'd begin a RSVP, "Oh, we're so sorry—we promised Jean-Luc we'd meet him tonight!" G-d is sometimes so generous in his match making. One of us is always the goofball who, in a predicament—say, our child loudly, publicly farting, or spilling the water carafe at a restaurant on to the lap of their grandmother—yells out, "Beam me up, Scotty," or "This is a job for Superman!"

Even with the pleasures of our shared geekdom, if Jim and I could have predicted the dangers that lurked ahead, all begotten by our nebbishy pastimes, if we could have caught a glimpse of the actual cartoonish quality our reality would soon become imbued with, we may have behaved differently. We may have buried our fondness for the melodramatic, father/son struggle between Luke Skywalker and Darth Vader; we probably would have avoided our philosophical dinnertime discussions around the existence and purpose of the "*Q*" in the Star Trek universe; and most certainly we'd have considered ripping up the movie tickets that allowed us to vicariously view (on a larger-than-life, 30 x 70 foot screen, no less), the daring feats of Spiderman, Superman, and any other Marvel character who had infiltrated our overactive imaginations.

◆　◆　◆

I pray every time I hear a siren. It's a little interchange I've had with G-d my whole life. On the road, at the beauty shop, or from my kitchen while I'm making French toast, when I hear the screaming pronouncement that something bad has happened, I close my eyes and entreat whatever powers may be that all ends up well, and that any harm that has transpired may be corrected. Those prayers became a bit more personal when my children weren't at home. I feared the sirens meant something had happened to them at the park, the arcade, the movie theatre, school, anywhere that I wasn't in control of the situation. I admit, I'm a worrier. And a control freak. But, when Michael began his journey into the big, bad world without me, my prayers became outright demands for divine intervention, complete with hand-wringing, hair-pulling, and tears. My fears weren't completely irrational; Michael had proved himself to be unreliable at best, and, at worst, a colossal tragedy waiting to befall us all.

It started out innocently enough. Given the normalcy of superheroes and sci-fi characters in my home, it wasn't exactly earth-shattering when Michael wanted toys to accompany our TV viewing, comic-strip reading, and regular movie nights. But the interest quickly escalated to obsession. At school he was known as "The Spiderman Kid." He has owned approximately a dozen different backpacks, thematically ranging from Spiderman, to Superman, to Batman, to Power Rangers, to Star Wars. He has sharpened a heap of pencils engraved with adages like "May the Force be with you" and "Faster than a speeding bullet!" He has never opened a notebook that wasn't adorned with a shiny, reflective depiction of some lycra-clad man zooming, soaring, rappelling, or destroying. He collected cereal box tops that advertised upcoming cinematic releases, along with the packaging to the literally hundreds of action figures and their vehicles which themselves are strewn across his bedroom. To top it all off—this is where we may have made a little mistake—Michael was the proud owner of two jumbo laundry baskets filled with every available, hero-themed Halloween costume sold at Wal-Mart over the past decade or so. Of course, his day-to-day apparel followed suit. On the bottom, Michael wore jeans or sweat-pants, but his shirts were invariably endowed with some artistic rendition of the visage, torso, or an acrobatic feat of Spidey, The Man of Steel, The

Caped Crusader, a Jedi Knight or Darth Vader. Our innocent family pastime became an all pervasive lifestyle for Michael.

I am—almost—ashamed to say that this infiltration of the heroic world was not exactly insidious; we all participated in its complete overthrow of Michael's psyche. Jim and I willingly shelled out the cash for all the hero-gear. We never really steered Michael to the Tonka Trucks and board games at Target, but rather allowed his auto-pilot to kick in and direct him to his aisle of idols. The schools were complicit; action figures were permitted to perch on Michael's desk and "help" him complete his CSAP (Colorado Student Assessment Program), by answering questions (think Charlie McCarthy) or cheering him on. For a desperate teacher, administering a CSAP test to a child with special needs justifies perching just about anything on a kid's desk that will facilitate the process: say, a German Shepherd, a stripper, a banana split, or a life-size, cardboard cutout of Princess Leia. At home, I would reward Michael with a grape Pez candy that plopped out of his Superman Pez Machine's mouth every time he correctly added 2 + 2, or spelled C-A-T. When Michael wanted to ask me for something he knew I might not agree to—like hot fudge sundaes for dinner or a trip to Chuck-E-Cheese for the third time that week—he maneuvered whomever the hero of the day was in front of my face and spoke in third person about his desires. "Michael wants to put maple syrup on his spaghetti, like in the movie *Elf*," Superman would inform me. And I, of course, carried on a full-fledged conversation with the little plastic simulacrum of Christopher Reeve twisting at the end of my nose. "Hey, Superman, tell Michael that he'll barf if he puts syrup on his spaghetti, and his mommy doesn't want to clean that up," I explained. Like I said, we're all responsible.

Many times, when my kids got a ride from another parent to some event, I ran out to the driveway and said a quick hello and offered my thanks. One such afternoon, when Michael was seven years old, I was chatting with my friend Dan Connell while our daughters sat in the back seat of his car, everyone anxious to get on the road to a soccer game. But they all seemed a little too anxious.

"Kathryn," Dan interrupted my banter about the girl's team's current stats, "I think you need to help Michael. Now."

"What are you talking about, Dan?" I answered. Dan stuck his head out of the driver's side window and pointed skyward, toward my house.

"Look!" he exclaimed.

I turned around and there, on the roof, running back and forth very, very, very fast, was Michael. When he realized he had us as a captive audience, Michael slid on his knees across the shingles, hooting and hollering the whole time, announcing his identity to the whole neighborhood: "I'm Superman! I'm Spiderman! I'm Batman!"

At that moment, I transformed into *Wonder Mother* and put all other heroes to shame with my uncanny ability to scream my child's name louder than it has ever been screamed before. I expertly slammed every door I encountered while traveling between my front yard and backyard, leaving a thick poof of drywall dust in my wake. I cursed the errant nitwit (Jim) who had left an upright ladder leaned against the house with super-words like "ass" and "dumbshit." I climbed said ladder without my feet touching the rails all in the blink of an eye— okay, in the blink of all the neighborhood eyes assembled to watch the spectacle. It wasn't really heroic, but it was sure impressive to watch chubby-ol'-me move. I retrieved Michael, climbed down the ladder, took a second to wonder if Super Glue might be the prescribed solution to keep the ladder remaining forever flat on the cement, went inside, plopped Michael in his room, and then, being the polite person I am, ran back out front and bid goodbye to Dan (now agape) and both our daughters (now giggling). No one in my house has since dared to leave out a ladder.

Over a decade or so, not a day went by where Michael didn't enact some heroic vision. Sometimes, when we took an afternoon stroll through Old Town in Fort Collins, Michael would suddenly and mysteriously disappear. I didn't panic. I knew that he was staked out in the nearest narrow alleyway, attempting to scale the brick walls, a la Spiderman. It was always the same routine. I'd enter the alley and find him sprawled against the wall, with one foot trying to find a toehold. He would see me, shake his hands and explain, "I'm out of Spidey web!" "Don't worry," I'd assure him. "You can try again another day." He looked dejected. There was—and is—a large part of Michael that believed if he wished hard enough, sticky strings would emerge from his fingertips and he would be able to adhere to objects at will and swing his way from the downtown toy store to the bustling Italian restaurant, out of human sight, above the mortal earth. All I could do was change the subject, and try to divert his attention from the lack of fantastical goop on his hands.

"How 'bout some ice cream?" I'd ask.

He'd brighten up and chirp out, "Can I have sprinkles?"

I observed Michael engage in such pretend play long past the age of ten, and twelve, and fourteen. It was real and in some ways pervasive. His book reports for school were on Early Reader pieces entitled *Spider-Man Versus Doc Ock* or *Batman: Trained and Ready*. His art projects were unique renditions of amoeba shaped figures clad in skin tight clothing or the outline of an action figure's body traced onto paper. Every month of the year, sometimes every day, Michael donned superhero Halloween costumes, posed in front of his bedroom mirror, and flexed his muscles. Dressed as Superman, he held a pretend microphone and sang along to an entire CD of songs from Pilot, the 1970s rock group. I have watched Michael slip on full Batman gear—utility belt and all—and jump our backyard fence to go scour the block for dastardly criminals. I thought it was all play. I was attentive to Michael's interests as sometimes dangerous and stupefying, but still, ultimately, I viewed them as play. I knew I needed to monitor ladders, roofs, and the sort until Michael could fully grasp the certainty of human limitations, but again, I treated it all as if it was only play. I was wrong.

♦ ♦ ♦

Michael had two favorite action figures out of the hundreds he owns. We never went anywhere without his four-inch Luke Skywalker, and a similarly-sized toy I nicknamed "Wiggly Spidey Guy." Luke is a tiny, molded Mark Hamill. Wiggly Spidey Guy is from a collection of amusements called Wacky Wall Crawlers, a variety of toys made of a gelatinous-like material. After getting Wiggly wet, Michael used to fling him against the wall, where he momentarily stuck, then he slowly crawled down, one wiggly foot after the other. I grew accustomed to the *SPLAT –THWUNK* noises that emit from Michael's room; I know that Wiggly was busy and Luke was probably posed on the bed, watching.

Wiggly Spidey Guy was not only a tremendous wall climber; he was a marvelous dancer as well. Michael has always found it great fun to manipulate the controls on his X-box and make the Spiderman image from his *Spiderman Two* game do the cha-cha. But, Wiggly! He was a live *danseur*, a tactile reality. Michael cranked up the boom box in his room, and made Wiggly disco down with *Hits from the Seventies*, hip-hop with The Backstreet Boys, mellow-out with Twyla Tharp moves to Crosby, Stills, Nash, and Young, and even made Wiggly channel Bob Fosse and finger-snap to the soundtrack from *Chicago*. Wiggly danced like a fool.

I have never been one hundred percent respectful of my children's privacy. I snooped through messy desks. I pried in cluttered closets. I accidentally read notes that miraculously unfolded in my hands. I eaves-dropped on phone calls, from the driver's seat of my car and through the walls, sometimes with a glass cupped to my ear. I rarely found out anything juicy. Michael is hardly immune to my well-meaning spying, but what I heard from Michael's room after one of Wiggly's dance parties gave me pause. Michael, Luke, and Wiggly often engaged in long conversations; but this was not typical play, with a child providing voices for inanimate toys. No. Michael was using Luke and Wiggly to voice his *own* thoughts. Wiggly commented, "I better tell Mom about not doing my homework." Luke piped in with, "I better tell Mom about the Frisbee on the roof and that I peed on the lawn like the dogs do." I played along when Michael had his toys speak to me in their respective characters, in different voices. But this was new. I dialed the pediatrician.

I found out that Michael was not doing anything out of the ordinary—not for a person with Down syndrome—and would probably continue talking, to himself, in his room, perhaps with toys, for the rest of his life. Quite simply, Michael was engaging in self-talk, not unlike the way I mumble out loud to myself in a parking lot when I can't find my car, or when I recite my grocery list in the dairy section so I don't go home without cottage cheese. Michael was reviewing his day and problem-solving. Wiggly and Luke were most likely the best speech therapists I ever hired; they allowed Michael to arrange his thoughts, to prioritize, to decide whether or not I really need to know that he took a whiz on the grass. Most importantly, they allowed Michael to practice the act of talking. His speech is not entirely comprehendible to people other than me; Wiggly and Luke gave Michael verbal confidence. What I heard while eavesdropping on Michael and his pretend companions was the first red flag that signaled Michael's preoccupation with heroes was much more than play. It was a flag that waved so boldly I was practically blinded. It was not to be the last.

In junior high, I installed a rule that Michael could not take his toys to school on a day-to-day basis; they were only welcome on state academic testing days. Teachers requested this rule because Wiggly Spidey Guy doing the Peppermint Twist on a desk was, without a doubt, much more interesting than multiplication tables or grammar. Luke Skywalker announcing the day's cafeteria menu, while standing on top of a chocolate milk carton, on a lunch table, can be a little distracting also. So, I promised Michael that Luke and Wiggly and the whole action figure gang would be waiting for him when he got home. I told him that if he got really lonely, he could look down at his shirt and say hi to whomever was gracing his wardrobe that day.

I was used to receiving phone calls from school to inform me that Michael was either having a fabulous day (he was on task, doing his work; he ate his lunch and played basketball at recess), or he needed to talk with me about his not so fabulous day (he's lollygagging, he spent forty-five minutes in the bathroom, or he got into a scuffle). These calls were splendid, until I got a red flag jammed into my skull, through the phone's earpiece.

Michael had asked for permission to leave his Social Studies class and go use the bathroom. He was allowed to go, and, somehow, snuck his backpack out with him. Social Studies was a struggle for Michael. I have fought mightily for inclusion, but it, like any other educational program, has its drawbacks. Michael was—and is—still learning time, money, reading, and simple math in his special education classrooms. Facts about the intricacies of historical events, their impact on humankind, and how deciphering the evolution of maps can explain an era—even with adapted lesson plans—did not make full sense to him. Still, I celebrated his participation in the regular classroom as a way to give him a sense of belonging, a chance for him to make friends in the typical population, and maybe even learn something we thought impossible. His teacher was open and accepting. What was there to lose?

Anyway, Michael returned from the bathroom and sidled back into his seat. Except, he wasn't exactly Michael. That morning, Michael had slipped a little something extra into his backpack. Now, sitting in the third row of 8th grade Social Studies, was Spiderman. Michael had changed into a complete Spiderman costume: masks, gloves, boots, and all. This old costume from the back of his closet was also about three sizes too small for Michael, and it emphasized anatomy that should not be emphasized in a junior high school classroom. His sweet, young teacher calmly announced, "My, my! We have a new student! Welcome, Spiderman." He brilliantly set the tone for the class to be accepting and not mock Michael's unusual actions. Michael/Spiderman looked up at his teacher and mentioned his intentions that day to ask his English teacher (a buxom, beautiful blonde just down the hall) to marry him. Michael's teacher let him down easy, changed the topic and said, "You know, I really miss Michael. Could you send him back?" Michael left the room, changed back into jeans and a T-shirt, then returned as himself.

Later that night, as I tucked Michael into bed, I asked him why he changed into his Spiderman costume at school.

"Because, Mom," he began, "I thought maybe Spiderman would understand everything." Red flags usually make us quickly veer in a new, safer direction. The next morning, I let Michael see me tuck Wiggly and Luke into his backpack.

"New rule," I said. "Luke and Wiggly Spidey Guy can go to school with you, but they need to stay in the backpack. Deal?"

Without hesitation, Michael smiled and echoed back, "Deal."

◆   ◆   ◆

When I first became sick and was delirious with fever, there was a moment when I felt as if I were flying. I remember wishing for my own superpowers, for some mystic intervention from the pages of a comic book. And Jim desperately wanted a silver screen moment where he could be Superman and "save the girl." We weren't sure from where our strength would come.

So, between the poking and prodding of nurses and doctors, I imagined implausible rays of vitality from G-d knows where infusing my broken body. I believed these magical thoughts, conjoined with my children's needs, would render me Herculean. That's how I recovered. I faked my way through it, assuring myself that I could transcend the meekness of being mortal. I could ignore pain, ignore exhaustion, ignore that life had changed. I could simply extricate myself from daily life, but still make sure daily life continued for everyone else. I could be content just observing. That would be my power.

Fifteen years and many more surgeries after my first days in the hospital, Michael and I were in the car getting ready to leave the

Safeway parking lot. It was a pitch-black and chilly fall night. As we wrestled with our seatbelts, an inconsolable Michael cried, "Mom! I lost Wiggly Spidey Guy! I can't find him!" We looked everywhere: under the seat, in the grocery bags, in our pockets, in my purse, on the floor-mats. We exited the car and searched the parking lot. There, in the cart return, underneath a lamppost, was Wiggly, lying face down on the ground next to a plastic bag and an empty Coke can. Michael practically collapsed from joy.

As Michael shouted for joy, I reminisced on a confrontation I'd had with Nathan near the same spot six years earlier. He was nineteen, home for winter break after his first semester of college. We had just gotten out of the car and were walking into Safeway for a late snack, him a few steps ahead of me in the typical teenage, "please-don't-let-anyone-see-me-with-my-mom" mode. I beckoned him to wait up, because I was having a pain episode and was momentarily doubled-over and derailed. He straightened his six-foot-frame, turned on his heels as if on a mission, stomped to my side and began an out-of-the-blue interrogation: "What were you thinking, Ma?"

Thinking? "Thinking about what?" I replied. And then came his unraveling.

"How could you have adopted Michael when you knew you were sick, when you knew how much pain you were in, when you knew how difficult it would be? Did you think you were Superman?"

The tears in his eyes mixed with tiny, random snowflakes that reflected the hot white glare of the parking lot lights. Trying to stay warm, our hands were stuffed in our pockets. We stared at each other.

"Nathan," I began, "Michael came *before* I got sick. No one knew I was going to get ill. It's just been so long that it's become all mixed up in your head. And, you know what? Michael saved my life. Dad kept bringing him to the hospital and insisted that Michael needed me. He helped me get well."

Nathan adores Michael. This was not *the* issue. There were, instead, multiple issues: his raw perception that I was in perpetual denial about my own disability; his grief based on his realization that all my children were a bit neglected because of my illness; his fear that I was delusional. I thought my explanation would ease his confusion, straighten the jumbled timeline of his childhood. I thought it would make him more appreciative of the big picture. Make him admire my steely resolve to leap over physical obstacles with a smile alone, since my body could barely hop. Make him forget I couldn't stand long enough to make a meal, couldn't go hiking, couldn't ski, couldn't play in parent-child soccer games, couldn't sleep, couldn't dance, couldn't carry the earth on my back and reverse time. Make him adore the image of me always waving goodbye as he and his siblings left for trips, or always waving hello to them on stages or on sports fields from my seats in auditoriums or bleachers, waving my hands because they, at least, continued to work.

Nathan interrupted my reverie of excuses and stammered, "What about the rest of us? Didn't you think we needed you too?"

There it was: the real question. Unprepared for his pointed retort, I choked out an insufficient answer.

"Oh, honey, Michael was the only *baby*," I explained. "At the time, in my incoherent state, I actually thought the rest of you would be better off without me. And, I've always been grateful that all of you have been so strong, so independent."

"You were wrong, Mom. We all needed you. We still do. Sometimes you just don't seem to understand how hard it is for you—for all of us. Sometimes you're so busy pretending everything's great and making sure we're involved in everything that you forget that all we want is for you to be there. To *really* be there."

"Oh, Nathan," I answered. "I should always share the whole story. How Dad brought all of you to the hospital. How I knew you all needed me. You all saved me."

Neither of us moved nor spoke under the light, in the cold, for a long time, until Nathan broke the silence asking, "Can we get some food now, Ma?"

Trudging into the grocery store that winter night, I felt broken, disconnected. Whatever fantastical image I had concocted of my possessing some amazing repository of secret powers bestowed by some unknown force, melted with the snowflakes that fell from my hair. I was wet, pathetically human, and eternally flawed. I was simply a worn-out mom with a battered body, shopping for chips and salsa at midnight. I wore no cape, and underneath my shirt was only an old, graying bra that needed to be replaced. I'd spent years pretending everyone was okay just because I radiated my make-believe vigor, spread my sermon of survival, and made sure everyone was busy. I was so overwhelmed by what *I* couldn't do, that I made sure everyone else did it all instead. I thought sending my kids off to adventures with the admonition to "have fun and be careful," would compensate for my absence, for my body that just refused to join in. I prayed they wouldn't recognize my lack of participation. Didn't Superman always fly away to the *Fortress of Solitude* after he'd saved the world? Well? Didn't he?

As I wandered Safeway's canned food aisle, I didn't need x-ray vision to finally realize that because I was limited, I'd hidden behind the imaginary. *Ah, limitations.* They can quickly beget a chimerical existence that only creates more limitations. But that night in Safeway, I acknowledged my pain with every step. I made vows. I vowed to read more books aloud to my children at bedtime. I vowed to celebrate James Joyce and finish reading *Ulysses* with Nathan. I vowed to sit in the snow and cheer on my kids as they whooshed down hills on sleds and skis. I vowed to braid my daughters' hair. I vowed to watch stupid movies with my sons. I vowed to pack picnic lunches and wait at the bottom of the hill for my family when they came back sweaty and happy from a hike. I vowed to dress up in superhero costumes with Michael and agree to put a Batman mask on our beagle. I vowed to accept that it was more important to do what I could, than to cover what I couldn't. I vowed to finally negotiate pain instead of ignoring its devastation. I vowed to be the person who began the standing ovation at my kids' performances—I vowed not to just sit and watch, not anymore. I vowed to stop assuming that surviving with fairy dust and heroic platitudes was good enough. My children needed more than that. That night, Nathan had handed me a chunk of Kryptonite and stopped me in my tracks. I was grateful.

So there, standing in the dark at the Safeway cart return with Michael, I truly did understand his relief at finding Wiggly Spidey Guy. I understood his desire to sublimate the messiness of constraints with, say, imagining capabilities of the absurd or claiming an action figure as a best friend. I understood that "anything goes" in the pursuit of a modicum of pleasure, to maintain a sliver of hope. Michael and I are the same, even though we will both forever be obviously different. As I watched Michael hug Spiderman, then make the darn wiggly guy do the cha-cha under the lamppost, and I remembered the snowy night stare-down with Nathan so long ago, I was overcome with a sad, weepy fear.

I feared that while my solution of retreating to my own fortress of solitude to cope with the ache of my life had been transient, Michael's chosen escape might become a permanent glue to hold his world together. I feared that Michael would never find his own voice and revel in its sound. I feared that Luke and Wiggly would forever order for Michael in restaurants, ask movie ushers which theater a movie was playing in, and talk to doctors when Michael was sick. I feared his endless parade of superheroes, action figures, and his sublime universe of the imaginary, might all forever, immutably set him apart. Forever is a long time.

◆   ◆   ◆

Right after the near-miss with Wiggly Spidey Guy, our new Border Collie puppy, named Elphaba, after the Wicked Witch of the West from the novel *Wicked*, lived up to her name. She retrieved Wiggly from the kitchen table, ripped his head off, and swallowed it whole. Michael was beside himself with grief. His companion, his friend, his *voice*, was beheaded. Luke was without companionship. Life looked dismal indeed, but I was still a little obsessed about that "forever, immutably set apart" thing. Maybe, Wiggly's sorrowful decapitation was a chance to wean Michael off of his dependencies. I tried to minimize the event and emphasize new opportunities for Michael to speak without a puppet. There was some success. At restaurants he did manage to order solo, and he reported misbehavior at school while looking me straight in the eye. But, he became an imp. He was a grump. He hollered at our dogs when they barked. His sleep was restless. He stomped a lot.

Michael took care of the problem. He replaced Spidey with a long, blue shoelace. He started waggling this shoelace in front of his face, almost as if in a trance. I'd seen him do this before, years back, with other strings and #2 pencils. At the time, I was told by medical professionals that the "dangling string" and "dancing pencil" were common events for kids with Down syndrome. They were a method of self-stimulation, both in times of tremendous stress, and as a possible alternative to engaging in excessive masturbation. Dumping the scenario of tremendous stress and excessive masturbation on Michael didn't make me feel like, well, mother of the year. I became convinced that forever was actually a bit shorter than it seemed to be in the Safeway parking lot. The image of a stressed child excessively masturbating in public quickly changed my parental outlook on just how truly problematic it was if I allowed toys to occasionally speak for Michael. And, frankly, toys seemed better than a dangling blue string. So I got on the internet to find a replacement Wiggly Spidey Guy. I could not find a single store in the United States that still carried Wiggly. Finally, I found an online vendor, and ordered an over-night delivery of six Spiderman Wacky Wall Crawlers from a toy company in Australia.

♦　♦　♦

Before Michael entered junior high, I tried to read a book to him that explained his Down syndrome and what it meant for his life. The book was positive and spoke more to the realities of learning at a slower pace than it did to the certainty or definition of distinct, non-negotiable limitations. Of course, Luke and Wiggly listened in on the story. I had barely read two or three pages, when Michael took the book from me, shut it tight, and whispered, "I don't want to read this." I asked, "Why not?" He sighed deeply, smiled at my naiveté, and replied, "I already know who I am, Mommy."

I think Michael is a stunning child. He has chocolate, almond shaped eyes that crinkle when he laughs. He has a perfectly round nose, with a tiny curve on the end that his glasses continually slip past. His skin is a deep olive and his hair jet black. He is perfect. Some children with Down syndrome have facial plastic surgery in order to lessen the appearance of the syndrome, to help them blend into mainstream society. They have had the size of their tongues reduced to make speech easier, their jaws reconstructed, their ears pulled back, their eyes widened, and, in some case, been given hair transplants to compensate for the sometimes sparse and wispy tresses these kids sport on their heads. It is a painful, painstaking process. Sometimes, these kids do end up looking "normal," whatever that means, but their behaviors remain unchanged. Only now, with eternal masks and costumes, there is no visual explanation to help keep the cruel world from being even crueler to these kids when they, say, inexplicably make a four-inch Luke Skywalker burp at a Bar Mitzvah. Maybe it is the rest of us who need corrective procedures to enhance our compassion, understanding, capacity for love and unconditional acceptance of our fellow human beings.

I hate to stereotype, but I do know a lot of kids with Down syndrome. They hug without prejudice. They are color blind. They couldn't care less if you're short, fat, tall, thin, black, white, green, purple, or have bad breath; if you're up to having a good time, you're A-okay in their book! They are honest. They love music and love to dance whenever the desire hits. Some of them are desperately, interminably in love with super heroes. Some even like dressing up and pretending they are someone else, but only every now and then. I don't think anyone wants to do that forever.

Sometimes, I carry little pewter angels in my pocket. I've named them Sylvia and Matilda. In moments of nervous tension, brought on by returning to college in my middle-age, I fingered them and recited silly prayers like, "Matilda, I'll kiss you five million times if you help me get an 'A' on Professor Marvin's Western Mythology test." It doesn't matter if I truly believe Matilda can help me or not. It just helps me feel better. Sometimes I wondered what would have happened if I took Matilda and Sylvia out of my pocket and let them hold my pencil during a test; or if I let them sit on the mamo-pad during my yearly mammogram; or if I let them dance every time I want to, but can't, because my body hurts too much. I wonder if the world would have stopped rotating if I told everyone to go to suck an egg, and allowed Michael to let Luke and Spidey out of his backpack and join his day, every day.

I didn't have to take that stand. It was sudden, yet Michael's days incrementally started to look a little different. In ninth grade, Michael was invited by a group of freshman football players to sit and watch the varsity game with them. It was unexpected, but welcome. Before Michael joyously left my side to be with the "cool guys," he handed me Luke and Wiggly and asked me to put them in my pocket. I was surprised. And I was sad. And I was elated. On warm days, Michael wanted to go to the driving range with friends and hit golf balls. Again, Luke and Wiggly stayed in my pocket while Michael yelled, "fore" as his ball rolled thirty feet. Like I said before, things change. The invitations continued and Michael's horizons expanded.

Michael knows who he is. I still think Luke and Wiggly will remain Michael's forever friends, even in his adulthood, but I no longer fear they will be his only friends. Michael will need his toys, from time to time, when the going gets rough. Just like I need my angels and Jim needs movies where good guys always save the girl.

◆　◆　◆

When he was in junior high, Michael told me, in no uncertain terms, he would be going to college with all his new, flesh-and-blood buddies. He also told me that when he went to college, he wanted me to come to his dorm every Thursday night at 7:00, bring some Wendy's chili and fries, and watch *Smallville*, the television homage to Superman, with him.

I didn't argue these points, because I've learned that I can't define Michael's limitations for him. The minute I do, the world will correct my arrogance, and something astonishing and incomparable will drop at my feet—like news of a wonderful skycoaster ride over an untamed river, or the chance to watch Michael sit amongst his peers at a football game, cheering "Go Lobos!" in harmonic tandem with all the other voices.

College has not turned out to be part of Michael's reality. Still, I suspect the world will continue to graciously bestow other gifts and surprises whether I interfere or not. For now, I'm finding it singularly satisfying to just love Michael with all my being, to watch the mystery of him beautifully unfold, and to watch my son, the superhero, fly.

Michael (8) at a school Halloween parade

Michael (14) seriously contemplating how to save the day

Dancing

I know that it is not appropriate to repeatedly scream out in agony when one of my children is performing in a sold-out, standing-room-only, high-school talent show. It could easily be misinterpreted as rude. Or as child abuse. I know this. That, however, doesn't mean I haven't done something like that. Or exactly that. I have. I am a middle-aged, overweight, perpetually dorky-acting, potty-mouthed woman who is often in pain, and sometimes, decency be damned, I slip.

For weeks, Michael had been rehearsing for his coveted role in the annual talent show at Rocky Mountain High School in the spring of 2009. It was his junior year, and we had been perpetually listening to the soundtrack from *School of Rock* as Michael put his body through his original choreographic moves behind the closed door of his bedroom, in front of his full-length mirror. Jim and I watched a couple of his rehearsals—we sat on his twin bed, underneath the life-sized Luke Skywalker/Han Solo mural. Michael's stage was the middle of his bedroom, and his music played from a boom-box on his nightstand. In typical Michael fashion, the choreography was . . . flexible—in other words, it was completely different each time. He went with the inspiration of the moment, and we oohed and aahed regardless of the exact steps. Michael had recently been propelled into a milieu that gave him a lot of inspiration.

Michael now had a girlfriend. *Casey Ann Lord: The inspiration.* Their romance began with a series of notes passed in class during his sophomore year and her senior year at Rocky. Casey also has Down syndrome. Her academic skills are solid. She can read and write well enough to navigate *Harry Potter* books and do research on Egypt and Russia, which are but two of her passions. She is beautiful. As in head-turning beautiful. She has lovely brown eyes, silky dark hair, a petite yet curvy figure, and a mega-watt smile that showcases perfect teeth. She is a beauty. After a brief spell of match-making initiated by Casey and Michael's teachers, Michael read Casey's introductory note: "Would you be my boyfriend? Maybe we can kiss." The actual note was longer. Much longer. Here are some snippets:

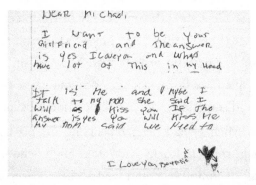

An excerpt from the first love note written by Casey, which was a full page long

What teenage boy in his right mind passes up the potential of getting to first base, right off the bat, with a beautiful girl? Not to mention the prospect of marriage? Michael replied with a simple and irrefutable, "Yes!" And so, that weekend, Jim and I met Casey's mom, Cindy, at a practice for Dance Express, which is a local dance troupe that brings together dancers with challenges and typical dancers to rehearse and perform. Both Casey and Michael were members, so weekend trysts were already built into the deal. We set up their first date and they have been together ever since.

◆ ◆ ◆

The night of Michael's junior year talent show, I sat in the audience with Jim, Cindy, and Casey. James, Casey's father, was in China on business. It was a typical high school talent show: guys on electric guitars living out rock star fantasies and girls at pianos channeling Alicia Keyes, agonizingly lame comedy routines, off-key renditions of Celine Dion songs, trumpet duets, and then . . . Michael.

This was not Michael's first talent show. His first foray into the world of dance performance for a public audience was during ninth grade at Blevins Junior High in their spring talent show. As Michael rehearsed for that talent show, Edie told me that I had better watch Michael's routine before the day of the actual show.

"Why?" I asked.

"Because," Edie replied looking at me like I was an alien, "He might take off his clothes."

That evening Jim and I watched Michael immediately begin a strip tease to the soundtrack of *Happy Feet*, the animated family movie featuring penguins.

"Whoa, whoa, whoa, whoa, whoa, Michael," I sputtered out, while Jim left the room to try and contain his giggles.

I should have seen this coming. Michael loved to watch MTV and BET where clothes did indeed come off during dancing.

Jim re-entered and suggested, "How about you wear two shirts, and just take off one during your dance?"

I am a very liberal parent, and I hate to interfere with my kids' creativity, even if it involves potential nudity, so this seemed like a reasonable compromise. We selected the two shirts—one to remain on Michael's body and the other to be ripped off—and Michael finished his rehearsal. It all seemed tame enough.

During the actual performance, Michael began with his back to the audience and then turned to face us within the first few beats of music. Immediately, the outer shirt came off and was lowered in between

Michael's legs for a brief exhibition of back-and-forth motions before it was thrown to the floor. What followed was spectacularly sexual. Michael gyrated his hips in ways I did not know were possible. Then he started toying with his belt buckle. Even though I am Jewish, I believe I said a Hail Mary at that point. His pants—thank G-d—stayed on. His crotch, however, was not untouched. When he finished, he receive a standing ovation. I will admit that my children—Michael's siblings— were also standing and whistling and shouting. Jim and I were, too. Later, the principal told me that had it not been Michael, any other student would have been pulled from the stage and given a three-day suspension. At that moment, I was thankful for the fickleness and ir-regularity of inclusion in my school district.

A tradition had been born. Michael's sophomore year dance per-formance at the Rocky talent show amped the sexuality even more. Michael and Casey were a new couple at this point, and she, her mother, and her father joined Jim, me, and Sean for the event. Dressed entirely in black, Michael bumped and grinded to Skindred's "Twist and Crawl" from the *Sky High* soundtrack. His hips were engaged in an endless series of Chippendale-worthy rolls. A shirt was shred. He even showed the audience a lovely music video movement, executed on the floor to suggest a horizontal tango from both top and bottom positions.

My parental pride mechanism was in a flux of confusion. "Wow!" thought my artistic, non-censoring parental side. "He's good! I am actually seeing some Bob Fosse moves. Awesome!" The oh-my-G-d-what-will-people-think-Jim-and-I-do-at-home-when-no-one-is-watching side, on the other hand, was prepping to run up on the stage, side tackle Michael, flee the school, and catch a plane to Mexico where we could hide for the rest of our lives. Michael's dance ended before I could react. He received another standing ovation, although Casey's father mouthed the words, "*We need to talk!*" in my direction while everyone else was cheering.

◆   ◆   ◆

The anticipation of Michael's junior year performance at the talent show was palpable. Would Jim and I finally be arrested? Would Michael be expelled? Would we see Michael naked? Would Casey's father rib me with another whispered, veiled threat? Jim and I had spent a year lecturing Michael on how to perform appropriately—sans portrayals of sex acts—and tried to provide Michael with alternative choreographic role models other than, say, Britney Spears. We enrolled him in a dance class at Rocky and we made sure he continued dancing with Dance Express. We monitored his at-home rehearsals and even made sure that there was some consistency in choreography. All seemed copacetic.

Michael's actual performance was wonderful. There were a few nods to stripper-inspired moves, but, for the most part, his dance to Jack Black's song "Fight," from *The School of Rock* soundtrack, was filled with some repetitive movements that appeared much like the chorus to a song appears; every two measures Michael's right arm crossed the body, he double tapped with his left foot, and then he let go a small hip swivel. There were a few "step-together-steps." His legitimate dance training was taking hold, and the emulation of the BET and MTV dance-masters was relegated to Michael's bedroom and his full-length mirror. Maybe later he could pursue a career as a Chippendale. He still got a standing ovation. But the evening had not yet ended.

The last act of the evening was a performance by the Latino Dance Club. At the end of their lively set of dances, they invited the entire cast on stage to learn some authentic Latino dance moves. Michael was there in a nanosecond. Jim and I held our breath. Michael took the stage—front and center—and danced his hips, I mean heart, out. Jim and I exhaled. It was sweet, and Michael was dancing with many people who were all engaging in silly attempts at Latino dancing. Jim recorded the moment on the video-cam.

In the middle of the community dancing, Michael sauntered over to the talent show emcee and whispered something in his ear. Jim and I held our breath, again. When the emcee passed over the microphone to Michael, Jim stopped recording, started panicking, and laid the video-cam, still running, on his lap. I sat forward on the edge of my seat. Michael held the mic to his mouth and asked for everyone's attention. The audience and on-stage cast members complied. A speech ensued.

"I just wanted to tell everyone how much I love my girlfriend, Casey Ann Lord. She is beautiful. She is a wonderful kisser."

At this point, Jim had become glassy eyed, and I was eyeing the exits.

And Michael continued. "Casey, my love . . ." he cooed as he dropped to one knee. "When I graduate, will you marry me?"

Jim, Cindy, and I sat staring in a sort of twilight zone trance. Casey, however, climbed over us, ran to the stage and planted a full frontal facial assault smooch on Michael—tongues and all—before she cried out, "Yes! I will marry you!" As Casey returned to her seat, the audience was on its feet screaming congratulations and applauding. Jim, Cindy, and I remained seated in what had become a coma-like trance.

Michael rose to his feet and, into the microphone announced, "I would now like to sing a song." And, G-d forgive me, I stood up and yelled—yes, yelled—"NO!" The reality for Michael and singing is this: *It is horrifying*. Really. He loves to sing. But Michael sings in keys of his own making, full of dissonances and flats and groans, and sounds that should only be emitted from a raccoon in heat. So, I yelled out, "NO!" But, "NO!" from a mother's mouth to a teen's ear turns in to the phrase, "Oh, darling child of mine, please do that incredibly stupid thing—I would love that!" So, Michael thoroughly ignored me and began to sing "You Are So Beautiful" into the mic. It was loud. And reverberating. I began to slide down in my seat and crunch over to, well, hide. This was a mistake, not so much because a mother should never show such blatant embarrassment over a child's actions, but because I should have known better than to try and contort my body. As I slid and crunched, I begot a cycle of incredible abdominal pain and muscle cramps that wracked my challenged physique. During Michael's rendition of "You Are So Beautiful," the audience could also hear me screaming, "Oh-ouch-oh-ouch-oh-ouch-oh-ouch-oh-damn-it-oh-ouch" as my body went into uncontrollable spasms. It appeared as though I was verbalizing the pain of hearing Michael sing. I'm not that bad a mother; I kept that particular agony inside. Cindy finally stood up and began to applaud before Michael could embark on the third verse. The audience rose to their feet again, while I was desperately trying to get my body back to some sort of position of comfort.

When I could finally walk, we exited the auditorium with new, un-anticipated roles: fiancés and in-laws all, we left to go to Applebee's and get a bite to eat. There were also unanticipated questions racking my brain: what is dance, really, without singing, even horrifying singing? On the way out (as has happened after Michael's other performances), people stopped, touched me on the shoulder and, with a wink and a nudge, said, "Did you teach Michael how to dance like that?" I always replied, "I used to dance. But not like that."

♦　♦　♦

When I was three years old, I stole a pair of brown tap shoes from a lost and found box and snuck into my older sister's dance class. At my mother's urging, the dance teacher let me stay for the duration. I didn't leave dance class for the next seventeen years. It was all I knew. It was all I wanted.

It helped me to have danced. It was the closest thing I had to prayer, that dancing. There in the memorization of steps and chanting of my body, was the forgetting of all that was disquieting; the human form is loud when it declares its intent to move. But, it was all for naught. In love with ballet, but not lovely at the art, was my circumstance. It happened quickly—losing membership in the itty-bitty-titty-committee sealed the deal; there are no swans with cleavage. My lack of talent, my inability to stay rail thin, and the breasts, all ended the reverie. Maybe, I thought, I would create dances instead. Whatever form it took, I knew that dance would always be part of my life. I knew that.

I made my kids dance. Some of my kids still haven't forgiven me. I insisted that Sean and Nathan take both ballet and clogging classes between the age of three and seven. *Clogging!* I was desperate to continue the legacy of movement. When Sean and Nathan's days of clogging and ballet come up during dinnertime conversation, they often disappear to the bathroom. Or Mars. They rarely return to the table. My daughters were not much more enthusiastic than their older brothers. I enrolled them in ballet, tap, jazz, and . . . clogging. They went—begrudgingly. It was short-lived, although in college both Joedy and Edie became enamored with African Dance. Michael has always loved to dance, and even though it is a constant source of joy for him, it is still absolutely an avocation, not a necessary obsession like it was for me.

Because I got sick after Michael's arrival, I have not danced in the typical sense in over twenty years. I always thought I'd be one of those trim, ninety-year-old women who go to ballet class with a tight chignon and a modest, black sweater draped over their leotard, place a wrinkled, elegant hand on the barre, and wait for Mozart and the downbeat, ready to plié in first position. That is not to be. I have had to redefine what dance is. Now, I see dance as something that transcends movement. It's true that none of my children can be defined in a dictionary sense as having "danced." Yet, they have danced. They have run barefoot in the grass, waded in streams, read books, written poems, and painted their toenails blue; they've suffered splinters from climbing trees, blisters from the hot pavement, bruises from cliff diving, and heartbreak from young love; they've weathered broken bones, cancer scares, diseases, conditions, and the trepidation of walking without a visible path or functioning compass. Each of them has laughed, each of them has cried.

♦   ♦   ♦

Michael is more malleable than my other children. He is highly impressionable. This personality trait often goes along with having Down syndrome. My life-long love affair with dance has rubbed off on him in unconscious ways. Whereas his siblings pleaded with me to take down the shrine to Gene Kelly I erected in our family room, Michael willingly sat and watched *An American in Paris* with me. And he loved it.

Michael has been dancing in front of mirrors since he could walk. I play music—loudly—at all hours of the day and night, so there was always something he could dance to: The Rolling Stones, CSNY, anything Broadway, Barry Manilow, Led Zeppelin, Barbra Streisand, Dan Fogelberg, Green Day, Stravinsky, Raffi. You name it, I have played it. Michael rarely danced alone. He has some consistent companions in the form of his three-inch action figures and movie character replicas. And boy can they dance! Woody, from *Toy Story,* does a mean twist and Simba, from *The Lion King* can do a wild monkey.

Still, no toy compares in the mastery of movement to the White Power Ranger. Michael and the White Power Ranger spent hours dancing together. Michael would "trip the light fantastic" while White Power Ranger, his position firm in between Michael's pointer finger and thumb, moved like a mad man. This White Power Ranger had legs that were attached to his torso in a way that graced him with hugely flexible hip sockets. He was quite supple. A mere wiggle of Michael's fingers and White Power Ranger's whole body would explode into an array of humanly impossible paroxysms and ripples of pelvic magic. It was downright nasty. But cool.

Michael was beside himself when White Power Ranger disappeared during an outing at the mall. I looked at every store I could think of, but the Power Ranger fad had ebbed, and I could not find a replacement. Finally, I went on eBay, and found, for a mere $19.99, what looked like an exact reproduction of Michael's original White Power Ranger. When I announced my purchase to Michael, he replied, "Okay." The day the new White Power Ranger arrived, Edie and I sat near Michael as he unwrapped the package. Michael peeled back the paper and then the layers of bubble wrap to reveal the new plastic toy. Michael held him up high—it was all rather ceremonious—ensconced the White

Power Ranger in between his pointer finger and his thumb, and moved his hand in a quick back-and-forth motion. New White Power Ranger's hips stayed completely stiff. Michael set White Power Ranger down, put out both his hands, palms up, in my direction, shrugged his shoulders, and raised his eyebrows. Edie and I tried to remain composed, but we started giggling and couldn't stop—as in fell over on the floor, tears rolling down our faces, gasping for breath, couldn't stop. Luckily, Michael saw the humor and joined in. New White Power Ranger never did limber up.

Michael has used dance to shatter social norms. At the end of movies—Michael adores the cinema—he used to run up to the front of the movie theater and dance to the music that accompanied the credits. This was not random movement either. Oh, no! This was on-the-spot choreography that reflected the mood of the score. A rap song? Michael would freestyle and crump. Classical music? Michael would grand jeté and pirouette. Jazz? The only thing missing for Michael would be gloves and a hat pulled down over one eye, a la Anne Reinking. Edie and Joedy would often join Michael, but his brothers, Nathan and Sean, usually bolted the minute the dancing began. Jim and I would clap and holler: "Go Michael, go Michael . . ." Quite a few people stayed to see the credits roll just to be part of Michael's extravaganza. I used to worry that I was allowing some sort of "Down syndrome" show, but I let go of that fear. I remembered that on my first date with Jim, he actually fell out of his seat and rolled in the aisle of a movie theater he was laughing so hard. We were watching *Silver Streak* with Richard Pryor and Gene Wilder, which is, well, fall-out-of-your-seat-and-roll-in-the-aisles funny. I was not embarrassed. Nope. Instead, I recall thinking, "I am going to marry this guy." Movie theater shenanigans are a tradition in the Hulings household. *"Go Michael, go Michael!"* What if we all got out of our seats, filled the aisles and the fronts of movie theaters, and danced while the credits roll and we find out who the assistant to the assistant to the assistant of hairstyles is? I think that would be grand!

Casey put the kibosh on Michael's movie dancing when they started dating. She said it wasn't grown-up; her family is a bit more reserved in public than we are. Casey hasn't yet seen Jim and me (both grown-ups) waltz through King Soopers or boogie down in the middle of Macy's. We also race each other down the frozen foods section at Safeway. Still, even if she does witness our sophomoric antics, her mind will not change. I am glad that Casey can offer things to Michael that Jim and I never can or will.

Dance for Michael began as sheer celebration of movement to the ubiquitous presence of music in our home. He could find the beat and rhythm in the soundtrack to *Joseph and the Amazing Technicolor Dreamcoat* (the Donny Osmond version, of course). He was a maverick and found value in the pop group Pilot, just by actually dancing to "Magic" instead of gagging at the inane lyrics and bubblegum beat. Michael has found kinesthetic meaning in every cadence he has ever heard. Michael and his sisters have joined the animatronic riff-raff at Chuck-E-Cheese and danced away while the rest of the crowd nibbled on pizza and birthday cake. I watched Michael join an African Dance troupe at a First Night celebration and in minutes, he had down the metrical swinging of his arms, tossing of his head, and of course, the manipulation of his hips. He was leading the dancers. It was magical. I've watched Michael dance to the soundtrack of *Hairspray* while imitating Harvey Fierstein's raspy, throaty singing (extremely off-key and horrifying, but still a rather dead-on impression). Michael could always find a reason to dance.

Michael did not, however, beget the genesis of dance as a lovely sublimation for sex. Let's be honest; the real social lubricant isn't alcohol. It is dance—the ultimate foreplay. Get close, cop a feel, squeeze a tushy, bump and grind, get *really* close—this is not artistic expression, folks; this is down and dirty. Even ballet is suggestive; those lifts require the touching and caressing of some rather private body parts. Ballet just makes the groping beautiful. And, if your mother allowed you to watch MTV and BET—like I did for Michael—there are even subliminal and overt instruction manuals. No one ever says, "Look! Here is a great way to get off!" But the human mind registers sexuality better than, say, repetitive learning of our times tables. It's a built-in survival mechanism. Dance as a come-on is not a new trend; we've been touching one another to the strains of music forever. And so, when Michael asked a waitress at Red Lobster "How you doin'?" he wasn't beginning a cordial, mannerly conversation. The inquiry into the waitress' health was followed by another, more pointed query: "Wanna dance?"

I haven't raised a Lothario. Many folks who have Down syndrome also lack certain inhibitions. While you and I might willingly attach social norms to our actions and refrain from asking out the waitress/waiter at Red Lobster in fear of appearing creepy, we still might be internally thinking something to the effect of, "I want to jump his/her bones." The difference is that Michael's inside voice can often become his outside voice. He meant no harm; he simply was agonizingly truthful. He thought the waitress was hot and he let her know. No harm, no foul. Jim and I have spent the majority of Michael's adolescence helping him develop an inside voice. "Michael . . ." we would begin. "You're right; our waitress is cute. But you don't know her. She is doing her work right now. We don't ask people we don't know to dance with us in a restaurant." In essence, Jim and I have lied to Michael. Ever ask a complete stranger to dance at a food and drink establishment? Uh-huh. But we figured that Michael would not be frequenting many bars in his lifetime, so we were able to reframe our instruction as educational and imperative. Lacking inhibitions might be refreshing, to a point. We have to guide Michael carefully, without squashing his genuine adoration of humankind or making the expression of sexuality a bad thing. Casey has helped with this process.

◆ ◆ ◆

Dance is the foundation of Michael and Casey's relationship. They were both members of Dance Express—the dance troupe that mixes all kinds of people in the practice and performance of dance—and so their relationship had a nonverbal component built in from day one. They could watch and contemplate each other's bodies without it being perceived as ogling. Casey and Michael were the youngest members of the troupe at the time (Michael was seventeen and Casey was twenty-one), and the supervision of their coming and goings was a bit lax. So lax in fact, that it was easy for them to extend a change of costume for a dress rehearsal into something a bit more interesting. The two of them locked themselves into a bathroom and slowly stripped for each other. There was no touching at this point, but there was a lot of looking. How do I know this? Because both Michael and Casey have kept us all fully apprised of all aspects of their relationship. I know almost every step of the progression of their "dance." Along with the limited inhibitions associated with Down syndrome is also a lack of shame in that which is normal and beautiful. The typical individual's inability to speak candidly and frankly about all things sensual is a problem, not an asset. If only we all could talk about the time we stripped down to nothing and took a good long gander at new and exciting body parts, I think we'd all be much healthier.

Dance Express is a wonderful organization, but the dances were sometimes a little dated. Cindy decided to choreograph a piece for Michael and Casey for them to perform at the spring recital. To the crooning of John Travolta and Olivia Newton John's, "You're the One that I Want," Cindy created a dance for Michael and Casey that had them portraying Danny and Sandy from *Grease*. It was both innocent and highly eroticized, not because Cindy is a sexual deviant (she's not) but because the two dancers—Michael and Casey—were in love and their dance became an expression of that emotion. Michael's hair was slicked back, and he was dressed in a tight black T-shirt and tight black jeans. Casey wore body hugging, black leggings and a leotard with a low scoop in the back. At the end of the actual performance, Michael pulled Casey in close and gave her a soft, but passionate kiss. The audience oohed and aahed in a "isn't that cute" sort of way. "Cute" was not the word I had in mind. Dance was taking on new meaning for Casey and Michael.

In Michael's junior year at Rocky (Casey had graduated the spring before) he was crowned Junior Homecoming King with massive support from the football team. Casey attended the pep assembly where Michael's win was announced. While Jim and I were grinning from ear to ear, Casey was frowning. When the assembly ended, Jim and I ran to congratulate Michael, and Casey stayed behind. I took Casey out into the hallway.

"Casey! What is the matter? We should be happy for Michael." She began to cry.

"Casey! What is wrong?"

Casey looked up at me and choked out her pain. "I thought that if Michael was King that I would be Queen. I thought that I would get a crown and a sash, too. And I don't want him to dance with any other girl."

I took Casey in my arms and let her cry it out. I got it: if tomorrow someone crowned Jim as King, I had better be the only Queen next to him. Later, after I explained to Michael why Casey was upset, he went out for pizza with his junior high teacher, Tracy Gefroh, and together they stopped at the Dollar Store and bought Casey a toy tiara and sash. Casey wore the dime-store combo for a week. At the actual Homecoming dance, Casey became quite the snit when Michael danced the obligatory dance with the lovely Junior Queen with flaxen curls who had a good four inches on Michael. Casey pretended Michael didn't exist (she went off and group danced with some old friends) and told me (I was chaperoning) to bug off. I pulled her aside, told her enough was enough, and to shape up. We all put on smiley faces and went out for some ice cream. Inside my heart, I knew that I would not be too thrilled watching Jim slow dance with some tall blonde chick, obligatory dance or not. No matter our chromosome count, we all covet our dance partners.

Navigating Michael's sexual maturation has been startling. It has been so very . . . public. Whereas I have always been open about sexuality—my oldest son, Nathan recounts that he was the only child whose bedtime books included *Heather Has Two Mommies*—I was not prepared for one of my kids to Howard Cosell all the minute details of each step of his sex life.

When Michael and I sat on a wrought-iron bench, during the dinner rush hour, in the front of our local Olive Garden, with our little red, "your table is ready" buzzer in my hand, and Michael loudly proclaimed, "Mom, I really want to have sex with Casey!" at least I had an out. I had never discussed sex with one of my kids with twenty, hungry Olive Garden patrons looking on, and I had to think fast. Thank G-d for dance. "Oh, Michael, I think you should wait until the two of you get married," I said. I had never uttered those words before in my entire life. I continued, "Until then, you can do other things together, like dance." When my little red pager buzzed, I jumped for joy. I have never been so happy to be seated at a restaurant. It had been easier to negotiate Michael's superhero antics as he, say, ran across roofs or shot pretend Spidey webs in alleys. But this was new—I had never before explained sex to a superhero.

Soon after the Olive Garden sex talk, Jim and I decided it was time to have the "real talk" with Michael. We were not convinced that Michael knew exactly what having sex meant. So, we sat together and told Michael that we wanted to explain sex to him. We pulled out a rather graphic book, written explicitly for people who have Down syndrome, that includes no nonsense anatomical drawings and drawings of people engaged in intercourse.[3] Michael was riveted. Just in case Michael did not truly understand, I took it upon myself to mime the sex act using my fingers. I created a hole with my pointer finger and thumb, and using my other pointer finger, I made it go in and out of the hole. Jim grabbed my hands and muttered, "I think he gets it, honey. Now stop." When our tutorial ended, Michael chirped in, "So can Casey and I do that now?" Jim and I simultaneously replied, "No." Michael jutted out his lower lip and whined, "But I think about it all the time!"

Michael and Casey found ways to cope with the parental decision to delay the consummation of their relationship. One evening, Cindy walked in on Michael and Casey in Casey's bedroom. They had draped a red bandana over the lamp for mood lighting, and Casey was pole dancing for Michael (with an imaginary pole) using a pink shawl as her feather boa. Michael lay back on Casey's bed, his shirt off and his hands behind his head, taking in every shimmy Casey offered. Cell phones and computers have also really enhanced their art of coping. By prying and peeking, I have seen more than one sexy dance video starring Michael or Casey cross the fiber optic cable lines. That and some pretty steamy notes between the two that usually include illustrations of stick figures doing some neat horizontal dances. There are text messages that are direct and to the point: 'Sex?" "Yes, sex!"; "You have grt bobs [*sic*]!"; and "Do you like whipped cream?" Dance: it has no real limitations.

Dance does, though, transcend the physical plane. In truth, Michael and Casey love dance. Casey wanted to go on *American Idol* and sing and dance her way to stardom. Casey's voice is less horrifying than Michael's is, but it is not exactly lilting. Casey's folks were beside themselves with figuring out how to explain to Casey that it was wonderful to sing and dance for fun, but that she was not material for *American Idol*. Finally, they decided to video tape Casey and then watch the tape together. Seeing herself on tape, Casey realized that she wasn't a star. The next day, Casey decided to show Michael the video. When it was over, Michael turned to Casey and said, "You have the most beautiful voice, and you are the most beautiful dancer, ever." Screw *American Idol*.

There are more videos of Michael and Casey dancing and singing. At homecoming. At the high school prom. At another prom, put on every year at a respite care facility for kids with special needs every year with sponsorship from Colorado State University volunteers. On Michael's bed as the two serenade each other with a medley of songs from *Dirty Dancing*. Each captured moment looks more like love and less like choreography.

◆ ◆ ◆

Michael (age 17) and Casey in their Danny and Sandy costumes
after a performance from *Grease* for Dance Express

Michael (age 18) crowned as Junior Homecoming
King at Rocky Mountain High School

A couple of years ago, on the way to purchase a new *Speed Racer* toy, Michael and I bought Casey a promise ring. It was a temporary, post-talent show proposal ring. The real thing, the big purchase, occurred during the spring of 2010, when Cindy and I went shopping at Zale's, in the local Mall, where we found the perfect engagement ring. We knew it was perfect because we both started crying. It was not because of the way it shimmered under the jewelry store lights or the cut of the diamond, it was just the image of it on Casey's hand. After we bought the ring, Cindy and I sat on a bench and sipped iced teas. Cindy's voice cracked as she said, "I never even thought Casey would go to prom." Passersby might have been worried about the two middle-aged women crying in each other's arms, on a bench, in the middle of the mall, but they shouldn't have been.

Michael presented the ring to Casey at Chili's a few nights later. The entire staff helped us celebrate, and we all got complimentary smoothies. I wanted to dance, but Cindy, Casey, and James get embarrassed when I act out in public. So I just let my feet wiggle under the table.

At that point, Michael and Casey's wedding was slated for the spring of 2012 with a guest list of about a thousand people. They wanted the wedding at our house, in the front yard, but that would have been complicated. Jim and I would have needed to mow, roll up the hose, and pick some weeds. Maybe, if we had some pretty, white Christmas lights and strung them from our front yard ash tree, it could have detracted from the overgrown verbena and the incomplete layer of siding and trim on the face of our home.

The actual date of Michael and Casey's wedding is currently undetermined. As time goes on, when we imagine the planning of events, we think the most likely site for the ceremony will be the sprawling estate of my good friend, and Michael's junior high teacher, Tracy Gefroh. In the end, it does not really matter where the wedding takes place. As long as we have dancing, it will be wonderful. And, if anyone hears me scream out "Oh, ouch!" it will not be because I'm in agony over my son getting married or the way he most likely will horrifyingly serenade his new bride. No. It will just mean that even though I knew it might hurt, I decided to dance my heart out anyway.

Michael (age 17) and Casey before Casey's Senior Prom

Waiting

As Michael approached his fifteenth birthday, he became energized by the upcoming promise of gifts and cake and maybe a party. His birthday is in February. In November, on a Monday, during dinner time conversation, Michael asked Jim how long it was until his birthday.

"Your birthday will be in eleven Mondays, Michael," Jim offered. Jim is an engineer, a scientist, and he can reduce everything to equations and numbers.

I glared across the table. "You're kidding, right?" I said.

"Eleven Mondays?" Michael piped in.

"No, Michael," I interrupted. "Your birthday is not for a very long time. Let's think about something we can do *today* that is fun, okay?"

"Wait," Jim said. "Hey, Michael, let's get out a calendar and mark the eleven Mondays!"

And so they did. Michael had a calendar with the eleven Mondays until his birthday marked with big, red, Xs. Jim went to work for the next eleven weeks and solved engineering problems that are versed in terms and ideas completely disconnected from the daily lives of most folks. I spent the next eleven weeks answering Michael's daily, sometimes hourly question: *Is it Monday? Is it Monday? Is it Monday?*

Michael has a very limited sense of time. His life moves in increments that are not consistently tied to where the hands on a clock have settled at any given moment. How Michael's chronologically led life unwinds, at least in fragments of hours, minutes, and seconds, is often determined by the whims and regulations of other people—people who are older, can be identified as "typical," and who are not living with the challenges of a developmental disability. In many ways, Michael's life echoes the five-year-old query, chirped out every five minutes of a twenty-hour drive from the backseat of a mini-van: *Are we there yet? Are we there yet? Are we there yet? Is it Monday?* Michael, however, is not five. He is in his twenties. It's complicated.

Now, Michael wears a large watch on his right wrist made by a company called Watchminder. This watch is huge. Its circumference is significantly larger than that of a silver dollar. This watch, the Watchminder Two, is considered assistive technology, meaning technological tools that provide guidance and cues toward successful self-care for folks who live with special needs. Jim has programmed Michael's watch to vibrate at specific times: when to eat breakfast, when to brush his teeth, when to go to work, when to come home, when to go to flag football, when to bathe, when to go to bed, and so on. The watch can hold up to sixty-five vibrating alarms accompanied by a written message that appears on the face of the watch. *Sixty-five.* I have tried to count the number of things I do every day that are necessary—personal hygiene, cooking, eating, grading papers, taking medications, writing, corresponding with students, calling my mother, exercising, laundry, cleaning, watching *Modern Family*, attending class, going to the bathroom, teaching, playing with my dogs, reading, paying attention to Jim, taking care of Michael, checking up on my other kids, driving all over town, emailing, shopping, and so on—and it is surprising how quickly the number sixty-five approaches. I wouldn't want to have a vibration in my pocket to remind me of all I must do. It would annoy me because sometimes I like to mix up my days and surprise myself with spontaneity, change the order of my responsibilities, or let one or two slide. But Michael has no choice. He gets vibrated all day and there are many people who watch over him; we all hover and wait and make sure he pays attention to that big old watch.

◆ ◆ ◆

Not long after Michael's eighteenth birthday, Jim, Michael, and I spent an afternoon at the Larimer County Courthouse participating in a ritual reserved for families who have a member with a special needs. I remember waiting to turn eighteen: *Emancipation! Freedom! Beer!* This was not quite Michael's experience. When a child who has special needs reaches the age of eighteen, that child's parents have two choices: 1) the parents can give up parental rights and hand the care of their child over to the state; or 2) parents can maintain parental rights, but they have to apply for legal guardianship through a lawyer and the court system. That's right—after eighteen years of rocking Michael to sleep, teaching him to read, feeding him, clothing him, kissing his boo-boos, and spending every waking minute making sure he was healthy and happy, the state of Colorado required us (and every other family in a similar situation) to apply for guardianship. I understand that the foundation of this decree is to ensure the safety—in mind, body, and pocketbook—of folks with special needs. I understand that the system is trying to make sure that evil adults (and there are some) are not just "parenting" in order to run off with whatever meager supportive funds their child with special needs might receive. I get all of this, but it still smarts.

And so, after reams of paperwork, lawyer's fees, and a visit from a court appointed social worker to make sure we were good people, the three of us stood before a judge, in court, seeking approval to be fit guardians for Michael. The judge had few questions.

"Michael," he started, "Do you like living with your parents?"

"Actually, Your Honor," Michael said, "I do not."

Your Honor? Where in the world did Michael learn that phrase? Could it have been from my addiction to all things *Law and Order*? I looked at Jim who had started to silently titter, his shoulders moving up and down in rhythm with his breathy tee-hees.

"Why don't you like living with your parents, Michael?" the judge asked, a slight look of concern filling the space between his brows.

"Well, Your Honor, they make me eat vegetables, and they don't let me eat fast food all the time. They make me clean my room. And I can't watch TV whenever I want," Michael explained.

"I see," said the judge, now biting his lower lip.

"Your Honor?" Michael continued.

"Yes, Michael?"

"Your Honor, I would like to live with Casey," Michael said with his chin jutted upwards and his gaze directly honed into the judge's eyes.

"Who is Casey?" the judge asked.

"Casey is my love. She is the best girlfriend ever. She is a great kisser. I love her very much, and I want to live with her and Cindy and James," Michael clarified for the judge.

I hung my head and shook it back and forth. Please, G-d, I prayed, let this be a sane and reasonable judge. Please, G-d, let Michael stop talking sooner than later. Please G-d, make Jim stop giggling.

"Who are James and Cindy?" the judge asked.

"They are my other mother and father," Michael said.

"Well, Michael, Cindy and James aren't here. And I bet they want you to stay with your Mom and Dad," the judge replied.

"Well, then, what about Jane?" Michael asked with his hands thrust out palms up.

That did it. Jim and I burst. We guffawed. It was very un-court-like. Jane is my sister and Michael's favorite aunt. She is fun, she always smells like summer and flowers, she is beautiful, and she has lots of cookies and games. Michael's favorite cousin, Zach, Jane's son, has toy collections from Heaven. Who wouldn't want to live with Jane?

"Who is Jane?" the befuddled judge queried.

I stepped in and explained Jane's identity. I wasn't suppose to talk, but . . . well . . . wouldn't you have stepped in?

"Well, Michael, Jane isn't here either," the judge reminded Michael. "I think she wants you to be with your Mom and Dad, too. Okay?"

"No, Your Honor. I don't want everyone to tell me what to do anymore. I don't want to have to wait all the time. I always have to wait for everyone else to tell me when I can do things. I want to get married to Casey," Michael spilled out.

"Michael," the judge explained, "You may have to wait a little bit longer for all those things. Your Mom and Dad will help you get to the point where you can do more things on your own. We all have to wait sometimes."

Michael gave a nod of agreement. Jim and I were asked if we accepted the role of Michael's official guardians, and then, with a quick signing of papers and some shuffling of a law clerk, the system reaffirmed that Michael was, indeed, ours to parent for as long as we saw fit.

◆ ◆ ◆

Michael was surrounded by "typical" school friends who were getting ready to go away to college, who took road trips with their buddies, and stayed out late at night. They were spending less and less time with their parents, and there we were reasserting our control and our ability to make Michael wait for an indefinite period of time for what was already at hand for his peers. It was confusing for him.

In fact, in the realm of special needs and developmental challenges, I have seen that the chronological development of the body and the mind in relation to societal norms and expectations of how we grow up rarely match up like some grand alignment of the cosmos. Michael graduated from high school at the age of nineteen. That may be the only similarity—though perhaps off by a year—that he shared with most of his peers who sat in CSU's Moby gym in 2010, in rows and rows of metal chairs, sweating in caps and gowns while listening to the band play "Pomp and Circumstance" and teachers give farewell remarks and platitudes. Most of Michael's peers had spent the past six months beefing up their resumes and sending out applications to college. Not Michael.

A funny thing happens as children with special needs get older in the school system. It becomes advantageous to make these kids look a bit more needy on paper than they might be in real life. This sort of representation ensures that there will be services for the child; the higher the need, the more likely the school will hire an extra paraprofessional. This is not on-the-books policy. It's the hush-hush talk that floats between parents at back-to-school night: "Don't make a big deal out of the fact that Michael is reading so well," says cautious, experienced mom #1; "Just say he still needs support," pipes in cynical, experienced mom # 2. The parents know the routine. We had spent much of Michael's high school years reconciling how to celebrate accomplishment, push for inclusion, and still make sure Michael got the services he needed. The process is frustrating and exhausting. Still, as we came to an end of Michael's high school years, the frustrating and exhausting predictability of working the K–12 system looked preferable to what lay ahead.

The few months before Michael's graduation, we once again sat at an IEP to discuss his post-high school future. By law, kids with special needs are serviced by the public school system until they reach the age of twenty-one. It is not a clear cut process. I usually went to IEPs armed and ready, but this time, I arrived with a blank notebook and a pen. I'd been trying to investigate the mysterious world of special education after the brick and mortar solidity of the K–12 journey. Answers were usually couched in an evasive, "Well . . . it depends . . ." At the IEP, I immediately asked, "What are the options?" The folks around the table squirmed and cocked their heads from side-to-side and tapped pencils and ran fingers through hair in obvious discomfort.

I don't remember who disrupted the palpable tension and outlined the details of Michael's potential future. I do remember being offered four choices: 1) call it a day, wave goodbye to the school district forever, and join forces with our local rehabilitation center and the State

Division of Vocational Rehabilitation; 2) enroll Michael in a program that was totally life-skills based and meant for folks with very high needs; 3) enroll Michael in program that was community based (visits to exercise facilities, the mall, restaurants, learning bus routes, volunteering, and dipping toes into workplace internships); or 4) apply to a program called Project Search that is a combined effort between the school district, a retirement/assisted living health care facility, and a national organization that emphasizes functional workplace literacy and places participants in three, ten-week internships with the goal of being hired as a paid employee—with benefits—at the end of the year-long program.

I should have been grateful. I should have kissed the feet of the professionals, parents, and politicians who fought long and hard for these opportunities. I should have. Instead, I felt a tiny crack in the middle of my heart grow and split and make simple the release of a torrent of grief.

"All these options," I stuttered. "They are contained. Oh, my G-d, they are contained. We have worked and struggled for nineteen years to make sure Michael has led a thoroughly inclusive life. We have made sure that he is part of, not apart from, the world. And now, now you are telling us that our choices all mean that Michael will spend his days solely with other people who have special needs? Really? *Really?* Is *this* what we have been waiting for? Is this it?"

Jim held my hand under the table and gave it a little squeeze—a signal that he loves me, a reminder to take a breath, and a cue to calm down. I stopped my spew of sorrow. The room was very, very, very quiet. I am not the first mom to break down in such a meeting; the veterans in the room knew that silence was the only option at hand. In the quiet, while others shuffled papers and took sips of coffee, I thought hard and fast. I reminded myself that this small group of well-meaning, hard-working people could not solve the inequities of the world at my son's IEP. I reminded myself that whatever decisions we made were not the end all, be all; Jim and I always took responsibility for Michael's well-being. We joined forces with the systems that interact with the realm of disability, but never before had we completely depended on any system to do *our* work. This time would be no different.

♦ ♦ ♦

We selected the Project Search option, deciding that Michael was ready to be trained for the workplace. There was a risk—by selecting Project Search, we were also signing up for one year of services instead of two. The program was a one-year shot, and there was nothing offered afterward. Michael also wasn't exactly consistent or dependable in his abilities; he was still social, dear, kind, and funny, but not necessarily a great worker. I tossed and turned with this decision, wondering if it was sane. In the end, my confusion was settled by outside forces. At the end of Michael's senior year, maybe a couple of weeks before graduation, Jim and I received a rash of desperate emails and calls. "Contact us quickly! It's about Michael!" "We need to talk about Michael!" "Time is of the essence! For Michael's future! Call! Soon!"

The big, hurried news was that all of Michael's teachers felt strongly—vehemently—that Michael was not ready for Project Search. They told us he did not have the stamina, did not have the work ethic, and needed two years to transition, not one. They figured this out after plans were in motion. In all fairness, they were right. I wasn't tossing and turning for nothing. This meant a new meeting with all the professionals at a table, this time adding the director of the community based program, which was the new suggested path. The community program was Cooper Home. Yep—Cooper Home. The same place Michael despised as a junior high student. The same place he was exiled from when he ran up and down the aisles of Safeway, during a Cooper Home field trip, infamously yelling, "I hate this shit!" As we sat at yet another IEP meeting, I, too, hated this shit.

What was it that I expected? I already knew that there were many kind, if not law-abiding citizens in my town. Everywhere we went,

Michael asked for a job application. Michael had witnessed his four, older siblings work at many jobs, go to college, and pursue careers. He knew the mechanics of the routine. Most of the time, without blinking, people complied, handed Michael a long, complicated form, and wished him good luck. Michael would then hand me the application and excitedly tell me that he had a job. I was left explaining the process of gaining employment. I had to explain that he couldn't be a lifeguard because it would hurt his ears to go deep under water; that he couldn't be a truck driver because he didn't have a driver's license; that he couldn't be a cashier because it might be hard for him to stand for many hours; or that he couldn't be a waiter because the trays were too heavy for him to carry. In other words, I lied. I never told him that he could never understand how to perform CPR, that he could never pass a driver's license test, that he could never understand the functions of a cash register and giving change, or that he could never write down peoples' orders for eggs-over-easy. I never told him that the world I imagined—the undivided one full of people with open arms, hearts, and minds, whose bottom net worth was not the driving force in their lives and, as such, would hire him as an act of humanity and as a long term commitment to training him and helping him create his future—does not yet exist. I have kept that understanding to myself. It could be said that I expected, and was waiting for, the impossible.

We were assured that Cooper Home had changed and was no longer involved with junior high and senior high students as a pull-out training program for washing dishes and sweeping floors. It was now a transition program, only for post-high school graduates, with the goal of meaningful movement into adulthood. We signed up and hoped for the best. It was, as it turned out, a very good year. Maybe the world I imagine is not as impossible as I assume.

Cooper Home was now run by Gayna Jobe, a no-nonsense, tell it like it is educator with years of experience and heart of gold. Michael's days were indeed contained in an exclusionary environment, but they were productive. With help, he created and typed a resume on the computer. He led his own IEPs using a PowerPoint. He learned about stranger awareness and healthy eating habits, and he cooked full meals. He went to Rockies baseball games and toured museums. He made dog biscuits and sold them for a fund raiser. He learned a bus route to a local gym. He tried to negotiate money and paying for things, and he practiced grocery shopping without running in the aisles screaming, "I hate this shit."

Michael was also hooked up with three internships in the real world. At Beaver's Market—a small, family owned grocery store—Michael stacked boxes of cereal. Michael loves cereal. So much so that one day he tried to steal three boxes of cereal from Beaver's by zipping them under his hoodie. We were fortunate that all parties involved used Michael's potential criminality as a teachable moment instead of an arrestable moment. "Michael," his work coach said, "If you want to get some cereal, you can buy it. Don't take it. That's wrong. You won't be able to work here if you take things." That's all it took; Michael's life of crime ceased and every time he went to Beaver's he had a few dollars in his wallet to buy a treat.

Two mornings a week, Michael also interned at The Egg and I, a local breakfast and brunch spot. He prepped and bussed tables. He did it thoroughly and perfectly and very, very, very slowly. To speed up his thorough process, they dangled a carrot in front of him—he could get a plate of home-fries at the end of his ninety-minute shift. Thank G-d for home fries. The staff and manager were supportive and would have been willing to hire Michael—for real—if he had proven himself to be ready. He was not ready. Speed is the name of the game in the restaurant business, and Michael was not moving at anything near a breakneck speed. He chatted with customers and staff and made folks laugh, but it took him five times as long as a "typical" worker to complete any given task.

We moved on. Texas Roadhouse agreed to take on Michael as an intern to bus tables and peel potatoes. The gig was after school hours though, so the district could not provide a job coach. This did not seem to faze Jimmy, the manager. On Michael's first day, I escorted him into the building and connected him with Jimmy, a stout man with a booming voice, a loud, easy laugh, and bulging biceps.

"Okay! Let's get going, Michael!" Jimmy said.

I started to follow them. Jimmy turned and stared me down with a smile.

"Michael is in good hands. You should go," he said.

And he ushered Michael away. I retreated to my car and marveled at what had just transpired. No job coach, no professional presence and no mom hovering. Just a good old-fashioned boss, peer pressure, and . . . normalcy. I was breathless. Michael worked at Texas Roadhouse for five months, two days-a-week, for ninety minutes a pop. He bussed tables and he became more and more efficient under the watchful eyes of his fellow workers. A few times, Jim and I popped in for a meal during his shift and we would see him back in the kitchen, sipping a soda and chatting it up with one of the cooks when he was supposed to be hard at work. He was also caught catching a few winks in empty booths every now and then. I never said Michael became a perfect employee; he became a better employee. He was not hired on at the end of his internship stint.

Still, Michael became part of a group that to this day, when we go there to grab a bite, welcomes him and celebrates his appearances. One night, over steaks and chicken fingers, a waitress asked Michael what he was up to these days.

"Oh, I'm busy at school, my parents are annoying, and I am going to get married to Casey," Michael replied.

"You're just livin' the dream, huh?" the waitress replied.

Michael nodded and smiled. When another waitress came to refresh our drinks, she, too asked Michael how he was. Armed with a new turn of a phrase, he lilted, "I am living *my* dream!"

♦   ♦   ♦

Michael's transition included more life changes than just learning bus routes, working at internships, and making dog biscuits. The summer before he entered Cooper Home we got a forecast of all things transitional that were to come. I was in my office, in the early evening, writing, when Jim shouted out, 'Hey—why is there a fire engine in front of our house?" The two of us stepped out on to the front porch and saw Michael coming round the corner, holding his cell phone with one hand and clutching his chest with the other, just as a police car and an ambulance joined the fire truck. Michael was jogging at a fairly decent clip. Jim and I didn't even know he had left the house. Michael greeted the fire fighters, paramedics, and police officers on our front lawn with a wave. "We got a call that someone was having heart trouble?" inquired one of the paramedics. "Yes," Michael said, still holding his chest, "I am having heart trouble. My chest hurts."

Jim and I remained on the porch; we both had our arms folded in front of our bodies, our lips were pursed—to the casual passerby we would not have looked like very concerned or caring parents. We looked mad. We were mad. Michael lay down on the lawn, and the paramedics took his blood pressure and his pulse. Jim and I beckoned another paramedic to join us for a little aside.

"He's fine," said Jim. "Could you please get out a really big needle and tell him you're going to stick him with it?"

Before the paramedic could call over a police officer to arrest Jim for suspected child abuse, I entered the conversation.

"Really, he is fine. I bet this has something to do with Casey, his girlfriend. They've been fighting today."

The paramedic nodded, and the three of us sauntered over to where Michael was surrounded by people in uniforms. I crouched down next to Michael who was now sitting, crying, and begging to be taken to the hospital to fix his broken heart.

"Michael, what happened?" I asked while Jim asked another paramedic if there was anything really alarming they could pull out of the ambulance and threaten Michael with it.

"Casey broke my heart," he sobbed.

"You guys been fighting?" I probed.

"Yes. And my heart hurts."

"Is that why you called 911?"

"Yes. I want them to take me to the hospital and make me feel better."

By now, all uniformed personnel were listening and were on the verge of breaking into a chorus of "Aw…" I glanced up and shot them all a "don't you dare" look accompanied by a sharp shake of my head.

"Michael," I reentered our chat, "We only call 911 when there is an emergency. Do you remember what an emergency is? Tell me."

"Fire? Bleeding? Can't get up? Can't breathe? Choking?"

"Right. Do we call 911 when we are upset and sad just because we had a little fight with someone?"

"Yes?"

"*No,* Michael. We don't. Right now all these people need to be ready to help someone who is really badly hurt or really sick. Please never do this again. If you and Casey have a fight, I bet your heart will hurt again. But Mom and Dad will talk with you. Or Sean, or Nathan, or Joedy, or Edie."

A handsome paramedic got down on the ground with Michael and put his arm around his shoulders.

"Michael," he confided, "Girls are gonna break your heart every now and then, buddy. But you can get through it, okay?"

"So . . . can you take me to the hospital?" Michael continued.

Jim stepped in with an adamant, "No! That's enough." He got Michael to his feet, and we all thanked Fort Collins' finest for their time and understanding. We make sure to donate to the Police and Firefighters Fund each year to show our appreciation for being so kind in this difficult situation. Then we went inside, where Jim took Michael's phone away for three days. Matters of the heart need at least that long to transition well.

The fall Michael entered Cooper Home, the 911 saga just a few weeks behind us, we all were aware that interwoven between the strands of Cooper Home rituals and intermediary steps toward adulthood, there also ran the titanium thread of the Michael and Casey story with its own rituals and intermediary steps toward adulthood. There have been so many eyes peeled on those two kids, watching and reporting on their every move. So very many eyes.

Soon after Michael graduated from high school, Casey's parents—Cindy and James—and Jim and I began to switch weekends having the kids stay with us. Every Saturday, Michael and Casey go bowling at a local alley with a Special Olympics program. There are reliable folks there who help and monitor the goings and comings of the participants, so, both sets of parents often choose to not stay. One weekend, which was designated a "Cindy and James" weekend, Cindy got a call from the recreational therapist in charge of Saturday's bowling.

"Cindy," she cautiously began, "Casey is ordering a beer—a Fat Tire—at the bar. She said she's had a hard day and really needs a beer. Can she have a beer?"

Cindy replied with an emphatic, "No!" peppered with a sigh and a chuckle.

Casey was of age (she was twenty-three). She could legally order alcohol. She had been watching adults order drinks her whole life; that Saturday, she was done waiting. It was her turn to throw back a pint.

Michael watched this whole Fat Tire saga unravel from the initial order to the phone call to the stern reprimand Casey received from Cindy on the way home. That did not stop him from ordering a beer a few weeks later when he, Jim, and I were at Old Chicago for a slice of pizza.

"Michael—you can't order a beer. You're too young!" I said as I cut short his foray into his first cold one.

"When I'm twenty-one can I get a beer?" Michael asked.

Jim looked at me from across the booth. "Yeah, Kathryn—when Michael's twenty-one, can he get a beer?"

"Well . . . I mean . . . I think . . . um . . . sure. Sure. Michael can get a beer when he's twenty-one. As long as I'm there with him. Now, where's our pizza?" I asked trying to redirect our attention.

Doesn't every young man want his mom along when he orders his first legal beer?

Michael and Casey rely on us for transportation as well as running liquor consumption interference. They are learning how to navigate buses, but there is always the nagging fear of exploitation and potential danger lurking on a bus. You just never know. Casey is far more cautious than Michael. She does the protecting—she will shun any stranger—and Michael does the talking and schmoozing—he'll ask for directions and locations when the need arises. But usually at least one set of parents is nearby. On restaurant dates, Casey and Michael get their own table, but some set of parents sit nearby, peeking over potted plants to see if they are eating a balanced meal. At movies, Casey and Michael sit alone with Twizzlers and Diet Coke, but we are either a few rows behind or in the theater next door, sometimes text messaging them to make sure they don't eat all the licorice and get tummy aches. When Michael and Casey go to Barnes & Noble to get a new book, DVD, or CD, there we are again, pretending to listen to a selection from a new CD release, headphones securely on our heads, but the volume is on zero, so we can eavesdrop on the lovebirds as they discuss what new entertainment to purchase.

It is not safe to venture too far away. During Michael's first transition year, I decided to leave him and Casey in the music area at Barnes & Noble while I perused the poetry aisle. I was gone no more than five minutes. When I returned, Michael was at the checkout with Casey, deep in conversation with the clerk. I quickened my pace, reaching the counter right as the young, male clerk was pulling a ten dollar bill out of his pocket and handing it to Michael.

"Hey, there!" I offered in greeting. "What's up?"

"Well . . . see . . . he . . ." the clerk explained, pointing to Michael. "He didn't have enough money, and I wanted to help him out, so I a decided to spot him a ten—"

"Oh, thanks—really—but no thanks," I interrupted before I turned to Michael whose chin rested on his chest and whose lip pouted down to his chin.

"Michael, we need to fix this problem, okay?"

I spent the next ten minutes figuring out that Michael had tried to pay for a *Harry Potter* movie and two more music CDs—for Casey—with an old gift card with no money left on it and a new gift card with about thirty dollars left on it that he dug out of his wallet. In his mind, the cards were money. And money is simply money to Michael. If he has a card—any kind of card—he can buy whatever he wants. And why shouldn't he think this? Jim and I pay for everything with a credit card. It's magic: we hand over our card, we sign a piece of paper, and we leave with a purchase. Michael recently left me a note to find when I woke from a nap that said: "I borwed yr deb it crd. Bk son. Luv, Michael." Thankfully, I woke up before he left and took a walk to Safeway, across the street, to buy G-d knows what. Some nights when we go out to dinner, Michael has taken out his library card to pay the bill, announcing, "it's on me!" Money is a conundrum. And so, at Barnes & Noble that evening, I only had one choice; I paid the difference that Michael owed, with a VISA card of course, and Casey got a nice treat.

On the way home, I listened to the backseat chatter between Michael and Casey.

"This is love," Casey cooed. "If you have a gift card, you buy me things. If I have a gift card, I buy you things."

"I will buy you whatever you want," Michael said.

"And then we will get married," Casey declared before they fell into a lip lock of epic proportions.

◆ ◆ ◆

I hope that Michael and Casey get married. Marriage is a weird institution to begin with, but considering it as part of Michael and Casey's future takes it beyond weird and into the realm of the almost supernatural. When I consider marriage for these two, I have to remind myself of some real life specifics: I still cut Michael grapes in half so he won't choke; Michael is still terrified of monkeys—so much so that he almost fainted when we went to see the most recent *Transformers* movie and a preview for *The Planet of the Apes* was shown, and the rest of the summer, I had to offer bribes (money, clothes, Thai food) to Michael to get him to the movie theater; Casey proclaims she is well, after a bout with a cold, by saying, "The bug crawled out of me;" at large gatherings and on long car rides, Michael and Casey pass the time by coloring in coloring books and playing tic-tac-toe; on the weekends, they take turns riding Michael's electric scooter, swinging on the porch swing while drinking smoothies, watching movies, playing X-Box games, crooning with a karaoke machine while strumming Michael's electric guitar, dancing to CDs, and snuggling on the couch in their pajamas; and during the week, they call each other at midnight to say goodnight. Michael and Casey are in their twenties. The chronologies of age and their expected behavioral corollaries are simply out of whack. At least some of them are. Some are in sync. Sort of.

In December of Michael's Cooper Home experience, he became sullen and morose. He would not talk, his eyes were filled with tears, and he curled up in a ball on the couch. I was panicked, because Michael is rarely unhappy, let alone sullen and morose.

"What's wrong, honey?" I asked.

"Nothing," his voice cracked.

"Something is wrong, Michael. Please tell me," I coaxed.

And the story spilled. Michael told Casey that he kissed another girl—his old, two-minute flame from junior high who was also at Cooper Home. Michael then told me that he was "a different kind of man," and Casey told him that "he was not the kind of man she thought he was and they needed to break up." Sullen and morose made sense, but nothing else did. Another girl? A kiss? "A different kind of man?" What the hell?

I called Gayna, the director at Cooper Home and asked if any hanky-panky had transpired between Michael and the other girl. Gayna investigated—thoroughly—and no such thing had occurred, at least not at Cooper Home. Remember: time has no real meaning for Michael. The story he told Casey was an ancient one. Yes—Michael and another girl stole a kiss in seventh grade, but not recently. I suppose guilt knows no boundaries of time and space. And the "different kind of man" line? Watch Michael Jackson's *Thriller* video, which my own Michael had been watching incessantly the weeks before he turned morose and sullen. Before he turns into a zombie, Jackson explains to his date that he, indeed, is a "different kind of man." Not unlike reciting lines from *Angels in the Outfield*, Michael was simply inserting found dialogue into what seemed like an appropriate context. I called Cindy and explained the whole saga so that she could somehow tell Casey that Michael was still the man she thought he was, and that he was just a bit confused by the passage of time and the meaning of an MTV video. I also had to explain to Michael that it is best to not tell Casey about past girlfriends. Not ever.

Michael and Casey enact most of the ins-and-outs and ups-and-downs of male-female relationships. More than once, I have glanced in the rearview view of my car and caught Michael fast asleep on Casey's shoulder while, for example, she talks about her grief over a dog that died. Michael is not the first man to doze off while his woman is talking. Casey is not the first woman to keep on talking anyway. Michael orders for Casey in restaurants, and Casey fluffs a napkin on his lap before they eat. They shop together and plan menus for the weekend. They go on dates. They have snits over whose turn it is to put the clothes in the dryer. And they have sex.

Hormones and desire did not pass by Michael and Casey. But, unlike many of their peers, they had to wait for permission to consummate their relationship. They never really could find a time to be completely alone. Some parents were always hovering, lurking, watching. Jim and I have always been open about sexuality with all or kids. We were open with Michael, too, but it was different. There were many things to consider. There was the knowledge that Michael could become fixated on things he enjoyed at the expense of other activities. It was not a stretch of the imagination to assume that sex might fall under the category of things Michael would really enjoy. There was the issue of birth control. Michael and Casey will be challenged to successfully raise a puppy; kids are not an option for this couple. We parents needed to figure out the best way to prevent pregnancy. Then there was the need to make sure that Michael and Casey understood the idea of sex as private and sacred and . . . well . . . how to actually do it.

Finally, during the Cooper Home era, on a fall evening, during a weekend at Casey's house, Michael and Casey were given the go ahead to make love. Cindy set electric candles and mood music in the bedroom and then closed the door. When Jim and I picked up Michael later that weekend, he bounded up the stairs, stood in the middle of the living room, in front of all four parents and Casey, and announced, "We did it!" I asked if everything went well. Michael and Casey held hands, touched heads, and smiled dreamy smiles. So much for needing instructions.

Today, Michael and Casey's room is directly below Jim's and mine, and it is audibly clear that their physical relationship is healthy and thriving. As such, I have petitioned for soundproofing, which Jim says is impossible. Michael and Casey consistently demonstrate that they feel no shame in their enjoyment of each other. A year past the "first time," on weekends at our house, Casey and Michael started to take baths together in the really big tub in the bathroom right off our great room where we watch TV. It is usually a very noisy bath. Sean, who is still playing the field, teasingly asked me if, when he gets a serious girlfriend, it's okay if he and she take a bath while Jim and I watch *CSI* or *Law and Order* or *Nightline*. I told him that if he could find a gal willing to take noisy baths while her future in-laws are right next door watching TV, then kudos to him.

◆ ◆ ◆

Who had Michael become? He was not the sickly baby who arrived at Stapleton with a bottle meant for an animal and a bagful of medicines. He was no longer the boy who ran and hid. He no longer believed he could fly. He was becoming an adult. After a year at Cooper Home, it was determined that Michael had built up enough stamina and work ethic to make Project Search and working in a local retirement community a reasonable option. This time, there was not a flood of phone calls to change plans; it was agreed that Michael was now entirely ready for Project Search. We moved forward with this final step, realizing this was our final year cushioned by the support of our school system.

The first six weeks of Project Search were iffy. Michael acted tired. He sat down a lot and spent inordinate amounts of time in the bathroom. I got worried emails from the staff about whether or not Michael could stay in the program. He told me that he hated old people and didn't want to be with them. But I waited. Michael has a strange internal clock when it comes to new situations. The first six weeks of his infancy, of his life, were fraught with illness, unpredictability, and constant movement. Who knows what sort of effect that has on the spirit? Throughout his life, the first six weeks of any experience have not gone swimmingly for Michael. And then, he turns; he gets the expectations, the routine, the rules of the game. There will ensue some hiccups, of course, but for the most part, things will coalesce and gel. At the six week point at Project Search, I requested a meeting with Michael's teacher and coach to discuss their concerns. "It's amazing," they said. "The past few days he has become a new person. It's just amazing." I have no earthly explanation for why Michael has this particular sense of time. I only know that if I wait six weeks, he and his inner clock will prevail.

Still, I am not a fool. Sometimes waiting six weeks will mean nothing. Not too long ago, we received a reverse 911 call at my home regarding an armed man on the loose. I was honest with Michael about the call, because I did not want him leaving the house for an unannounced walk or bike ride or jaunt on his scooter.

"Should I put on my Spiderman costume?" Michael asked.

"Oh, no, honey. This is real. The real police will take care of it, okay?" I answered.

Michael smiled a tiny smile that almost told me was he teasing. Almost.

I know that Michael is becoming well-practiced in the family art of teasing and kidding. Sometimes, though, I need to remind myself that his understandings of life are quite literal and are not nuanced with winks and nudges. I got just such a reminder at our local mall. Michael's two sisters both got married the summer before Project Search. I was dragging Michael around with me all summer to the mall and various other stores getting wedding stuff. One such afternoon at the mall, Michael was lollygagging while I was moving with purpose, as quickly as my old body could move.

"Michael, hurry up!" I called to him. "Catch up!"

"Mama, Mama, Mama, I really want something!" Michael told me when he reached my heels.

"What do you want?" I asked.

"I really, really, really, want one of those necklaces with a plus sign!"

I looked back to where Michael had been dilly dallying. He had been loitering at a kiosk that sold necklaces with crucifixes and other religious icons.

"Oh, honey. That's not a plus sign. That's a cross," I explained.

I started to tell the story of the cross, thought better of it, and simply said, "It's something Christians wear, and we are not Christian. We are Jewish. Okay?"

Michael shrugged his shoulders and said, "Okay."

We went on shopping. Later, when I told Jim about the experience, he quickly informed me that I missed a great line. "You should have told him that he could get something way better than a plus sign," he jested. "You should have told him that he got a star!"

Also during the summer before Project Search, we enrolled Michael in a private reading program to boost his workplace skills. The room where he was tutored had a small viewing window. I watched and listened as he stared intensely at his books, slowly spitting out the words. Each visit, he began the lesson by writing a journal entry, usually about Casey; he loved writing about their time together or their wedding plans. His second most intense interest, after writing about Casey, was in learning about money and getting a debit card of his own. So at his sessions, he and his tutor worked primarily on the language of money and work. I wondered if he was learning anything that made sense in his reality. On the way home from a reading session, I asked Michael what he wanted to do for a job.

"I want to work in a bank or in technology," he said.

"What would you do in the bank," I asked?

"I would count money and then I would put it in the tube and watch it go down the tube and then the people in the cars would catch the money."

"And what about technology?"

"I would go to work with Dad and I would sit at a computer and I would research about Spiderman."

At Project Search, instead of banking or technology, Michael served juice and snacks to elderly people, cleaned computers, and stocked shelves. It was not the stuff his dreams were made of or what he waited and worked for all these years. Still, Michael brings something to the workplace that I know many folks with PhDs are incapable of doing. One time, while Michael was serving juice, one elderly man expressed that he felt dizzy. Without coaching or prompting, Michael helped the gentleman lie down, lifted his legs into a comfortable position, covered up the man with a warm blanket, and sat with him while he finished his juice.

I get it. Michael doesn't fully understand time or money or religious symbols. He is both aware and unaware. He is both wise and completely innocent. He knows himself and he doesn't know himself. So? If we are honest, we are all like Michael in one way or another.

♦ ♦ ♦

I owe my mother-in-law, Alice, a long, overdue apology. I love Alice. I do. But I used to think that she was sort of a buttinsky when it came to Jim. She had many suggestions, and I ignored most of them. Sometimes Alice would walk away from me making a little *humph, humph, humph* sound under her breath. Not too long ago, I went out to lunch with Casey—just the two of us—while Michael was at school. The realization of my own impending mother-in-law-hood hit me like . . . well . . . a mother-in-law. During lunch, I even made a couple of *humph, humph, humph* sounds under my breath. Over Subway sandwiches, Casey filled me in on the vicissitudes of life.

"Michael steals the covers," she complained.

"Oh, really?" I replied.

"Yes. He bothers me at night with silliness and I can't go to sleep," she continued.

I wanted to tell Casey about my favorite nighttime game. It's called, "Does this bother you?" I used to sneak into my kids' rooms, or lay next to Jim at night, and do something really annoying, like wiggle my fingers in front of their faces, or lightly pull on one single hair on their heads, or make some low, barely audible sound really close to their ears, and I asked, "Does this bother you?" I know it's not normal, but it's fun. It was like a competition to see how far I had to go before one of them yelled, "Yes! For the love of G-d, yes, it bothers me! Stop it!" It also delayed the inevitable hour when everyone would be asleep but me, and I would be left to toss and turn with pain. I also wanted to tell Casey about my other favorite game called "I can make you laugh by the time I count to five." This game also works well at night when someone has gone to bed grumpy. There's nothing like having your mother come into your room, announce that she can make you laugh by the count of five, and then, say, do an imitation of Arnold Schwarzenegger, or stand on her head, or hip hop dance. Casey also might have been interested in the way I used to get Edie and Joedy to stop fighting at night. It was simple. I had them sing the words of their fight to a nursery rhyme. It is very difficult to stay mad at someone when singing "You ruined my shirt," and then replying "I did not," to the tune of "Three Blind Mice." Silliness at night was a Hulings tradition. I thought that maybe Casey needed to understand this and start playing along.

"I really need to get to sleep at night," Casey kept explaining, "He is silly when I am with him, and he calls me late at night when I am at home!"

I wanted to rebut Casey's insistence that Michael allow her a modicum of sleep. But I quickly had to remind myself that Michael and Casey needed to find their own patterns of night and day that would make them happy. And, if truth be told, I was the only one who ever really liked playing "Does this bother you?" For everyone else it was just a pain, but they knew I needed some laughter and entertainment before I entered my long nights. So I told Casey that I would talk to Michael and tell him that she needed her sleep, and they could be silly at other times. In my heart, I wondered what night games Alice had let go of and didn't impose on my family, in favor of letting Jim and me find our own blueprints for life.

Plans matter. Jim and I have fashioned the garden level of our tri-level into an apartment for Michael and Casey. They have a large family room with a fireplace that is never lighted, comfy sofas, and bookshelves to hold games, movies, and books. Jim gutted and remodeled the downstairs bathroom into a spa-like space with a shower that has handheld, wall-mounted, and ceiling-mounted sources of water spray. I selected the linens in the bedroom, and the rest of the décor is decidedly "early love nest." Pictures of Casey, Casey and Michael, and more of Casey cover the walls and furniture surfaces, with an occasional stretch of space filled with a *Spiderman, Star Wars,* or *Smallville* poster, and Michael's high school graduation certificate. Right now, we all share the upstairs kitchen, but a downstairs eating area is being constructed.

Casey's folks have done the same with their lowest level. Casey has a large studio apartment space that is divided into a bedroom and family room—where she and Michael have matching recliners—and a kitchen area with a refrigerator, microwave, cabinets for cereal and potato chips, and a dinette set for two. Casey's décor is similar to Michael's except she has *Harry Potter* and *Twilight* posters.

Casey and Michael pay rent to their respective parents. At eighteen, many folks who have special needs begin to receive a monthly stipend from the government, much like Social Security, but that money comes with rules. It must be used for rent, food, and personal expenses. It cannot be saved—if Michael or Casey were to amass more than about two thousand dollars in a bank account, they would lose their benefits. Yearly, we must prove that the money is not stashed somewhere—we must show receipts and budgets and statements that prove the money has been used properly, like to buy *Smallville* posters or *Harry Potter* memorabilia. Folks who receive these funds are also limited in how much money they can earn through the workplace. If they go above a wage that would place them above the poverty line, their benefits are also lost.

Receiving supportive services—therapies, shopping buddies, workout partners, life skills trainers—as an adult with special needs is also not a given. Michael has been on a waiting list for such services for over seven years. His number might come up in a year or two, but Federal and State funding are neither predictable nor reliable. Casey's family moved to Fort Collins when Casey was close to twenty years old. Casey will probably be on the waiting list for years to come. I am constantly torn: I am thankful to live in a society that sees fit to provide benefits for citizens who cannot provide for themselves, *and* I am frustrated that that very system sets up multiple roadblocks that get in the way of true independence.

Even if there are no roadblocks, I do not know for sure that Michael and Casey will achieve true independence. I used to think without hesitation that Michael would live independently. I am no longer completely convinced. I believe he will continue to learn and grow and his life will continue to unfold in mysterious, unpredictable ways. I don't think, however, that scenario includes a life free from some degree of supervision and observation. I have become a bit of a realist. I think that Michael and Casey will live with their two respective families for many years to come. I still dream of buying them a condo and setting them up with services that assure their safety, health, transportation, recreation, work, friends, and time alone. I am quite sure that no one needs a mother-in-law lingering around all day, watching and commenting and imprinting her plans. I know that one day we will kick the bucket, and we need to make sure Michael and Casey are left with a good life. I know that both of them have siblings who will not let anything bad ever happen. Still, they deserve a space of their own, away from all of us and away from constant surveillance. I'm just not sure that will happen.

◆   ◆   ◆

In the summer of 2011, Michael's sisters, Joedy and Edie, got married to some really great guys—Dave and Jeff. Both weddings were full of love and equitable vows and had very little to do with tradition. Edie's wedding took place in August at the Sunrise Amphitheater in Boulder Colorado, on top of Flagstaff mountain. Before we traveled up to the summit, we gathered for pictures and a pre-ceremony ritual at Chautauqua Park for pictures. As we headed out to a little scenic patch of grass and rock, I noticed that Casey was stomping as she walked.

She had set up a little rhythm to match a little, repetitive chant: "Joedy was first-Edie is today-and Michael and me are next." I am not sure how to define "next" for Casey. She and Michael may have to wait to get married longer than they realize.

The same system that has beset benefits for people who live with special needs with rules and regulations has also integrated itself into the realm of marriage. The laws are complex, but in a nutshell, it is very possible that if a couple who has special needs gets legally married, one of them will automatically lose some of their benefits. *There—another roadblock to independence.* It makes no sense. It's not like the couple would become millionaires with the meager benefits afforded them. It could mean that one of them could be rendered devoid of medical services, or housing assistance, or therapeutic interventions if needed or if they ever get off the waiting list. When the time comes for Michael and Casey to formally commit to each other, I bet that a few lawyers will be on board to pave the way. For Michael and Casey, that time cannot come soon enough.

Cindy and I are very close. We are similar on many levels and, thank G-d, we both have an intact sense of humor. I know that I can count on her for anything. Still, on the topic of Michael and Casey's marriage, we come to a bit of a fork in the road. I am of the opinion that a wedding *today* would be grand. I am not sure what we are all waiting for. The way I see it, these two kids are in love. Their relationship is a miracle. I have seen the loneliness of their peers who have not yet found a partner. Companionship is hard to find and nurture when a million eyes are watching, when everyone has a stake in the outcome. And Michael can actually become physically ill—stomach pains, throwing up, 911-worthy chest pains—when he and Casey are apart. I do not see a wedding as changing anything that already is and will be for years and years to come. We would still need to help them with jobs, life skills, grocery shopping, and debit cards. The big change would be Michael and Casey's emotional health. They would feel validated as a grown-up couple. They would feel like Joedy and Dave, Edie and Jeff.

"I'll know it when I see it," Cindy has told me when I ask her exactly what she needs to transpire before she will give Michael and Casey the go-ahead for a wedding. Cindy wants to see two people who are self-sufficient in cooking, cleaning, laundry, jobs, transportation and are engaged in adult activities. All that, from my point of view, *may* happen, but a very long time from now. I am not even 100 percent self-sufficient in all those areas. Who is? The future I see for Michael and Casey, which I am fine with, does not take away Michael's action figures or Casey's obsession with all things *Twilight*.

I am not sure Cindy is comfortable with allowing these things to remain, and I'm not sure it's our business how Michael and Casey entertain themselves and find joy. Cindy has also admitted that she doesn't want to give up the lure of a wedding as leverage. When Michael and Casey hit a lull in paying attention to their responsibilities, Cindy will say, "people who do not do their laundry are not acting like adults. And, only adults can get married. If you want to get married, you need to do your chores." I have to admit that she may have a point there.

I know what Cindy is doing, and I love her for doing it. She is doing the best she can to make sure her daughter has a meaningful life and a future that celebrates her as an individuated person, even if it means possibly delaying gratification. I want the same things Cindy does, but I often get lost in the moment and can't see past the beating of hearts singing out for time to stop and vows to be made. I suppose Cindy and I balance each other out the same way Michael and Casey balance each other out. In the end, it will all come together just fine. See? A miracle.

Casey is prepared for her wedding regardless of its timing. So prepared that, early in the fall of 2010, she sent out an email announcement, unbeknownst to Cindy, to everyone she knew that she and Michael were getting married on October 27, 2011. Needless to say, Cindy was thoroughly confused when she started getting congratulatory emails. Congratulations for what? Chagrined, Cindy replied to all with a brief explanation that Casey had jumped the gun a bit and, of course, when a real date was set, they would receive an invitation.

Casey has not been deterred from planning. She has filled two or three black and white composition books with wedding details. She visits wedding websites and copies down templates for writing vows, invitation etiquette, and how to select a cake. I eavesdrop on her conversations with Michael about matrimony.

"This is what marriage will look like," she says.

"Yes, dear," Michael responds.

"My dreams are coming true. But there are the things we need to work on. We can't be rude to our parents. We need to always be honest. No lying! We need to do our household chores, and we must not fight."

"Yes, dear."

It's a good thing that Michael has learned to say, "Yes, dear," because Casey has already made up her mind about many details. I read one of her wedding planning composition books and noticed there was hardly any mention of Michael's side of the family. "Casey—why is Michael's family not in included in your book?" I asked.

"Oh, you're in there. All of you get to watch," she said.

"Oh. Well, that needs to change, honey. We want to participate," I retorted.

It seems that Casey has acquiesced to my demands. At a visit to my folks' home in Littleton, Casey sat on the sofa with my mom and she shared every page of her most recent wedding plans: the theme is white; the reception will be at Chili's; it will be held in a "Jewish church;" Casey will be dressed like a fairy princess with a fairy princess up-do; Michael will have five best men and they will all wear tuxes; Casey will have three maids of honor; the current guest list stands at about five hundred people who will all fit in Cindy and James' backyard (the most recent designated wedding locale); Casey will buy one more *Harry Potter* game, and then she will save money for the wedding; and the honeymoon will be in Mexico—Cindy and James will have one room, Jim and I will have another, and in between our two rooms, Michael and Casey will have their own room strewn with rose petals. My mother told Casey that she was very proud of all her planning before she left the sofa and joined me in the kitchen.

"Oh my, Kathryn. They need to get married soon," Mom whispered. "Very soon."

In many ways I have given up predicting the future. I have no idea what lies ahead. None of us do. Still, I prepare for the possibilities. I still advocate for Michael, and I help him practice reading, cooking, cleaning, and laundry. I keep trying to coach Michael in the use of a debit card. Other than that, I wait for Cindy to give her wise blessing for a formal announcement of Michael and Casey's wedding date. I have only two requests as that time grows close. One, we need six weeks to plan and practice. And two—I would really love for the wedding to be on a Monday.

CASEY ANN LORD
—AND—
MICHAEL TAL HULINGS

WHO HAVE WAITED A LONG TIME
TO MAKE THIS ANNOUNCEMENT,
ARE NOW OVERJOYED TO INVITE
YOU TO THEIR WEDDING

WHEN: VERY SOON
WHERE: SOMEWHERE BEAUTIFUL
TIME: WHEN IT'S RIGHT
RSVP: TO THEIR MOMS

An imagined invitation to Michael and Casey's future wedding of the century. Reprinted by permission of Northern Exposure Photography. Artwork courtesy of Edith Marie Hulings.

Wondering

On the evening of March 20, 2011, the stage in the Timberline Church auditorium was graced with human beings who carry with them a parade of diagnoses. *There*—the girl whose arm hung stiffly, in a permanent right angle at her side. *There*—the boy whose head stuck out far beyond his neck. *There*—the girl whose short stature had no balance with her limbs. *There*—the girl who merely stood and stared when the music played. Gathered on that stage was an amalgam of birth defects, genetic mutations, the outcomes of accidents and injuries, and mysterious, still unnamed conditions that simply "are." I could have made educated guesses as to the scientific labels and conditions assigned to most of the cast members of the show. The only diagnosis, though, that I would have been one-hundred percent accurate on would be for those individuals who have Down syndrome.

I know that something unexpected happened to Michael's chromosomes before, during, or after his conception. It was silent, it was unstoppable, and it was unknowable. I was not there—as Michael is adopted—so I have often tried to construct and crystallize and hypothesize my son into existence. Whatever the circumstances, I assume there was an abundance of love. I have no proof this is true, but my heart needs this to be a part of the story.

I do know that one of a few explainable events occurred. In layperson terms, one possible scenario is that a *translocation* may have occurred during cell division, where part of Michael's 21st chromosome broke off and attached to another chromosome. As such, even though he would have 46 chromosomes, each one would carry an extra part of the 21st chromosome. Imagine it as a mutiny where a few mavericks of fortitude and fearlessness jump ship in search of a commingling with some new vessel, or where maybe a lonely traveler hitches a ride with a friend willing to provide transport. Translocation can be inherited from a parent who may carry what is called a *balanced translocation* that does not affect the carrier's health in any way. In other words, the mother or the father had always harbored within their own genetic codes the possibility of having a child with Down syndrome.

Or, something called a *nondisjunction,* might have occurred, when, prior to conception, the pair of 21st chromosomes fail to separate in the sperm or the egg. The embryo then has three copies of the 21st chromosome in every cell in the body, instead of the normal two. Here, I imagine the personified sperm or egg selfishly saving an extra copy of a piece of life and in the uniting expressing a replicating exultation of three. A specific type of nondisjunction is a called *mosaicism,* where the nondisjunction occurs in some but not all of the cell divisions. Having the mosaic form of Down syndrome does not necessarily mean that the condition will be expressed in fewer or less obvious ways. After birth, there are tests that can be done to determine the type of Down syndrome an individual has if such knowledge will help the family.

Whatever the cause of Michael's Down syndrome, in the instant that it occurred, this new genetic configuration immediately determined that Michael would have some degree of an intellectual disability. This new genetic configuration also began to determine Michael's physical appearance. If Michael's birth family could have witnessed Michael's development in utero, they would probably have been able to spot nuances and unfolding differences. They would have seen the beginning of traits that now make possible a visual identification of Michael as a person who has Down syndrome. I wonder what it would have been like to have peeked inside Michael's amniotic sac and pointed at each new characteristic with wonder and an exclamation of *there! There*—the onset of a single crease down each stubby hand; *There*—eyes up at attention in a smiling slant; *There*—Lilliputian ears folded down on top, listening closely to a reverberating secret; *There*—from the vestige of a tiny mandible, a lolling tongue licking an impossibly short thumb nested in the curve of a second simian crease; *There*—a flat nose, the face's compliment to the swept up eyes; and *There, There, There, There*—a thickening in the neck, a harbinger of what was to be. *There!*[4]

♦ ♦ ♦

Jim, Casey, James, Cindy, and I entered Timberline Church to watch Michael perform in the first annual *Changes in Attitude Showcase of Talent*, sponsored by the Arc of Larimer County and in honor of National Disability Awareness Month. Michael was performing with Dance Express, the same Fort Collins, Colorado, dance company where Michael and Casey's relationship began. We all knew from past performances that whenever Michael dances, it is, indeed, a "showcase of talent."

The emcees for the show, Brooks and Adrienne Yates, were members of Timberline Church, and they urged the audience to sit back and enjoy. Brooks filled any time lags with magic tricks—his linked fingers as magic rings—and Adrienne dutifully rolled her eyes. They knew they were not the main attraction; they were simply there to introduce the stars of the night. Dance Express was first to perform. This particular evening, the dancers were only those who had obvious developmental challenges. They were not performing in tandem with typical dancers, the ones who do not walk around with preconceived labels attached to their foreheads that declare their challenges: i.e., "has a messy desk"; "chews with mouth open"; "farts in public"; "cracks knuckles incessantly"; or "mixes plaids with stripes." Each dancer was cloaked in a silky, dolman-sleeved tunic, each tunic was stitched from a varying jeweled-toned swath of fabric, and each body was swathed

in black pants that brushed the laces of black-shoed feet; emerald, ce-
rulean, ruby, purple, and fuchsia filled the stage. Tamara, who is in her
early thirties and has Down syndrome, and Michael stood center-stage,
a step or two in front of the rest, and with the cue of taped music lilting
from the church's sound system, they led the troupe in a cadenza of
movement—deep pliés, eternal stretches of arms toward invisible yearn-
ings high in the ethers of the church's high ceiling, hands that swept the
dimensions of unseen diamonds in the air, heads that leaned back while
hands grasped hearts, and then, myriad solos all at once, as each dancer
moved according to his or her own plan, and Christina Aguilera's voice
rejoiced with a celebration of individuality in her song, "Beautiful."
With their final pose, each dancer looked out at the audience and willed
us to hoot and holler in appreciation. But they were not done.

After the applause died down, Jessica, who has Down syndrome,
took center-stage, and the rest of the dancers formed a straight line
behind her. To the hip-hop strain of Jamie Foxx's "Gold-digger," Jessica
began to work the stage, *girlfriend,* swaying her hips and shimmying
her shoulders. All the dancers, now completely donned in black, broke
out of the line and were breaking it down and busting a move, as their
bodies gyrated, popped, and pumped. Michael repeatedly winked and
pointed—in musical rhythm, of course—at Casey. Tamara did a cheerleader leap. So did Jessica, in between leaning over and whipping her
waist-length ponytail in furious circles, then miming the actions of digging with a shovel. Everyone else rocked out, rocked out, rocked out,
including Michael, in a black leather jacket. *That's my boy!* By the time
the dancers returned to the orderly line behind Jessica, the audience
was as breathless as they were.

◆   ◆   ◆

Before more folks were invited up on the Timberline Church stage
to perform, there was a brief, PBS-type fundraising moment from the
Director of the Arc of Larimer County, which serves and advocates

for people who have developmental disabilities and special needs. She presented us with a metaphorically beautifully gift-wrapped treat by reminding us of the recent passage of Rosa's Law, the bill that United States President Barack Obama signed into Federal law on October 5, 2010, that "removes the terms 'mental retardation' and 'mentally retarded' from federal health, education and labor policy and replaces them with [the] people first language 'individual with an intellectual disability' and 'intellectual disability.'"[5]

It seems like such a simple thing to me, this idea that we should not demean one another with a careless use of language. Years ago, when I was very young, I never thought we would need to create such a law. My parents referred to people only by their names, not with any sort of labels—not by race, by disability, by job, by illness, by gender, or by sexual orientation. Just names. Whenever my siblings and I made the mistake of misusing language to demean anyone, it was a punishable offense. Later, in my teens, I learned how some thought that calling someone or something "retarded" was funny or an acceptable use of pejorative language. Now, as a parent of a child who has Down syndrome, I have adopted a vow of non-silence regarding hateful words, and I readily invite those who casually use the "R" word to find a new adjective.

Not long ago, Jim, Michael, Casey, and I were eating at one of our favorite Mexican restaurants. We were seated near a large table of rambunctious college-aged students who were also enjoying an evening out. One of the young men at the table kept repeatedly yelling out that everything was "retarded." Michael and Casey are not immune to the meaning of this word in its misuse. It hurts. They were quickly losing their appetites. Michael put his hand over Casey's. They both stared at their plates of tortillas, refried beans, and tacos. I often embarrass my family. This evening was no exception.

"Hi there!" I offered to the young man in question as I sidled up to his table and sat down in the empty chair right next to him. The table of young adults went silent.

"Hi?" he responded cautiously.

"I would love for you to do me a favor," I proposed.

"Okay . . ." he muttered as his eyes grew wider and wider.

"Look at the table behind you. The one where I was sitting."

He looked at the table. Then he looked back at me.

"Do you see *who* is sitting there?

He nodded an abashed yes.

"Good. Now, I invite you to find another word to replace the five, loud 'retardeds' you have yelled out this evening. Okay?"

He nodded again.

"Great! Have an excellent evening," I called over my shoulder as I returned to my tacos and enchiladas.

Upon my return, Michael and Casey looked up from their plates and smiled at me. "Let's enjoy our dinner!" I urged, and my table returned to eating and chatting. The table of college students continued eating, but their conversation became subdued and barely audible. I take the use of language very seriously. It influences perceptions. It influences decisions. It influences actions.

◆ ◆ ◆

The Director then asked us to recognize the auspicious origins of the evening: National Disability Awareness Month. There was a slight trickle of subdued laughs from the audience. I can say with absolute certainty that nary a soul sitting on one of Timberline Church's numerous chairs or waiting in the wings to go on stage needed an enhanced awareness of disability. For the family, friends, and performers gathered at Timberline Church that evening, disability was a twenty-four-seven, forever-and-a-day reality. All those who live with or are intimate with a life touched by special needs, are *aware*. We are daily entangled in a system of red tape so convoluted that it enforces such statutes as the one that lawfully reduces government support for one partner from a couple with disabilities who choose to get married. We daily rejoice the smallest of steps achieved: a spoon not dropped before it reaches the lips, a bus schedule mastered, a communication board purchased. We daily embarrass our families as we sidle up to restaurant tables full of young college students and invite them to stop using the word "retarded" and to pay attention to the powerful influences of language. We daily educate professionals at school board meetings as we try to foster classroom inclusion. We advocate for diversity and accessibility at city council meetings. And we explain to neighborhood playgroups why our children are not yet potty-trained. We daily celebrate birthdays that we were told would not be met, words that come tumbling out after years of therapy, and every smile that meets our eyes. We are acutely *aware*.

As the Director spoke, I looked around, and I wondered. I do that a lot, this wondering. I wonder, and I wrestle with angels, both as incessant, life-long habits of mind. I wondered why it was that in my pursuit of equity for people who have developmental disabilities, my circle of familiarity and love seemed to grow smaller and not wider. I had known almost everyone in the audience, some for twenty years. I recognized others from all the other get-togethers we shared (picnics, meetings, fundraisers, forums, panels, conferences), which were thematically linked by their focus on the realm of disabilities. *We* are linked. I wondered how my circle could expand. There, in Timberline Church, the Director preached to the proverbial choir. Even there, in the effort to call attention to and raise awareness of disabilities, we were entangled, rejoicing, inviting, educating, and celebrating, but still somewhat alone.

♦   ♦   ♦

The show resumed with a singing duet by Jenna and Shannon. Dressed in their Sunday best—Jenna in a cotton skirt, light cardigan, and blouse; Shannon in corduroys, a sweater vest and button down shirt—the couple stayed in one position for the entire song. Jenna stood facing the crowd, her eyes shadowed by large circular framed glasses and her dirty-blond hair. Shannon, also bespectacled, angled his skinny body toward her, impossibly close, their shoulders touching, holding both her hands in his. The strains of Aaron Neville's tenor trill singing "Don't Know Much" filled the space, and Shannon and Jenna sang along. Every time Neville offered a verse, Shannon and Jenna would almost imperceptibly whisper a fleeting echo of the lyric into the microphone in front of them. It was, by far, the most beautiful rendition of that song I have ever heard.

The show was on a roll. Tamara showed us that she most definitely had the funk as she booty bounced, flipped her hair a la J-Lo, and led the audience in a raucous round of clapping to George Clinton's insistent song, "We Want the Funk." In the end, really, isn't that the truth? I know I want the funk! After Tamara ran off the stage, high-fiving Brooks and Adrienne as she went, the whole of Timberline Church hushed and the rafters seemed to whistle as Tammy maneuvered her electric wheelchair up the ramp to the stage. I've seen Tammy over the years at school functions and community events; she has always been quiet. Her features suggest that perhaps her challenges extend beyond her paralysis. Her brow is prominent, her eyes unmatched in their depth and spacing, and her mouth is set awry. As soon as Tammy positioned her wheelchair in front of the microphone, the angels I wrestle with took my head in their hands and did not allow me to avert my gaze as Tammy sang—garbled and strained, but singing nonetheless—along with Lady Antebellum's, "Hello World." The lyrics were mostly out of Tammy's control—her mouth and tongue would not cooperate—but I have learned never to underestimate the workings of a determined heart. When the words got lost in her throat and her brain, they were enunciated instead by the passion in her eyes and the quivering catch in her breaths.

Act after act brought more fun. Ryan rapped and aped each and every one of Weird Al Yankovic's silly scenes in the video, "White and Nerdy"; Ryan got the joke. In his bowtie and pants belted somewhere near his breast bone, he hammed it up as he enacted mowing the lawn, typing on his laptop, and precisely parroting every single word. Like Weird Al, Ryan concluded his rap with Spock's famous "Live long and prosper" hand sign. A Trekkie! Ryan was one of my beloved people! The audience screamed in approval and rose to their feet. LeAnn and Becky sang "You are My Sunshine"—my Grandma Belle's favorite song. Jessica pirouetted her way through a modern ballet number replete with twirls, leaps, and spins. Unashamed, she became one with Isadora Duncan, Martha Graham, and Twyla Tharp. James took the stage, with "I'm Kind of a Big Deal" plastered in large font on his t-shirt, and sang along with Michael Jackson's "This Is It." James tossed off his hat, swung his hips three counts to the right, three counts to the left, and then let loose an intricately choreographed robot routine.

As I was clapping wildly for James, Jim tapped me on the shoulder.

"Kathryn," he said in a low voice, "Why is Michael standing against the wall, near the stage, wearing his leather jacket and shades?"

Michael was not scheduled to perform again since he had decided not to compete in the individual talent portion.

"Oh, G-d," I sighed. "Go check it out. Now."

As Jim snuck off to have a little chat with Michael, Cindy leaned over and tapped my other shoulder. Whenever people start tapping my shoulders, I know that something big is about to happen.

"Michael is wearing *my* good leather jacket," she complained, her eyes wide and twinkling. "How'd he get my jacket?"

"He probably went into your closet and got it out," I replied. After Cindy threw a teasing glare in my directions, I added plausible deniability for my sake, saying "But, really? Is that *your* jacket? Hmmmmmm . . . I just don't know!"

Jim returned, a smirk on his face, and began readying the video camera. "He entered himself as a solo act. He's dancing."

I sat on pins and needles through the next few acts. Alva sang along with the Backstreet Boys, "I Want it That Way." Chrissy stuck one hand on her hip, stared down the audience, and belted out "That's What Love Is For" along with Amy Grant. Elizabeth wore a sparkling black shirt and looked radiant; for most of her performance, she just hummed and swayed along to Dionne Warwick's "That's What Friends are For," but without exception, she fully and robustly sang the chorus.

Two more acts and then it would be Michael's turn. The Wildcats Pom and Cheer Squad, a dance group of young ladies who have developmental disabilities, strutted their stuff to Michael Jackson's "Black and White," turned cartwheels, and copied every move of their coach who did the routine below the stage, providing a canvas which the girls could mimic and then recreate as their own masterpiece. Tiffany and Taylor—a married couple—who both have Down syndrome, two-stepped their way through George Strait's "You'll Always Be a Fire I Can't Put Out," the two of them exchanging enough "come hither" glances to have set Timberline Church on fire.

Finally, it was Michael's turn. Brooks announced to the audience that he had been waiting all night for this moment; I wondered if Brooks' rear-end was as sore as mine from sitting on pins and needles that, as the evening progressed, had morphed into daggers and swords. I knew Michael's dancing was magnificent. I also knew that Michael's dancing could be unpredictably erotic. And we were in a church. A big church. We were a Jewish family in a big, conservative, evangelical church.

Michael began his dance with his back to the audience. To the contagious beat of Kenny Loggins' "Footloose," Michael began what has become his signature first step: slowly, and smoothly, he stripped off his leather jacket (which, we later found out was Michael's sister's, not Cindy's) and then turned to the audience. After the leather shenanigans, Michael got the audience going in a clapping frenzy as he sashayed, spun on the floor, unhinged his hips, and, finally, ended his dance in a Burt Reynolds' pose a la *Playgirl* (although Michael was clothed, thank G-d). Running off the stage, he fist bumped with Brooks, who declared, "You're the man!"

◆ ◆ ◆

Science can make real the dreams of mortals. And what science can offer in the care of individuals with Down syndrome is, in fact, miraculous. As a parent of a person who has Down syndrome, I have a heightened awareness of how science has made healthier and more fruitful the lives of my child and many others who live with Down syndrome. Before Michael came to us, we met with a pediatrician who warned us about the potentially short lifespan of a person with Down syndrome. She was right in one sense; years ago, as recently as the turn of the twentieth century, a baby born with Down syndrome had a life expectancy of nine years. But today we can expect most babies born with Down syndrome to live to age sixty and beyond. A lot has changed.[6]

Along with outward physical manifestations, Down syndrome also carries with it a host of possible health problems including congenital heart defects, respiratory issues, thyroid dysfunction, intestinal malformations, visual impairments, leukemia, and Alzheimer's. That small snafu of the 21st chromosome can mightily affect multiple body systems. Luckily, our society has evolved to the point of not only embracing but actively pursuing the ideals of inclusion and civil rights for people with disabilities. Think of the special education mandate passed in 2004, The Individuals with Disabilities Education Act, which the US Department of Education explains as "ensuring services to children with disabilities throughout the nation, [governing] how states and public agencies provide early intervention, special education and related services to more than 6.5 million eligible infants, toddlers, children and youth with disabilities."[7] Think of the Developmental Disabilities Assistance and Bill of Rights Act Amendments of 2000 that, according to the Administration on Intellectual and Developmental Disabilities, are meant "to ensure that people with developmental disabilities and their families have access to community services, individualized supports, and other forms of assistance that promote: self-determination; independence; productivity; integration and inclusion."[8] Now, our attention has also turned to making better the health and medical lives of people born with complicated genetics or developmental disabilities. In 2008, the Prenatally and Postnatally Diagnosed Conditions Awareness Act was enacted; this bill, as stated by Govtrack.us, "amend[s] the Public Health Service Act to increase the provision of scientifically sound information and support services to patients receiving a positive test diagnosis for Down syndrome or other prenatally and postnatally diagnosed conditions."[9] This act argues for a positive, hopeful, supportive, well-informed outcome for families facing a diagnosis of disability.

As recently as the late 1970s, people with Down syndrome were institutionalized and were called "Mongolian idiots."[10] Remember the power of language? Words can influence perceptions, decisions, and actions. These people, referred to as "Mongolian idiots," were given little care in the areas of nutrition, fitness, therapies, or human interaction, let alone life saving interventions. Now, however, for people who have Down syndrome, the world has become a wonderful place. Heart defects are diagnosed early, sometimes even in-utero, and pediatric cardiologists have become skilled at successfully treating them. Visual problems are corrected with glasses and specific surgeries. The administration of antibiotics alone has saved the hearing of individuals with Down syndrome, who may be predisposed to inner ear infections. Thyroid issues can be treated with replacement therapies. And, as our treatments for leukemia have advanced, people with Down syndrome who become ill with the disease also have a better chance of fighting it.

Science can also tinker with dreams. The same realm of science that has saved and improved the lives of people with Down syndrome has also provided the means by which to stop such a life from ever entering the world. Prenatal screening is available for pregnant woman of all ages to help determine the likelihood that they might be carrying a baby with some sort of problem or chromosomal disorder, like Down syndrome. Somewhere between the fifteenth and twentieth week of pregnancy, the *Triple Screen and Alpha-fetoprotein Plus* tests, which measure the levels of alpha-fetoprotein, human chorionic gonadotropin and un-conjugated estriol, can be performed as a simple blood test. When the measurements are added into an equation that considers the mother's age and perhaps other contributing factors, science has enabled doctors to at least estimate the chances of carrying an affected baby. Heightened levels of these substances might suggest that a chromosomal abnormality may be present.[11] The mother's age is part of the equation because, historically, evidence shows that the chance of having a baby with Down Syndrome increases with the mother's age. At the age of forty-five, a woman has a one in 30 chance of having a baby with Down syndrome. At thirty-five, the chances are one in 350.[12] A more recently developed screening test relies on the use of high-resolution ultrasound. The *Nuchal Translucency Screening* (NT), performed between eleven and fourteen weeks of pregnancy, looks at the fold of skin at the back of the baby's neck and the amount of fluid accumulation there. Increased fluid accumulation indicates that a baby may have Down syndrome.[13] Again, these measurements are mixed into an equation, which includes the mother's age, to calculate the risk of the baby having Down syndrome. These tests—the alpha-fetoprotein and the NT—are not definitive; a positive test does not mean for certain that a baby has a birth defect. Likewise, a negative test does not mean for certain that a baby does not have a birth defect. These tests are like red flags on the highway that urge us to slow down and take a very close look at our surroundings. These tests only suggest caution and perhaps further testing.

If a woman sees such red flags, she and her doctor can move beyond the screening tests and pursue diagnostic tests. *Amniocentesis*, performed between fifteen and twenty weeks of pregnancy, uses a small needle that is inserted through the abdomen, into the uterus, and then a sample of amniotic fluid is withdrawn. The cells from the fluid are cultured, and, in about two weeks, the results provide an extremely accurate diagnosis regarding whether or not the baby has Down syndrome (and/or other conditions). *Chorionic Villus Sampling* (CVS), which can be performed between ten to twelve weeks of a pregnancy, involves going through the abdomen or cervix with a needle to obtain a sample of tissue from the placenta. Again, the cells are cultured, and a report arrives within about two weeks. Both amniocentesis and CVS come with about a 1 in 100 risk of miscarriage.[14]

Currently, the risks of testing may have become a non-issue, but the ethical stakes have increased. Stanford University scientists have developed a blood test that detects various chromosomal disorders, including Down syndrome.[15] This maternal blood test can be done very early in pregnancy, which can be a blessing or a curse.

None of these tests can even remotely predict the extent to which the baby will be affected by Trisomy 21. The range of possible effects is huge, and these diagnostic tests are not capable of determining the future cognitive or physical abilities of the baby, nor can they determine the therapies, actions, educational, and medical interventions of each respective family. These tests cannot predict the influence of love. These tests cannot predict what dance or song the child in question might perform twenty years later, in a talent show, at a church, maybe even while wearing a leather jacket and very cool shades.

These tests only provide a simple "yes" or "no," which leaves the mother with a not-so-simple decision. Some will decide to keep the pregnancy and begin setting up early interventions, proper medical care, and becoming knowledgeable about the condition, schools, our legal system, and how to connect to that small, linked circle I talked about earlier. Some will decide to terminate the pregnancy. It has been indicated that 90 percent of women who receive a positive diagnosis of Down syndrome choose to have an abortion. This number has been disputed with other researchers who cite figures closer to 60 percent.[16] But the numbers do not change the experience. I imagine that it is an incomprehensibly quiet, painful, and private moment for each of these mothers. Dreams are shattered. The image of a child and a life wished-for is irrevocably altered. I will not say that I know this pain; I do not. But still, I wonder.

I wonder if the knowledge that science brings must cause dreams to shatter. I wonder if a normal genetic test, one with no obvious defects, automatically translates into a charmed life. I wonder if our souls, our intents, our purposes in life are defined by our genetic markers. Are we nothing more than the physical manifestation of codes and equations? I wonder. When I first looked upon Michael, when he was almost seven weeks old, I traced the curvature of his flattish head, his almond eyes, his puckered lips, his strong neck, and his grasping hands. I looked, and I saw his tongue, rolling in and out of his mouth, and I gave him the word his tongue was seeking: *Mommy*. I did not see his genetics. I looked at him with wonder.

What makes a life meaningful? Do strands of DNA mark our station any more than the soil of our origin? Is the human of clay or the human of a Petri dish—both miracles—a simple amalgamation of sequenced traits, of inevitability? I hold my son—I have held him for years—and I eschew the predictable; I know I cannot metamorphose the make-up of inheritance or nondisjunction or translocation, yet I know I can—I do and I have—jazz a synapse in my son's brain into the riff of a raucous symphony of discovery. He dances, he sings, he reads, he writes, he loves, he makes love, he walks the dogs, he works, he talks with his hands (like me), he tells bad jokes (like Jim), he rides his bike, he makes PB&Js for lunch, he goes to school, he lives for pizza, and his DNA never converts.

The cells from a Petri dish could not have predicted any of this. My son stands before me, a cyclone of cells and synapses and sinew and mischief and helix and canted eyes and stout neck and tenacious tongue; all cede his conjectured blueprint, but cannot touch the profundity, the still uncharted odyssey of his identity.

♦ ♦ ♦

An awards ceremony ended the evening. While we waited for the judges to tally their votes, The Two Man Orchestra: The Gary and Emery Show, filled the time. Emery lives with some sort of developmental delay; he has difficulty forming words. He was introduced as a twenty-plus-year employee of Foothills Gateway, the local Rehabilitation

Center. He played the harmonica, while Gary played the accordion, shook bells on his shoes, and blew into a whistle tube. Everyone from the evening's cast was called on stage, given an instrument/noisemaker, and was invited to play along. Michael held maracas. With a downbeat, the cacophony ensued. It was hardly Mozart. It was better.

Brooks and Adrienne came out onto the stage, envelopes in hand, ready to announce the winners. The two large performing groups were all given a prize. The top three winners, who each won an iPod Nano, were, in no particular order: Ryan, Tamara, and Michael. Michael looked out at the audience and smiled broadly. Everyone, actually, was smiling broadly.

As we headed to the car, I silently blessed the cast of thirty-four. I blessed the audience of one hundred sixty. I prayed that casts and audiences everywhere would keep creating ever-widening, dynamic circles of familiarity and love. Then, Jim, Michael, and I drove to IHOP and stuffed ourselves full of pancakes. Michael actually had mashed potatoes and hash browns. I watched my family eat and laugh and figure out how to program the iPod Nano. Everything was perfectly, beautifully, insanely normal. It is possible, as science progresses and offers more and more ways to definitively diagnose Down syndrome and other conditions before birth, that people like Michael may cease to exist. I wonder about this. And I weep.

Wrapping

Sometimes, from my upstairs bedroom, at any given time of day, I can still hear Michael talking to himself. I remember how I used to run downstairs and glue my ear to his closed door, worried that something was terribly wrong with this scenario. I recall how I was informed that nothing was wrong and that some people with Down syndrome just have a tendency to let inside voices escape outside more often than typical folks might. Now, when I hear Michael having a chat with himself, I don't run downstairs anymore. I want to, but I don't. Just because Michael lets his private thoughts slip into the ethers for me to hear doesn't mean I should invade his personal space and listen. He's under enough close, constant scrutiny as it is. I am not entitled to any of my kids' clandestine thoughts. They will share with me what they wish. Michael included.

I'm not sure I ever had a clear entitlement to write this story of raising Michael. I did it anyway, convincing myself that it was necessary. I wanted to show the world how wonderful Michael is. I wanted to show how wonderful—how resplendently complicated—he has made my life. Now, however, it has become plain that it is time to wrap up this story, not because it has ended, but rather because I can no longer justify some carte blanche privilege to chronicle Michael's life. He is no longer a little boy. He is in a committed relationship, and he is working hard to be included in the workforce. He has a calendar chock full of recreation activities in the community and responsibilities at home. His life sounds a lot like his siblings' lives, and I would not write about the foibles and exaltations of his siblings' adult existence. That's personal. It's not for me to interpret or expose. The same must apply to Michael.

Jim and I have entered what we call the "popcorn phase" of parenting. We are still there, but we are not necessarily always in the picture. Instead, we have popped a humongous, bottomless bowl of buttery popcorn, plopped on a big old sofa, and we are enjoying watching the show continue, to unfold without our constant, tangible presence. Of course, we both carry an almost too-heavy-to-handle safety net in our back pockets so we can catch any child who may errantly fall or hit hard times or need an ear to bend. We haven't disappeared. We still get late night phone calls asking for advice and we still all regularly get together to share meals, company, and holidays. We are, by default, more visible in Michael's life, but even there, we are being incrementally phased out.

Recently I was told by a gentleman—a fine human being, prolific writer, and gifted teacher—that the main character in this story is not Michael. Rather, I was told, the main character is me. At first, I balked at this. Why would I want to write about myself? I'm boring and pedestrian. The exigency for writing this came not from anything remarkable about me, but, instead, from the extraordinary lives of all my children and my husband, and the gifts Michael has brought us all. Without those people, without Michael, there would be no story.

On second thought, I realized that maybe this is partly about me. Maybe this story is about what has become of the me formed long ago while, as a small child, I read about Dale Evans' angel; or while I sullenly witnessed bullies taunt, and adults ignore, kids with special needs in the hallways of my schools; or while I taught life skills classes at a residential facility; or while I studied to become a Recreational Therapist in Boulder, Colorado. Maybe this story is about the grown-up me who still dreams of a world where everyone finds and is extended joy. Maybe this is a story about finally understanding how I define feeling whole: Michael came, and I got sick, and along the way of taking care of him and his siblings and getting well, I realized that I am silly and unusual, that I know how to love completely, and that I matter very much to my family because I can and do help their lives be good. Goofy, but good. Maybe that's not something to balk at. Still, I insist there is no story without Michael and his siblings and Jim.

♦　♦　♦

Like all his siblings, Michael has a trunk full of memorabilia: pictures, drawings, awards and ribbons, all to be placed in a scrapbook, one day, when I have the time. Each of my offspring also has a plastic box crammed full of school souvenirs and t-shirts from swim meets, basketball teams, soccer tournaments, family reunions, vacations, performances. In a special container, I have the outfit my biological children wore home from the hospital folded neatly beside the dress I chose for their naming ceremonies at the synagogue. Michael also has a naming ensemble, but instead of finding space near a token piece of swaddling, it was gathered next to the blue duffel bag full of all the things he arrived with.

During my summers, I spend time sorting through all my kids' old stuff. In the past, I removed too-small items from their closets and drawers to go to Goodwill. I am still reorganizing keepsakes and preparing for all the artsy-craftsy plans I have in store. I calculate how to commence the process of making them t-shirt quilts so they can, on cold nights, cover themselves in memories. Recently, I sat on the floor of my office, surrounded by boxes and tees, photographs and popsicle-stick-frames, paintings of blob people who say "I luv my famlee," and that blue duffel bag of Michael's things. I unzipped the bag, unopened for many, many years; it smelled musty, old, unused.

I sat with that bag in my lap for a very long time, but took nothing out; I had no compulsion to feel the buttons, no need to rub the fabric against my cheek or inhale the imagined scent of my baby. I sat with the open bag, hoping it would swallow my guilt and broken promises:

I never gave Michael the Star of David or put the miniature red Torah under his pillow as Michael's female relative, his escort to Colorado requested; they both are safe in my jewelry box, in my top, right-hand dresser drawer. I sat with the bag, knowing I'd only answered a few of his escort's letters and included some pictures we took at Sears, but I never initiated communication on my own. Michael's birth parents made finalizing the adoption very difficult (their grief, I'm sure, was paralyzing) and, in the process, I lost my sense of trust, even of the escort who brought me my son.

The escort wrote me a few years back that her family had adopted their own child. I sent a gift—a couple of lovely outfits that matched and would fit—and then, our correspondence stopped. I think the escort came full circle; she finally replaced the baby she'd witnessed being let go with a baby who needed catching. Still, this escort is with me every day, in my prayers.

♦ ♦ ♦

Michael has not asked questions about his own conception. Michael has a foggy notion of what the word adoption means, yet he still does not know that he is adopted. It's not an issue of shame. What Jim and I decided a long time ago was that if Michael ever became capable of comprehending the beginning of his life, we would tell him. That day has not arrived; I don't know when it will, if ever. At least for a while longer, I sense that all that information would provide is extreme, immeasurable confusion. Michael has enough challenges. He knows that I am his mommy and Jim is his daddy and Casey will be his wife and that he is adored. That seems to be enough. For now.

And so, I sat with the blue duffel bag of Michael's things until I stood up. Then I bundled it in an old blanket and placed it deep in the Goodwill pile. The contents of that bag did not belong in Michael's t-shirt quilt. They were not mementos of joy, but of the unknown, of the weeks I was not his mommy, the weeks he didn't hear my pulse, the weeks he was ill on a kibbutz I'd never seen, in a city whose streets I'd never walked. They were the rags of my sorrow. And so, I determined that the "family sleeper" would be called Michael's coming home outfit, which in a very real sense is a genuine fact. I wrapped up its contents and ceded the bag to someone else less fortunate than Michael.

Michael's t-shirt quilt, I decided, would be a patchwork of truth; if I included the relics of his arrival, there would have to be an accompanying lie to explain their meaning, to legitimize the "I Love New York" shirt that never showed up in any baby picture, which was an artifact that made no sense; Michael never spent any real time in New York as an infant. Michael will not miss that bag or that shirt; he never knew either existed. And I did not need them to remember. The miracle of my child and the gift of his life are permanently intertwined with the sweetness of secrets and the necessity of my own betrayals, my own lies of omission. All that constitutes the genesis of Michael is tightly wrapped in a mixed-up and powerful existence smack in the center of my heart.

Sibling photo taken at Joedy's wedding (Left to right: Sean, Jeff Fryer [Edie's husband], Edie, Joedy, Dave Kaplan [Joedy's husband], Nathan, Casey Lord, and Michael [age 20]). Reprinted by permission of Kelli Nixon Photography.

Progressing

About two years ago, if anyone had told us that Michael would soon be gainfully employed and working ten hours a week, with little to no supervision, Jim and I would have appeared decidedly doubtful. I would have bitten my lip and cast my eyes downward, the way I do when I am about to cry because I feel like I am stuck in the middle of a bad joke at the expense of an innocent being. Jim would have crossed his arms in front of his chest and repeatedly cleared his throat, the way he does whenever he gets nervous or is trying to formulate a counter-argument. Eventually, one of us would have murmured something to the effect of, "Hmmm. Well. Maybe. We'll see."

What we now see is extraordinary. Somehow, between making errant 911 calls about his mean mom or his broken heart, performing sanctioned erotic dances at talent shows, posing as Spiderman, charming his way through school, and figuring out how to be a proper boyfriend/fiancé to Casey, Michael actually got the hang of not only how to navigate, but enter the work world. By the time he graduated from Project Search in May of 2012, he had already been hired by a Fort Collins retirement home to help maintain kitchen supplies and machines AND by a city recreational facility to help with maintenance in their weight room.

At his graduation, Michael and his fellow Project Search graduates each presented a PowerPoint chronicling their accomplishments: There was Michael cleaning the coffee machine. There was Michael filling salt and pepper shakers. When a picture of Michael grinning at the camera showed up, Michael turned to the audience and said, "That's one good looking guy!" At the end of the ceremony, Michael asked to control the microphone, and, in keeping with tradition, Jim and I held our breath, not one hundred percent sure what he might say.

"I just want to say," Michael began, "that my teacher, Marilee, is the best teacher in the world. I want to thank everyone and my family for everything."

Marilee, Jim, I, and many others in the room all mouthed the words, "You're welcome."

Then Jim mouthed another very special message: "That's enough, Michael. Go sit down!" It wasn't a good moment to press our luck.

As a reward for performing a miracle and getting a job, we got Michael a debit card. *A debit card!* We were acknowledging to Michael that he was indeed a grown-up, doing grown-up things. This debit card has opened the door to new lessons about money management and deciphering the difference between needs and wants. Not long after receiving his debit card, I saw that the screen saver on Michael's computer was covered with over twenty pictures of the same exquisite diamond ring. I was curious.

"Michael, what's up with the pictures of this ring?"

"That's the ring Casey wants for her birthday."

"Hmmm . . . Casey already has a very pretty engagement ring from you."

"But she wants a 'carrot' ring. This one has 'carrots.'"

And so it did. Many, many, many carats. The same number that might show up on the finger of a princess or a movie star.

"Michael, that ring costs $35,000. It costs more than both our cars. We cannot get Casey that ring."

"But, Mom," Michael interrupted, "I *can* get her that ring. I have a debit card!"

Our job as Michael's parents is far from over. We had to help Michael break the news to Casey that she was going to get a flower, a card, and a gift card to Barnes & Noble for her birthday instead of the $35,000 ring. There were some tears and slammed phones, but it was all short-lived. A few nights after the great carat debacle, Michael, Jim, and I went out to dinner, and Michael ordered a beer. Jim and I looked at each other and, in tandem, said, "Oh, G-d. He's twenty-one!" We let the scene play out. Michael showed the waitress his state ID, she brought him out a Bud Light, and she poured it into a sleek glass. Michael took a long sip, shuddered, looked at us, and proclaimed: "Yuck!" Jim and I finished the Bud, and Michael hasn't ordered a beer since.

Michael still makes some big, honking mistakes. Even superheroes stumble. Not too long ago, he visited his beloved teacher at the middle school he attended. He visited her weekly, on Tuesday—his one day off of work. Outside of the school, on his way home, he approached two female students, a sixth grader and a seventh grader, and asked them for their phone numbers so he could "date" them. The two terrified girls told their parents, their parents told the school, and thankfully, because they know and love Michael, the school was able to explain to the parents that Michael was not dangerous in any conceivable way. Still, Michael is no longer allowed to visit the school, per the students' parents' request. Not ever again. This could have been a wonderful step forward for humankind—the girls and their parents could have come to a new understanding of some of the manifestations of disability, trusted that Michael would not repeat this error, and Michael could have continued visiting his alma mater. But I am a realist, after all. In the grown-up world, I realize—and agree with the fact—that twenty-one-year-old men should not make weekly visits to their old middle school. I empathize with the parents request—it *is* odd for a grown man to hang out at a middle school. *There: a new idea for me to accept—Michael is now a man.* I must make sure he is a good man in the real world.

And so, I was left to sternly—in a very mean voice, and with a few fangs exposed—explain to Michael how grown men do not ask children for their phone numbers or date them, and how all people in schools are children, even if they look older. Michael does not yet have the filter to differentiate a thirteen-year-old girl who looks twenty from an actual twenty-year-old. *There: a new skill I must teach him.*

I had to explain that grown men who have fiancées don't ask any girl, of any age, for her phone number, that it is called cheating, and that he hurt Casey when she found out about his betrayal. Casey found out because Michael told her. The filter that most men in committed relationships begin to develop—the one that stops them from doing something really stupid—is also not yet fully developed for Michael. He sensed that what he was doing was less than okay, but he did it anyway, and then he confessed and apologized. I had to explain that sometimes apologies just don't cut it, and it might take a while for Casey, and me, to trust him again. *There: another new set of skills for me to teach.*

I took Michael's phone from him and told him he could no longer go anywhere by himself, except for work, because he was not acting like a grown man. I didn't tell him that I had to make him wait to venture out solo until I knew, beyond all doubt, he fully understood all these new lessons because I have learned that the world's understandings of Michael will lag far behind his acquisition and mastery of new skills. I must keep him safe from the world's misunderstandings. *There: I must also teach the world.* I called Cindy, Casey's mom, and explained the whole chronology of events. Then, I curled up on my bed, ate Pop Tarts, and cried.

Later that evening, Michael explained to Jim and me that Drake, from the TV show *Drake and Josh*, asks girls for their numbers so he thought he could, too. Jim explained that TV is pretend, that Drake is a young teenager, and that Michael is a grown up man with a fiancée. *There again: the list of new skills for me to teach grows and grows and grows.*

And so, Michael's concerns have become "adult." His thoughts—and mine about him—are occupied by work, money, beer, handling the female desire for jewelry and, now, learning that he cannot be friendly toward everyone, that there are some relationships that are just plain not okay. There are other grown-up steps being taken. Michael plays exclusively in the adult leagues in Special Olympics, and he competes alongside other athletes more than he "performs" silly stunts for spectators. His dancing is showing more nuanced choreography alongside the standard hip thrusts and shoulder rolls. He is anxious for us to finally finish the kitchen area of his downstairs apartment so that he and Casey can dine in private and fully claim their own clandestine space. And, even past "noticing" other girls, he still wants to get married.

"Mom, when can Casey and I get married? Huh? When? I have a job. I'm an adult. I have a debit card," Michael often implores.

"Oh, Michael," I sigh. "Things are progressing so very well. Let's just enjoy each day and see what happens." Each time my answer is the same. Yet, inside my head, I plan and ponder all the ways I can make sure things keep going well.

"What does progressing mean, Mom?" Michael asks. Each time his confusion remains. And, I wonder what's inside his head, what he really thinks, what he really comprehends.

I begin to explain. "Progressing? That means that there is still much to learn, and that with every new day, and with every new thing you understand, you grow to be even more wonderful than you were the day before." Then, I hold my breath, and I hope this singular truth will suffice for Michael. I hope it will also suffice for the world that I dream will finally and fully understand—*will cherish*—who Michael is.

Michael (age 22) working hard at New Mercer Retirement Community

Thanking

I gladly offer my heartfelt thanks to the following people, without whom I would not have been able to complete this book: my adored husband, Jim Hulings, who has the patience of Job, and my beloved children and their significant others, Nathan, Sean, Joedy & Dave, Edie & Jeff, Michael & Casey—the nine of them are my life and my muses; my parents, Marsha Udevitz and the late Norman Udevitz, my sister, Jane Miller, and my brother Andrew Udevitz, who all taught me how to see, cherish, and celebrate both a simple moment *and* the big picture; my mother-in-law, Alice Hulings, and my late father-in-law, Russ Hulings, for helping me believe I could write; Cindy and James Pursel for unyielding friendship; Casey Lord for bringing Michael the miracle of her love; all my dogs who, at the end of the day, still think I am grand even if I haven't written a word; Professor John Calderazzo, a gem of a man, who daily inspires me and countless others to do things we never thought possible; my dear friend, Janelle Adsit, for sharing her laughter with me; Professors Pam Coke and Karla Gingerich for giving me their care and advise; Patryica Hatten for bringing play, light, and joy to our lives; Foothills Gateway Inc. for providing ongoing support for people with disabilities in Northern Colorado; the Poudre School District staff and administrators at Barton Early Childhood Center, Moore Elementary School, Blevins Middle School, Rocky Mountain High School, Cooper Home, and Project Search for understanding why inclusion matters; Poudre School District teachers Amy Fristoe, Tracy Gefroh, Molly Kechter, Chris Rosazza, Emilie Ring, Kim Nigro, Greg Brigham, Gayna Jobe, Marilee Boylan, and Derek Gumuchian of The Center for Community Partnerships in the Department of Occupational Therapy at Colorado State University for giving Michael an individualized, loving, incomparable education; the football and swim team coaches and players at Rocky Mountain High School; the Village Green Swim Team and the Village West/Lexington Green neighborhood for being Michael's extended family; all of the Northern Colorado Special Olympics teams' coaches; Fort Collins Parks and Recreation for providing inclusive programming and the wonderful Funtime program; Mary Elizabeth Lenahan and Dance Express for giving Michael a place to dance; The Columbine Health Care System and EPIC of Fort Collins for enacting the ideals of inclusive employment; the University of North Texas Press—especially Director Ron Chrisman and my editor, Susan Thomas—and the Mayborn Literary Nonfiction Conference for making my dream come true; and, finally, wherever they are, Michael's biological mother and father for giving my family the greatest gift of our lives.

Appendix

Further Down Syndrome Resources for Infants to Adults

GENERAL

AAIDD: American Association on Intellectual and Developmental Disabilities

501 3rd Street, NW, Suite 200
Washington, DC 20001
http://www.aaidd.org

"AAIDD promotes progressive policies, sound research, effective practices, and universal human rights for people with intellectual and developmental disabilities."

Global Down Syndrome Foundation

3300 East First Avenue, Suite 390
Denver, CO 80206
http://www.globaldownsyndrome.org/

"The Global Down Syndrome Foundation is a public non-profit 501(c) (3) dedicated to significantly improving the lives of people with Down syndrome through Research, Medical care, Education and Advocacy. Formally established in 2009, the Foundation's primary focus is to support the Linda Crnic Institute for Down Syndrome, the first academic home in the United States committed solely to research and medical care for people with Down syndrome. Since Down syndrome is the least-funded genetic condition in the United States, fundraising and government advocacy to correct the alarming disparity of national funding for people with Down syndrome is a major goal."

National Down Syndrome Congress

30 Mansell Court, Suite 108
Roswell, GA 30076
http://ndsccenter.org/

"Founded in 1973, the National Down Syndrome Congress is the country's oldest national organization for people with Down syndrome, their families, and the professionals who work with them. [They] provide information, advocacy and support concerning all aspects of life for individuals with Down syndrome, and work to create a national climate in which all people will recognize and embrace the value and dignity of people with Down syndrome."

National Down Syndrome Society

666 Broadway, 8th Floor
New York, New York, 10012
http://www.ndss.org/

"The mission of the National Down Syndrome Society is to be the national advocate for the value, acceptance and inclusion of people with Down syndrome."

MEDICAL

Denver Adult Down Syndrome Clinic

The Medical Center of Aurora (TMCA)
MCPN Clinic
700 Potomac Street, Suite A
Aurora, CO 80011
http://www.denverdsclinic.org/

"The mission of the Denver Adult Down Syndrome Clinic is to provide quality health care to adolescents and adults with Down syndrome, education for the families and care givers, and consultative services for their health providers."

Linda Crnic Institute for Down Syndrome

Research Complex 2
Room P15-4014
Mail Stop 8608
12700 E 19th Avenue
http://www.ucdenver.edu/academics/colleges/medicalschool/
institutes/lindacrnic/Pages/lindacrnic.aspx

"Mission: Significantly improve the lives of all people with Down syndrome: Eradicate the ill effects associated with Down syndrome (having an extra chromosome 21)

Vision: Provide the world's first 'cradle-to-cradle,' fully integrated institute for Down syndrome with the highest quality basic, translational and clinical research, clinical trials, therapeutic development, medical care, education and advocacy in the pursuit of the mission: Change the paradigm of how people with Down syndrome are perceived by society: Serve as the Anschutz Medical Campus gold standard for translational research for Colorado and the gold standard worldwide."

EDUCATION AND COMMUNITY ACTION

The Arc

1825 K Street NW, Suite 1200
Washington, DC 20006
http://www.thearc.org

"The Arc promotes and protects the human rights of people with intellectual and developmental disabilities and actively supports their full inclusion and participation in the community throughout their lifetimes."

Best Buddies

Global Headquarters
100 Southeast Second Street, Suite 2200
Miami, FL 33131
http://www.bestbuddies.org/

"Best Buddies® is a nonprofit 501(c)(3) organization dedicated to establishing a global volunteer movement that creates opportunities for one-to-one friendships, integrated employment and leadership development for people with intellectual and developmental disabilities (IDD).

Human Animal Bond in Colorado

1586 Campus Delivery
Colorado State University
Fort Collins, CO 80523-1586
http://www.habic.cahs.colostate.edu/about/whoweare.aspx

"HABIC'S mission is to "improve the quality of life for people of all ages through the therapeutic use of companion animals." Within this mission are the goals of:

Service/outreach—providing animal-assisted intervention services and programs (animal-assisted therapy, and animal-assisted activity) in partnership with: public schools; long-term care and rehabilitation; hospitals; hospice; mental health; youth corrections; residential treatment; the Veterans Administration and other health and social services organizations in Colorado.

Teaching—educating students and professionals on the human-animal bond, the therapeutic use of companion animals, and animal-assisted interventions.

Research—conducting research in the human-animal bond field and animal-assisted therapy/activity interventions; evaluations of the animal-assisted therapy model/approach with "at-risk" students in schools."

IDEA: The Individuals with Disabilities Education Act

http://idea.ed.gov/

"The Individuals with Disabilities Education Act (IDEA) is a law ensuring services to children with disabilities throughout the nation. IDEA governs how states and public agencies provide early intervention, special education and related services to more than 6.5 million eligible infants, toddlers, children and youth with disabilities. Infants and toddlers with disabilities (birth–2) and their families receive early intervention services under IDEA Part C. Children and youth (ages 3–21) receive special education and related services under IDEA Part B."

Peak Parent Center

611 North Weber, Suite 200
Colorado Springs, CO 80903
http://www.peakparent.org/index.asp

"The mission of PEAK Parent Center is to provide training, information and technical assistance to equip families of children birth through twenty-six including all disability conditions with strategies to advocate successfully for their children. As a result of PEAK's services to families and professionals, children and adults with disabilities will live rich, active lives participating as full members of their schools and communities."

Project Search

Cincinnati Children's Hospital
Medical Center 3333 Burnet Avenue, MLC5030
Cincinnati, Ohio 450229
http://www.projectsearch.us/

"The Project SEARCH High School Transition Program is a unique, business led, one year school-to-work program that takes place entirely at the workplace. Total workplace immersion facilitates a seamless combination of classroom instruction, career exploration, and hands-on training through worksite rotations."

R Word: Spread the Word to End the Word

http://www.r-word.org/

"Spread the Word to End the Word is an on-going effort to raise the consciousness of society about the dehumanizing and hurtful effects of the word "retard(ed)" and encourage people to pledge to stop using the R-word. The campaign is intended to get schools, communities and organizations to rally and pledge their support."

LEARNING TOOLS

Love and Learning

9828 Melrose
Livonia, MI 48150
http://www.loveandlearning.com/home.shtml

"[Their] technique and materials (DVDs, audio cds, books and computer programs) help children with Language and Reading development. [They] originally developed these materials for [their] daughter with special needs. Maria exceeded [their] expectations by being able to speak, read and understand 250 words at 3 years of age and over 1,000 words at 5 years of age. [They] offer an easily do-able, loving manner of teaching that values the individuality of each child and helps nurture self-esteem."

Signing Time

870 East 7145 South
Midvale, UT 84047
http://www.signingtime.com/

"[Their] award-winning Signing Time DVDs will help you and your child learn basic American Sign Language (ASL) vocabulary words. Signing Time truly makes learning sign language easy, entertaining and fun for children of all ages. The format of Signing Time includes an adult (Rachel Coleman, co-creator) to model each sign, supported by footage of Alex and Leah (real kids, cousins in real life, Leah is deaf and Alex can hear, and Leah is Rachel's daughter), as well as footage of children and families demonstrating each sign in the proper context. Two to four thematic songs are sprinkled throughout each volume to help bring together all that you've learned . . .[e]vidence is also mounting that children with special needs, such as apraxia of speech, autism, or Down syndrome who have difficulty with speech can make great strides in their communication development when *Signing Time* is part of their regimen. The multi-sensory approach of *Signing Time* engages visual learners, kinesthetic learners, and auditory learners of all ages and abilities, while making sign language easy and fun."

TouchMath

5445 Mark Dabling Blvd., Suite 200
Colorado Springs, CO 80918-3850
1-800-888-9191
http://www.touchmath.com/

"TouchMath is a multisensory program that uses its signature TouchPoints to engage students of all abilities and learning styles."

Zoo Phonics

950 Ferretti Road
Groveland, CA 95321
http://www.zoo-phonics.com/home.html

"The Zoo-phonics Multisensory Language Arts Program is a kinesthetic, multi-modal approach to learning all aspects of language arts, including vocabulary development and articulation, based on phonics and phonemic awareness. The principle of Zoo-phonics maximizes understanding, memory, utilization and transference to all areas of the reading, spelling and writing process in a playful and concrete manner. . . . It is excellent for ELL/Transition/Special Ed students—a total physical response at its best because of the concrete Animal Letters and Body Movements."

ADOPTION

Reece's Rainbow Down Syndrome Adoption Ministry

PO Box 4024
Gaithersburg, MD 20885
http://reecesrainbow.org/

"The mission of Reece's Rainbow is to rescue orphans with Down syndrome through the gift of adoption, to raise awareness for all of the children who are waiting in 25 countries around the world, and to raise funds as adoption grants that help adoptive families afford the high cost of adopting these beautiful children."

RECREATION

Special Olympics

> 1133 19th Street NW
> Washington, DC 20036-3604
> http://www.specialolympics.org/default.aspx

"The mission of Special Olympics is to provide year-round sports training and athletic competition in a variety of Olympic-type sports for children and adults with intellectual disabilities, giving them continuing opportunities to develop physical fitness, demonstrate courage, experience joy and participate in a sharing of gifts, skills and friendship with their families, other Special Olympics athletes and the community."

ToysRUs Toy Guide for Differently-Abled Kids

> 1-800-ToysRUs(800-869-7787).
> http://www.toysrus.com/shop/index.jsp?categoryId=3261680

"As a company that loves all kids, Toys"R"Us, Inc. has a long history of supporting the special needs community. For nearly two decades, [they] have published the annual Toys"R"Us Toy Guide for Differently-Abled Kids, an easy-to-use resource featuring specially selected toys that encourage play for children with physical, cognitive or developmental disabilities."

LEGAL

ADA: Americans With Disabilities Act

U.S. Department of Justice
950 Pennsylvania Avenue, NW
Civil Rights Division
Disability Rights Section–NYA
Washington, DC 20530
http://www.ada.gov/

"Information and Technical Assistance on The Americans With Disabilities Act"

Source Notes

1   "Learn," Dolphin Human Therapy, January 20, 2013, http://www.dhtgc. com/learn.html; "Dolphin Therapy," Dolphins Plus, January 20, 2013, http://www.dolphinsplus.com/dolphinswim-programs/dolphin-therapy/.

2   "About Down Syndrome," National Down Syndrome Society, accessed April 3, 2011, http://www.ndss.org/Down-Syndrome/.

3   Terri Couwenhoven, *Teaching Children with Down Syndrome about Their Bodies, Boundaries, and Sexuality,* (Bethesda, MD: Woodbine House, 2007).

4   "About Down Syndrome," National Down Syndrome Society.

5   "Rosa's Law," Special Olympics, accessed April 3, 2011, http:// www.specialolympics.org/Regions/north-america/News-and-Stories/ Stories/Rosa-s-Law.aspx.

6   "About Down Syndrome," National Down Syndrome Society.

7   "Down Syndrome Human and Civil Rights Timeline," Global Down Syndrome Foundation, accessed January 16, 2013, http://www.globaldownsyndrome.org/about-down-syndrome/ history-of-down-syndrome/down-syndrome-human-and-civil-rights- timeline/.

8   Ibid.

9   Ibid.

10 OC Ward. "John Langdon Down: The Man and the Message." *Down Syndrome Research and Practice.* 1999; 6(1); 19–24. doi:10.3104/ perspectives.94.

11 Kathy Massimini, ed., *Genetic Disorders Sourcebook* (Detroit, Michigan: Omnigraphics, 2000), 53–68.

12 "About Down Syndrome," National Down Syndrome Society.

13 "Diagnosis and Management of fetal nuchal translucency," NCBI, National Center for Biotechnology Information, accessed March 29, 2013, http://www.ncbi.nlm.nih.gov/pubmed/9800243.

14 "About Down Syndrome," National Down Syndrome Society.

15 Josee Smith, "Prenatal test raises ethical questions," *The Stanford Daily,* March 8, 2012, accessed January 16, 2013, http://www.stanforddaily.com/2012/03/08/prenatal-test-raises-ethical-questions/.

16 Darrin Dixon, JD, "Informed Consent or Institutionalized Eugenics? How the medical profession encourages abortion of fetuses with Down Syndrome," *Issues in Law and Medicine* 24.1 (2008 Summer): 5–8.